Cherry Angels and Earthly Predators

My Life Among Dangerous Wild Animals

By
Angela Harter

CENTRAL PARK SOUTH PUBLISHING

Copyright © 2021 Angela Harter

Photography - Ellen Martin Chester, Ellen's Animal/Wildlife Art

All rights reserved. No part of this publication may be reproduced, distributed or transmitted in any form or by any means, without prior written permission.

Publisher: Central Park South Publishing
Website: www.centralparksouthpublishing.com

Publisher's Note: Although some names have been changed, the people and events depicted in this book are real. This story actually happened.

Book Layout – Mark Mázers - alienartifacts

Cherry Angels and Earthly Predators by Angela Harter - 1st ed. © 2021

ISBN-978-1-7370777-4-9

Dedication

For Dr. Don Burton and Professor Ron Forsythe, always faithful, and Linda Langton, who saw beauty and truth where everyone else saw madness and depravity.

INTRODUCTION

Whores and Saviors

Here's the funny thing about the truth: if someone doesn't say it out loud, it dies; however, speaking it always comes with consequences, and consequences can kill truth, too. A lot of what follows in this story will probably sound reckless, scandalous or shocking to you. Regardless, it is the truth, no matter how outrageous or disturbing it might seem. I also understand, of course, that the truth can be subjective, particularly years afterward. Many of the incidents in this book happened decades ago, and my memory is as imperfect as anyone else's. However, what's in this book is exactly how I remember things.

I grew up feral in the slums of Columbus, Ohio, running the streets with hoodlums, stealing, drinking, getting high. I was repeatedly molested as a child and started trading sex for things I needed – or wanted – before I was even a teenager. When I was 16, I began stripping in clubs and bars. I also lived in a mansion for 10 years with a man who was so wealthy that we spent our summers in Europe and our winters in Aspen. I also pedaled my ass to buy food for massive predators that could kill me with a casual swipe of a paw. I also communicated with a murdered mountain lion.

I know that last part makes me sound bonkers, but as I said, it's the truth, whether you want to believe it or not.

As Angela Harter, I owned Rescue One Exotic Cat Sanctuary, in Lancaster, Ohio, for 16 years. Beginning in the mid-1990s, I saved and cared for scores of abused and neglected tigers, lions, cougars and leopards. During that same time, I was also Heather Smith, proprietor and only employee of Cherry Angels, an escort service. Heather specialized in well-to-do older men and spent their money to care for beautiful animals that people had treated like garbage, or worse.

In my tumultuous life, I've had two major paradigm shifts; both of them involve a cougar named Jewels. I bought Jewels totally by mistake during a drunken lark with some friends at an exotic animal auction in Mt. Hope, Ohio. Once I sobered up, I saw the barbarity of that auction – hundreds of exotics torn from their mothers and sold to anyone who had the cash to pay for them. That sick farce was enacted three times a year and wasn't even the only exotic auction in Ohio.

The "Mid-Ohio Alternative Animal and Bird Sale" was finally shut down, but to this day, similar auctions in Indiana, Texas and Missouri pimp exotic cubs to fools who think it would be nifty to watch a 500-pound carnivore romp with the grandkids; traveling "photo-baby" operators who drag cubs across the country and exhibit them for 12 hours a day so morons can have their pictures taken with them; owners of "canned hunts" who sell the privilege of shooting defenseless adult cats; and slaughterhouses that harvest and market skins, blood and body parts. The exotic-animal business is nearly as profitable as dope or illegal guns and a lot less risky.

When I started Rescue One, it was completely legal to own exotics in Ohio and in many other states; believe it or not, the federal government still has no comprehensive laws governing private ownership of big cats. Ohio was the Wild, Wild West of exotic ownership. There were thousands of privately-owned big cats in the state, perhaps as many as 20,000 in America, and the majority of them were treated inhumanely.

That freewheeling neglect eventually led to the infamous Zanesville Massacre, in which a man named Terry Thompson allegedly released 56 dangerous exotics and then shot himself. Cops killed all but seven of the animals. I visited the Thompson farm three years before that terrible night in October, 2011, and was appalled at the misery I saw there.

Once I realized the extent of the problem, there was no going back for me. I couldn't bear the thought of such majestic animals suffering so terribly, so I began to rescue them from hellholes. I tried to find permanent homes for them in other sanctuaries. However, there are few legitimate exotic rescues in the United States, and most of them are overwhelmed with castoffs. I had no choice but to keep dozens of big cats that I was unable to place.

Every animal cost approximately $10,000 a year to keep healthy and safe. I had to pay for food, secure caging, daily maintenance, medicine and specialized veterinary care. When I founded my sanctuary, I was a semester short of my degree in philosophy and psychology and jobless. Rescue One was not a municipal zoo or shelter. Neither the government nor animal rights organizations support private exotic rescues – not with a single dime. I refused to breed my lions, tigers and cougars and sell the cubs or to charge the public to gawk at them. I'd learned as a child that my only asset was my looks, so that's what I used to protect my cats.

The relationship I had with my animals isn't nearly as one-sided as I'm making it sound, though. The metaphysical benefits of animals are tremendous. They are spiritual beings who can guide, protect and heal us – *if* we foster kinship with them. People who don't will never understand the profound joys. It's this simple: My animals were my kids.

I don't want to minimize the risks I took, however. Whether Angela was transporting a pissed-off black leopard or Heather was locked inside a motel room with a horny, coked-up pervert, my life was damned hazardous. My days and nights were all about predators and prey. Animals attacked me. People attacked me. How I've gotten this far in one piece is a miracle.

My survival depended on paying attention to body language, to tone of voice and to the eyes – always the eyes. Take it from someone who knows, the devil is absolutely in the details. During those years, I slept only 10 or so hours a week. To enhance my hyper-awareness, I began gobbling Tramadol – synthetic codeine used to treat pain and anxiety. The drug helped me stay awake and alert.

The stress, of course, was unrelenting, and I dealt with it in the worst possible way – by binging and purging junk food.

Those awful sessions sapped my energy and undermined my concentration. Bulimia made my life exponentially more dangerous.

The other thing that protected me was my belief in God. I know it seems strange for a hooker to say this, but I'm definitely a child of God, who is blessed with all the faith and fuck-ups that come with that title. To be clear, though, I'm spiritual, not religious. I don't reject the belief; I reject the contrived artificiality of the ceremony. Manmade institutions, including organized religion, are evil and dangerous. People who hand over their divinity to an institution are dumbasses. On the other hand, anyone who doesn't believe in a higher power is a damned fool. I call that power "God," because I don't have another name for it. God allowed me to survive over a decade and a half of perpetual risk, maybe because I saved so many of his magnificent creations. Let's just say I'm all about love and salvation, not judgment and damnation, and I have the scars on my ass – and on my heart – to prove it.

My second paradigm shift occurred after someone poisoned Jewels. Through an eerie set of circumstances, I woke up and realized that the dead are dead only to those who are blind to the fact that they are still here. There is another world functioning alongside our daily 3-D existence; however, most people ignore or reject it. Through Jewels, I learned to embrace it.

I was forced to surrender Rescue One – and all my kids – in 2012, when the state of Ohio reacted to Zanesville with incredibly strict and outrageously expensive new regulations for dangerous wild animals. For all the time I ran the sanctuary, Heather Smith, Cherry Angels, sexual abuse and bulimia were my most deeply held secrets. Bringing them into the light now is like running naked through the streets of Columbus at rush hour. Finally saying the truth out loud is worth it, though, if I can help lay bare the consequences of child abuse, expose the cruelty of the exotic animal business, help one suffering big cat or change the life of someone who is fighting an eating disorder as severe as the one I live with. Besides, it not like half the world hasn't already seen me naked.

You can make of this story – or me – whatever you will, of course, but know that it is the truth.

CHAPTER ONE

A Cappuccino, A Camel and A Communication from The Universe

For the same stupid reason that has gotten me into trouble my whole life – I can't say "no" – I was trapped in a nightmare. A police detective was shouting through a bullhorn, and people in Hazmat suits and guys geared up like Navy SEALs and a team of grim veterinarians were dodging spooked-out horses and ponies that were galloping wildly around us, snorting and screaming and rolling their big eyes, terrified.

I was standing beside my red Mitsubishi 3000 GT VR-4 sports car on a farm in Zanesville, Ohio, that belonged to a couple named Terry and Marian Thompson, but I felt like I was in some foreign hellhole. Mitzi was the last vehicle in a line parked on a long driveway leading uphill to a shabby, one-story brick house and two sprawling barns surrounded by junk. Rusty chain-link cages covered with creeper vines and ripped blue tarps lined the driveway. The stench of shit and piss and rotting animal carcasses gagged me.

The property dropped off from where I was standing, so I couldn't see what was down there, but I heard lions coughing and snarling and tigers roaring. They were right there. They were dangerous and desperate. I felt that off those animals – desperation.

The smell grew even worse. I was holding a cappuccino I'd bought at a gas station on my way to Zanesville. I sniffed the lid, wondering if the milk was spoiled. Something wet and rough pushed hard against my neck and the back of my head.

I thought I was finally losing it completely. I hadn't slept at all the night before. I was exhausted and stressed from working two jobs and living two separate lives. During the day, I was Angela Harter. Angela wore ball caps and flannel shirts and chukka boots and took care of Rescue One Exotic Cat Sanctuary, the rescue for dangerous wild animals I'd operated for almost 12 years. At night, I became Heather Smith, proprietor and sole employee of Cherry Angels escort service. As an exotic dancer, Heather didn't wear much of anything; as an escort and prostitute, she put on or took off whatever her clients paid for.

That morning, I was neither Angela nor Heather, or both of them; things often got confusing. I'd rushed home from my night work, stripped off my black Joan Jett leathers, wiped my black lipstick on a paper towel and grabbed the first clothes I saw. I was wearing Angela's boots, khaki cargo pants and cotton jacket, but my hair was still curled and sprayed atop my head, my long, curved nails were painted black and I was blushed and rouged and doused in perfume. A fright mask of mascara was smeared around my eyes. I knew I looked like a bizarre hybrid of two very different women, but I was in a hurry to get to Zanesville. I raced toward the Thompson farm in Heather's Mitsubishi, a 322-horsepower roadrunner that responded to every caress of my naturally heavy foot and would get me there a lot faster than Angela's blue Land Rover.

I'd owned exotic cats since 1998, yet I didn't know anything about Terry and Marian Thompson. 'Hey, do you know that guy out in Zanesville?' people would ask. 'Why does he have all those animals? Is he rich? Does he just collect them? Is it a private zoo? Can I visit?' It was legal to own exotics in Ohio at the time, so I figured the Thompsons were just semi-wealthy weirdos who kept some animals on a lot of property right along Route 70.

I was headed there only because my United States Department of Agriculture representative, Dr. Clara Markin, asked me to do an unofficial evaluation of the Thompson farm. The USDA regulates privately-owned exotic animals in America; however, at the time, if you didn't exhibit them to the public and charge admission, you didn't need a USDA license. The Thompsons didn't exhibit, so the USDA had no official interest in them. Dr. Markin had heard a lot of rumors, though, so she was hot to know what was up in Zanesville. She asked me to check it out for her.

I didn't allow the public to see my animals, either, but I'd registered with USDA anyway, after a hassle over my first big cat, a cougar named Jewels. As soon as I did, my information landed on the internet. Calls poured in about lions and tigers and cougars that people wanted to dump. I couldn't stand the thought of those beautiful kids living in hellish conditions, so I started saving them. The animals found me one by one and claimed me. I tried to rehabilitate them and locate safe places for them to live out their lives, but not many legit people want a full-grown apex predator who's a mental mess after being abused her entire life by a dirtbag.

All the animals arrived with their own issues; the one thing that was consistent was how unbelievably expensive they were to keep. I owned dozens of big cats, each of which cost $10000 a year in meat, daily maintenance and specialized veterinary care. If my animals were going to survive, someone had to pay for it all, somehow. I inherited nothing from my messed-up family but my looks. I'm short, more gymnast than runway model, and wasn't born with great boobs, but my butt has always been round and firm, I have muscular legs and abs, my hair is thick and naturally blond and lots of guys have told me my face is the prettiest they've ever seen. To protect my kids, I went back to the life I lived when I ran away from home at 16: stripping in clubs and hustling gullible older men.

I was in a rush to get to Zanesville that morning because Dr. Markin had arranged for me to meet local cops, officers from the Bureau of Alcohol, Tobacco and Firearms and vets from The Wilds, a conservation center near Zanesville, who were doing a joint raid. I arrived early. No one was around. I sat in the Mitsubishi in front of a locked gate. Although it was almost summer, it was chilly. My breath fogged the windows. I sipped cappuccino to stay warm and gazed up the driveway at the house and barns, half asleep, until a SWAT officer rapped a knuckle on my window and hand-signaled me to be quiet and move my car because I was blocking the gate. I did as he ordered, and a cop yelled through a bullhorn, "Terry, it's the sheriff's department! This is Detective Steve Welker! Come down to the gate, or we'll have to come through!"

When no one answered, they snapped the lock and rolled up in a convoy. I followed them, parked and got out. The Hazmat people scrambled one way, the SWAT guys, holding machineguns across their flak jackets, went another. The madness – guns, yelling, stink, frightened animals – freaked me out so bad that I froze with my car door open, holding the cappuccino under my nose.

Whatever was behind me licked my hair again and slobbered down my neck. When I turned around, I was sure I was hallucinating. A massive, triangular head stared down at me from a long stalk of neck. I thought a dinosaur was attacking me, but after a second or two, I realized it was a camel. He stuck out his gooey tongue, attempted to get at my cappuccino. I tried to push him away, but he really wanted it. He was cute and sweet and batting the longest lashes I've ever seen. He also smelled putrid, and gunk was seeping out of one of his eyes. He nosed my arm. I was too wrung out to wrestle with a smelly camel over a cappuccino while an armed invasion swirled around me. I took the lid off the cup and let him lap from it while I awoke to what was happening.

I quickly realized that the Thompsons were backyard breeders of exotics. I'd seen the same stupidity and cruelty hundreds of times. Around the house and barns, small, filthy, dilapidated cages held animals. There were three female cougars, one without a tail. There was a bear with a cub and an Asian black leopard whose ears were chewed and ripped. She was 35 pounds, at best, in midlife or a little older, starved out and puffing and pacing in a gross cage, without food or water. At least 10 junior lions were crowded into a tiny enclosure, maybe 15x10x10 – little guys, two months or so. One of them had a tumor as big as a softball on his elbow. They were hungry and thirsty and covered in their own filth and biting each other. There were dozens of other animals, all of them suffering and frightened. I felt their fear.

The little lions looked up like they expected me to do something for them; they thought deliverance day had finally arrived. As an "unofficial observer," I couldn't do jackshit. Helpless and irate, I thought, 'This fucking place is so terrible that these little guys can't even off themselves to escape.' I was trying to be professional, but the animals suffering in those horrid conditions pushed me over the edge. I flung the cappuccino aside and walked up on Det. Welker and some people who were huddled around him.

"Arrest these assholes! Arrest them!" I shouted. "They're crazy! We've got to get these animals out of here right now!"

Welker barely glanced at me.

I got louder: "These animals are in trouble! They need food! They need water! We have to help these little guys! We've got to get to work *now*!"

"We have to follow procedures," Welker said, flatly.

"This is the worst neglect I've ever seen!" I fumed. "What're you going to do about it?"

He ignored me and turned around. No one else there cared what a raving, skanked-out amateur zookeeper had to say. I shoved the USDA evaluation form I'd brought with me into Welker's hands and said, "I'm leaving! I'm calling Dr. Markin!"

He didn't even look at the form. I bailed. Thank goodness my car was last in line. I backed down the driveway so fast I thought I was going to blow Mitzi's transmission. I called Dr. Markin, screaming. She was enraged, too, but she couldn't do much more than I could.

"Ang, I have no answers," she said. "I'll get back to you."

I called Jack Hanna, director emeritus of the Columbus Zoo and TV personality. I left a message: "Use your power. Do something!" I never heard from him.

I returned to my two insane lives. Every day, I managed Rescue One, where a needy predator could snap Angela Harter's neck just by "playing" with her; every night, I did reckless things for money in bad places, where a crazed john could do the same, or worse, to Heather Smith.

For months, whether Angela was scooping lion shit or Heather was running to a gig, I hassled people about the Thompsons' animals. Some said they didn't have jurisdiction; some obviously didn't give a damn; some changed their numbers. Det. Welker insinuated that if I didn't stop bothering him, he'd charge me with interfering in a police investigation.

Even Dr. Markin became aggravated with me. Everyone acted like I was the problem.

That whole winter, those kids in Zanesville never left my mind. They were freezing and starving, and no one would do anything about it. 'Can you imagine being starved out in that hell, and no one's coming to help you, and you have to go through winter?' I thought. The only thing that made me feel better was picturing the Thompsons' faces when they showed up on the Other Side and realized that animals really do have souls, and those tormented kids had been waiting there for them.

I found out later that as soon as the raid began, Terry Thompson fled out the back of the house, and the cops grabbed him up. When they burst in, they found Marian in the kitchen, naked. They put a t-shirt on her, cuffed her and kept her beside the pool. As a result of that raid, Terry Thompson was sentenced to a year in jail for possessing illegal weapons. Marian wasn't charged with any crime. Of course, the Thompsons got only a slap on the wrist for the appalling conditions at the farm.

When I heard Thompson had gone to prison, I thought, 'Good for you, dirtbag. I hope your ass rots there.' I had no idea that when I was standing beside Mitzi, looking at his place that morning, I was actually seeing my own future. I'd run my sanctuary for more than a decade. I thought I knew everything about owning dangerous wild animals. However, I was about to find out just how treacherous and unforgiving the exotic world can be.

The universe was trying to communicate with me that morning in Zanesville, but my head wasn't opened up enough to hear the warning. By the time I figured things out, it was too late for me, for Rescue One Exotic Cat Sanctuary and, almost, for my kids.

CHAPTER TWO

The Enchanted Castle

I didn't choose exotic animal sanctuary owner – or whore – as a career. When I was little, I thought I would grow up and things would fall into place and I would have postcard "normal" – family, friends, holiday dinners around a big table. I don't know where I got that idea, because the craziness that has filled my life started even before I was born. My family shouldn't have been allowed to breed. My mother had me when she was still a teenager. She worked nights as a bartender at a place called the Peppermint Tiger – weird as that sounds. She was gone all night and slept all day. My father, John Harter, was a policeman.

Most of the time, my mother left my brother, three sisters and me with my dad's hag mother in a place called Lockbourne, a very bad little joint on the south end of Columbus, right outside of Rickenbacker Air Force Base. Lockbourne was a low-class, lost-in-time hick ghetto of hellraising, brawling, rowdy bonfires, junkers rusting away on cement blocks, outlaw bikers and dope dealers. Hardly anyone worked. People burned trash in their front yards, dirty kids ran wild, hillbillies bet on chicken fights in abandoned garages and drunks beat their wives and girlfriends and kids on weekends, just for the fuck of it.

From jump, no one paid attention to me. One day when I was three, I was outside, unsupervised, and a homeless psycho snatched me out of the yard and took off with me. Luckily, he ran right into two cops who were spending their shift napping behind a gas station. Even those idiots knew that there was something not right with a guy dressed like a scarecrow running through an alley, carrying a struggling blond toddler. The cops cornered him and took me back.

It's weird that I ended up dedicating my life to animals, because my first serious experience with an animal was straight out of *Cujo*. Not long after the homeless guy stole me, I wandered out of the yard. The dog next door was eating his dinner. I went over to pet him and play with him. He probably didn't get dinner often, so he was serious about eating. He attacked me.

I remember being rushed into the ER and then down a hallway on a gurney. A bright light's in my eyes, and I'm scared.

A cop keeps asking, "What the hell happened to this kid?"

A doctor's yelling, "We've got to get this kid into surgery now!"

I remember the blood. I see it. I smell it. I remember people dressed in white. They're pushing me down on a table. I see panic on their faces.

The dog put more than 300 stiches in my face and shattered my right eye. To this day, when I try to see out of it, it's like I'm looking through a kaleidoscope. People have often said to me, "What are you looking at?" Not like a threat, but like, 'What are you looking at through those unfocused eyes that no one else can see?' At least my face wasn't permanently mangled. The scars are there, but they're faint.

The Hag despised my mother and hated me, too. She barely fed me, but she made sure to beat the piss out of me every day. She bought plastic scrub brushes by the gross and whaled on me with them; they broke easily, and she wanted to have a spare handy to keep the rhythm of the beatings going. Some of the worst whippings came when she caught me looking for food in the fridge or kitchen cupboards without permission.

Despite my experience with the dog, animals were my escape from that awful fairytale. As long as I obeyed their rules, animals didn't judge or threaten me. I trusted them way more than I did the humans tormenting me every day.

People frequently abandoned dogs and cats in Lockbourne. I took in puppies and stray cats and kittens, even a little groundhog. I nursed every injured bird I ran across. I found a baby raccoon next to a muddy creek in a little stand of trees one day. The woods were boxed in by streets; his mother had probably been killed by a car. Charlie was incredibly cute and cuddly. He was old enough to eat cat food, and that's exactly what he behaved like – a cat. No one paid any attention to me, anyway, so he stayed in my tiny bedroom and slept with me and squealed happily when I flipped him on his back and tickled his belly.

When he got older, Charlie wouldn't leave my side. He was curious and smart and could open cupboards and drawers. He tore everything up, and he wasn't litter trained. When Mom and

The Hag got mad, I started putting Charlie outside every morning, but I left the bathroom window open so he could climb in and hang out with me at night. After about a year, he hit puberty and became outright aggressive. One of the many "uncles" who came and went from the house all the time drove him out into the country and dropped him off.

The Hag sent me to school in dirty hand-me-down clothes, bruised all over, hungry. Because of my bad eye, reading gave me terrible headaches, so studying was out of the question. I was a loser who didn't fit in anywhere. Kids teased me relentlessly. I didn't go to dances, and I wasn't a cheerleader or anything. During lunch, everybody socialized. Not me. I hid in a bathroom until it was over.

To have decent clothes, I stole them from laundry lines. When people hung them out to dry, I ripped them off. I didn't steal because I wanted designer jeans. I thought that if I looked more like the other kids, they'd have one fewer excuse to torment me.

The only highlight of my time in school was a story I wrote about our cat. Tar Baby was a beautiful black bruiser who ruled the neighborhood, kicking dogs' asses, chasing anyone nervy enough to walk past the house, lying in the middle of the street so cars had to drive around him. I wrote "Tar Baby is the Baddest Cat in Town" for a state-wide contest. The kids who wrote the best stories in Ohio would take a field trip to the home of James Thurber, a famous dead writer, and spend the day at the museum named for him. My story was one of the winners of the "Celebration of Writing."

The field trip was amazing. In the garden across the street from the beautiful brick home, there was a bronze statue of a unicorn and in another garden, five quirky stone dogs. I learned that just like me, Thurber lost an eye in a childhood accident, had a whacky mother and liked animals more than people. He wrote a lot about animals and drew funny sketches of them cooking and writing and playing cards and hanging out with humans.

Our guide said the house had been built on the site of an insane asylum that had burned down and was haunted by a patient's ghost. It was an eccentric home, with lots of narrow passageways and tight, winding staircases. I sat at James Thurber's desk and ran my fingers over the keys of the typewriter he used to write books like *Thurber's Dogs* and *The Beast in Me*. I loved it there; it was like an enchanted castle.

Too bad it was only one day and one visit. Back in the real world, Angela Harter was a dead-end kid with a sucky home life who was destined to be a nobody. School administrators came to the house because I'd shown up with a black eye or I refused to listen to anybody or didn't have lunch money.

"Oh, we don't know what happened to her," The Hag would say, innocently. "The poor thing must've fallen down."

When the school people left, she got out the scrub brushes. I tried to tell Mom about it, but she wouldn't listen.

The Hag treated my sisters Patty and Dawn like crap, as well.

She was totally different with my sister Tabby and my brother, Johnny, the youngest child. She doted on Johnny, fussing over him and giving him anything he wanted. It made me mad, but Johnny was so adorable that I couldn't be angry at him. Although I was only two years older, I treated him like my baby boy. We sat for hours in the bare-dirt front yard and fought imaginary battles with his GI Joes or walked down to the market for snacks. He could be ornery when he took a notion, but I loved that little boy dearly.

When he was six or seven, a woman named Cathy moved in with some hick across the street. She started showing up at the house at Christmas and on their birthdays with presents for Johnny and Tabby, but not for Patty, Dawn or me. I had no idea who she was or what was up, until I came into the house one day, and Johnny rushed in after me and blurted out that John was his and Tabby's father, but not mine, and Cathy was his real mother. I could tell by how the adults there reacted that he'd let the cat out of the bag.

The Hag and I were actually not related at all. I realized then why she doted on Tabby and Johnny, and why they had olive skin and dark hair, while I was fair and very blond. From that day on, Johnny changed. He moved in with Cathy and wouldn't come back.

CHAPTER THREE

Feral

The Hag didn't have to worry about being blamed for my problems, because everyone blamed me for them. The grownups acted like I was another incorrigible hoodrat, not a victim of a doomed, sabotaged childhood – suspensions, scolding, lectures, detentions, truant officers, special classes in special rooms. I protected myself the only way I knew: by going feral. There was no way to control me. No one could get their hands on me. I was too wild – an alley cat prowling the streets with a pack of hillbilly hoodlums who wore leather jackets and Doc Martins, drank, got high and didn't give a damn about school or anything else. They told me I had to stand up for myself. On the streets, no one would do it for me. Never take shit from anyone, they said. If someone jumps in your face, you jump back. If you don't, they warned, the streets will chew you up and spit you out.

We loved to get drunk on Little Kings Ale and taunt two sawed-off bumpkin sheriff's deputies who messed with us when we were on the streets at night. They did a lot of yelling and threatening but were too fat and lazy to get out of their cars and chase us on foot.

I was roaming around with my buddy Chucky – who I called "Fuckles" – one night. We came up with an ingenious idea.

Those deputies were easy to goad. Our plan was to get them to chase us down the alley behind Mayor Shirkey's house, which was lined on both sides by old-time metal trashcans. Fuckles and I waited until night and wove clear monofilament fishing line from one side of the alley to the other, through the handles of the trash cans. In the dark, our spider web was invisible.

We devised bailout routes, created commotion to get the Dumbass Twins' attention and took off. They tore into the alley behind us, right into tangle of fishing line, dragging trashcans down the alley, making a racket that sounded like a high-speed pile-up on the interstate. They never chased us again. That prank made us heroes.

Lonely, embarrassed over my crummy clothes, terrified that a teacher would make me read in front of the class, I rarely went to school. I stole and got drunk and smoked as much weed as I could get my hands on. I swiped my mother's car and rode around all night with my friends, getting high, terrorizing Lockbourne. Once, after I dropped a tab of acid, I sat behind the wheel at a four-way stop for I don't know how long, waving cars around me and watching the Sun-Maid Raisins high-kick back and forth across the hood like a line of Ziegfeld girls. Once the rush finally subsided, I drifted the car to a stop in front of the house, snuck back inside and pretended to be asleep. Finally, I stopped coming home for days at a stretch. No one seemed concerned that I wasn't around.

I was like a modern-day female Peter Pan – watching darling families through the windows of darling homes, flitting off at the first sign of any adult, followed always by the faithful bunch of Lost Kids who'd gathered around me.

A plump, smartly-attired older woman with coiffed red hair and a perfectly made-up face parked her car outside one afternoon and marched toward the house as if she had a serious reason for being there. The Hag stopped her at the fence. They faced off and immediately started arguing. The woman was composed and polite, but she didn't back down to The Hag. For a moment, I thought she was from child welfare. Not about to go into any foster home, I tensed to make a run for it. Then she said she was my real grandmother, Alice Flowers, my mom's mother. Apparently, she'd been watching the train wreck from afar.

That's enough," she told The Hag. "I'm not leaving without Angela."

The Hag didn't put up much of a fight. I think she was happy to get rid of me; Mom probably was, too.

Granny took me home to live with her and Grandpa on the West Side. She sat me down and told me the whole truth: Patty and Dawn were actually my half-sisters. None us had the same father. Granny said my father had been a racecar driver. He was in a bad accident, and my mother ordered him to quit racing. He wouldn't stop, so they split up. Mom had never mentioned him – or her parents – to me.

"You'll always be loved here," Granny said. "You'll always have your own room. I'll cook for you and do your laundry. Please, just stay out of trouble."

CHAPTER FOUR

High Priestess of The Stage Witches

Granny and Grandpa were totally unlike anyone I'd ever known – warm, happy, kind and responsible. Grandpa, a Navy veteran who'd been badly wounded at Pearl Harbor, managed a dry-cleaning store. Granny was the center of an extended family of screw-ups who all expected her to fix their problems. They'd already raised 10 children, grandchildren, nieces and nephews. Granny was so kind and gentle that I never wanted her to see how messed up I really was. I smiled and brushed my hair, kept my elbows off the table, cleaned up after myself and even behaved in school.

That was my taste of normal, but it didn't last. The West Side was a rough area, too. I soon fell in with the same kind of hoods I ran with in Lockbourne. A few of the older ones knew dancers and bouncers who'd look the other way, so I started hanging around the strip clubs with them. The all-nude places were smelly, rowdy dumps filled with belligerent drunks looking for trouble and bored junkies wriggling around on cruddy stages cluttered with overflowing ashtrays, beer bottles and watered-down booze in plastic cups. Other clubs were far more upscale. They had plush furniture and gleaming fixtures and dramatic lighting for the highly-orchestrated pasty and panty shows. They offered expensive lap dances and VIP rooms and magnums of champagne. Either way, the clubs were a thrilling new environment stoked by free-flowing cash and the raw energy of men who'd checked out of Sheep World for a night of wildness in protected sex reserves.

The real pro strippers were awesome. They were gorgeous, wore expensive clothes and acted like movie stars. They seemed to float above Sheep World. I wanted to be just like them, and, Lord knows, they responded to admiration. They loved me. The Stage Witches became my family, my role models, my teachers. Those hardcore battleaxes knew every trick in the book. They schooled me on how to dress, do my makeup, dance and scam money from guys. They taught me that you don't have to force men to do anything. You initiate a hint of something in their heads, tinker with their imaginations, sell them their own illusions and grab every dollar you can. Forget about the best-looking or loudest dudes in the place, they told me, you want the most vulnerable men with the most cash.

The undisputed High Priestess of that coven was a woman whose *nom de danse* was "Silky." She was tall, her long, fine hair was as glossy as black silk and her skin was milky. Silky was also wise beyond her years, keen and confident and a mesmerizing dancer. She called guys "mushrooms." When I finally worked up the nerve to ask her why, she said, "Because you should keep them in the dark and feed them shit."

One night, Silky took me into a bathroom. The other Stage Witches were already crowded inside. One of them locked the door. Silky knelt in front of a toilet. Another Witch pulled her hair back from her face. The rest of The Stage Witches formed a circle around the toilet. I took my place among them. No one said anything. It was like we were gathered at an altar for a sacred ritual.

Silky stuck the fingers of one hand deep into her mouth. She gagged and choked and retched until she pulled the hand away and began heaving into the bowl.

Like a liturgy, the others chanted, "Get it all out. You're not done yet. I saw you eat that slice of pizza. Get it out of there. I want to see it. Go until we see the color. Get it out. Where's the color?"

Silky finally stood up and wiped her mouth and eyes with toilet paper.

She pointed at me and said, "If you're going to be a dancer, you have to stay thin. This is how you do it."

"What's 'the color' mean?" I asked.

"You bring food up in the reverse order that you ate it," she said. "The first thing you eat in the day should be something solid and colorful, like some carrot sticks or a couple pieces of celery. When that color comes up, you're done."

She looked at me silently until I realized what she wanted. I knelt in front of the toilet.

As Silky gathered my hair, she said, "If you're going to become one of us, you have to learn to balance your pain."

"What do you mean 'balance your pain?'" I asked, looking up at her.

She said, "Someday, you'll understand" and waited for me to complete the ritual.

Genuflecting before the alabaster altar, the circle of strippers chanting around me, I prayed the Stage Witch prayer.

CHAPTER FIVE

Heather Smith

By 16, I was stripping, too. I was no pole-climbing acrobat. I worked with what God – or my screwed-up gene pool – had given me. The Stage Witches told me never to forget that the customers are spectators, so everything has to be orchestrated to make them participate in the fantasy. They showed me how to locate the money in the room, bust out my best smile, make eye contact and create a personal connection with it. The key was control, they said. Control the fantasy and you control the man and his money. Give the boys a thrill, they said, make them feel good, but never forget that the ultimate goal is to get into their wallets. I soaked up every lesson, unlike when I went to school, which was happening less often all the time.

Since I was underage, I had to perform by a stage name. I have no idea where it came from, but I called myself "Heather Smith."

Heather was dancing at a place in Hilltop called Sugar Babies. The neighborhood wasn't the gutter, but if you went there, you better belong there. Some of the girls at Sugar Babies knew an older lady named Darla, who booked them extra gigs. Heather met Darla and started stripping outside the club, which, of course, can be very dangerous.

Darla called one night and said, "Okay, Heather, you're going to do a female review strip at this bar down by the West

Virginia border."

The show wasn't supposed to start until 10 o'clock, and it was a haul down to the venue. We'd be gone most of the night, so I knew Granny would be upset. The pay was really good, though.

"All right. The hell with it. I'll do it," I said.

"They'll pick you up in the parking lot at Sugar Babies," Darla said. "You'll have a bodyguard who'll also be your driver."

It was me and two girls I didn't know. They didn't look half-bad, but they were losers – already torching up in the car and drinking cheap wine from a bottle and giggling. I sat in the front seat, ignoring them, and we hit the road. The driver, a doughball with a mullet, long sideburns and a scraggly prison-pussy beard, got hopelessly lost. I was annoyed at myself for taking the gig.

We didn't make it to the place until almost midnight. We'd been told to expect a regular bar and a dozen guys. It turned out to be a crummy biker dive, a warehouse that had been converted into a clubhouse. The bikers were drunk and mad as hell; there weren't any dozen of them, either. When we pulled up, 50 or 60 of them oozed out of that beaten-down brick building.

Doughboy cracked the car window and said, "No, there's too many of you. We're backing out of this."

The bikers surrounded the little four-door and rocked it and pounded on it. Doughboy was as nice as could be, but he wasn't going to help us in that situation. The loser girls were in the back seat, trembling and crying and holding each other. 'These guys are going to beat the hell out of this idiot, and God knows what they're going to do to us,' I thought.

"Dude," I said to Doughboy, "it's the middle of the night, we're stuck in BFE, we're staring at bad numbers and they're all drunk. There's no way to protect us, and we can't leave. Hell with it, I'm going to do the gig, or this is all going to end very wrong."

I opened the door and stepped out, wearing my work clothes: black cowboy hat, fringed Western-cut jacket, black bustier, assless leather chaps, high-heeled cowboy boots with chains dangling all over them. Wide eyes and open mouths surrounded me. It was no time to show fear. I waded through a sea of testosterone, chromed-out motorcycles and beer sweat right up to the entrance.

The place was windowless and dark and stank of cigarette smoke, stale beer and unscrubbed toilets. There was a long bar, like a runway, with dance poles on each end. I put my purse on the bar and introduced myself to the three bartenders. They looked at me slack-jawed, like, 'Oh, my God! This girl is going to die tonight, and we can't help her.'

One of them shook his head, took my music cassette, put it in the stereo, swallowed hard and introduced "The Sensational, Sexy Heather Smith of Columbus, Ohio." The other two hoisted me up on the bar and stepped back to watch the gang rape.

The music was so loud it rattled the bottles on the shelves. I danced down the bar, unzipping and pulling at my clothes. I twirled around on the pole and sashayed back. I threw my jacket and my hat and shook my thick blond hair free. The music was pounding, and I was doing my job. I stripped down to my G-string and boots.

The bikers were totally cool. All they wanted was what they were paying for. I didn't even have to stroke them for tips. They cheered and pumped their fists and ran up to the bar and slapped down bills. The bartenders did what Doughboy was supposed to do: collect my clothes, scoop up my tips, keep the music going.

I danced for about an hour and made a pile. When I finished, the bikers handed me clean towels from the bar to dry off.

They escorted me to the car, chanting, *"Hea-ther! Hea-ther! Hea-ther!"*

CHAPTER SIX

z28

Against Granny's wishes, Grandpa bought me a used Camaro z28. She knew I couldn't handle having my own car, but Grandpa loved making me happy. In his eyes, I could do no wrong. When I got the chance, I drove across town to see Johnny. It didn't matter to me that we didn't share the same blood. He was the only person from Lockbourne I missed.

Johnny was hardly ever around, but I knew enough of his friends to track him down. He'd become best buddies with another boy, Luke*, who was just as cute and just as naughty. By coincidence, Luke's sister, Arletta*, had been one of my best friends in Lockbourne. When I bothered to go to school, we all rode the bus together. Once or twice a week, we walked their two dogs a mile and a half to the only store around, the Red & White. Arletta and I hooked up again through the boys.

I'd find Johnny and Luke, smoke a doobie with them and take them to McDonald's. The boys always ordered so much food that the drive-through attendants looked around like they were wondering where the tour bus had parked. I'd get my small salad with no dressing and unsweetened iced tea and hold my breath while I read bills that unfurled from my fingertips to my elbows. I never got away without dropping a couple 20s, but watching the boys enjoy themselves made me as happy as they were.

I wasn't happy about what I was doing to Granny, though. I was hurting that poor woman all the time. I felt terribly guilty, but by then, the streets had grabbed me; there was no going back to normal. A husband, children, holiday dinners, vacations at the lake – I couldn't force myself to do any of it. Something had to give. I could barely read. Graduating from high school, which I probably wasn't going to do anyway, and finding a lameass job in Sheep World meant nothing to me. I would miss my grandparents and Johnny and Arletta, but I had to get away from Columbus.

One night, I started the z28, shifted into first and headed west. My plan was to strip my way across the country – stop at a city, find the best club, talk my way onstage, work a few weeks, party my ass off with the locals and move on. I would use my looks to make a bundle and have a lot of fun.

I didn't stop to think that being beautiful comes with a downside – more people want to fuck you.

CHAPTER SEVEN

Heather Rising

Sneaking off in the middle of the night was the cruelest thing I could've done to my grandparents, but I had another good reason for running – Heather. Granny and Grandpa had rescued their abused, neglected granddaughter, Angela Harter, not an untamed creature named Heather Smith.

At first, Heather was a character I stitched together from bits and pieces of different Stage Witches and some other tough street chicks I knew or saw in movies: a badass curl of the lip here, a vulgar expression there, a fetching toss of the hair, a smoky burr in the voice, a come-hither rasp in the laugh, a cool way to light and smoke a cigarette, a defiant pose. It was pure Method acting. Once I conjured Heather up, though, she wasn't going away. In fact, I could feel her becoming more than an alias.

Heather and Angela were nothing alike. Angela never wore make-up or tight clothes. She was friendly and kind-hearted. Anyone could approach her. If a guy stared at her, she ran. Heather slathered on mascara and blush and dressed in plunging tops, tight jeans and spike heels. She wouldn't be caught dead without lipstick. She wriggled her ass provocatively when she walked, always creating an illusion – 'Maybe. What if?' Anyone who didn't approach Heather carefully might get punched, though. Unlike mild-mannered Angela, she had an explosive temper. Unleashing Heather on two innocent old people just wasn't fair, so we hit the road.

Heather dragged me into expensive gentlemen's clubs, rowdy strip joints and sleazy T&A bars from Columbus to Jackson Hole. Getting gigs was easy. If you look the part, speak the language and know how to behave in that environment, all you have to do is introduce yourself to the owner and act gamey. They handed me the keys every time. The other girls got pissed, but I didn't care. As soon as the spirit moved me, I followed the mile markers and road signs to the next city and the next club.

I kept my Stage Witch apprenticeship in mind and developed my show as I went along. I made my own soundtracks and practiced my routines after hours. Every club keeps a list of seamstresses on hand, so I had costumes made. Sometimes, I walked on stage in an ultra-conservative administrative assistant's business suit – sexy but aloof, my hair pinned up, glasses on a silver chain – and went around cracking dudes with a ruler, like I was saying, 'Excuse me. How dare you look at me like that? What do you think this is?' Then, of course, just when I knocked the customers off-guard, I let my hair down, stripped off my jacket and started the manipulation. Other times, I strutted out in a high-glamour, sequined getup, complete with lame cape, stacked heels, spangly headband and choker. It was straight out of a disco wet dream, just full on: 'Who dares?'

Normally, I had a three-song set. Nobody wants a constant fast show, so I kept the break-in song light. Maybe I'd wear my

Catholic schoolgirl uniform and act coy. That first song was the time to be gentle and get familiar, take it slow and see who was at the bar and what kind of money I was dealing with. I didn't want the boys up screaming on the edge of their seats just yet.

I worked the second song to grab all the cash I could. I didn't get too raunchy, but I wanted the boys amped up and spending. I had a devil costume that I liked to wear for the second song. I put dudes uptight with the naughty fantasies that dragged them into the club – the devil in all of them: 'Oh, I think I saw her pussy'; 'Oh, she put her titties in my face.' That was the time to tear into the crowd and clean house.

The third song slowed the action down again. The stage darkened. I had a few seconds to change, dry off and put my hair up. I had a satin comforter that was tan on one side, blue on the other. While the lights were down, and I was getting my shit together, I had a bouncer put that comforter in the middle of the stage. That third song would be a slow, sensual one, something to calm the crowd while I cleaned out their wallets. I crawled out onto the comforter in my angel outfit and played off of all those nasty fantasies guys have – girls with their hands in their panties, rolling back and forth on their beds, pivoting, doggy-style, moaning like they're in heat.

That's what the boys are paying attention to. What I'm paying attention to is the money. Who's got the cash? Who should I focus on? I had to clean up on my way out, or the next performer was going to get my money.

The Stage Witches told me that only years of experience

could teach me how to target the right dudes in the crowd, but Heather had an instinct for spotting vulnerable men with money. I swear she could smell what was in their pockets. She was also very good at manipulation and suggestion. She liked the loud, macho assholes best, because sending them home broke was so easy. She encouraged them: "Oh, aren't you something? I'll bet you have a *big* cock. Can you use that big hard thing, baby?" Just when they thought they were all that, she made fools of them, took their money and sat them down.

The cash rolled in. I didn't even bother with laundry. I left my clothes behind in motel rooms and hit the malls for new ones. I'm sure I made a lot of housekeepers very happy. I was a like a dragonfly blown along by the wind.

I went to work in a gentleman's club called Showgirls, in Ft. Wayne. Showgirls wasn't elaborate, but it was hopping. It was a shotgun place, like an elongated box. When you walked through the doors, the bouncers were sitting right there. The bar was on your left. The stage was a rectangle in the middle of the room, with one pole. The pool tables and customer tables were on the right side.

There were rules: no complete nudity; no raunchiness on stage; pasties on your nipples. The crowd was mostly mannerly businessmen who tipped well. I worked from 8 o'clock to three or so. Even on a slow midweek night, I could guarantee 500 bucks in my purse. The club didn't charge dancers a stage fee to perform, like some places did, so we spread our tips around to the bartenders, waitresses and, especially, the bouncers.

The money was so good – and the venue so calm – that I decided to stick around. I moved into an apartment with another dancer named Lori. When he found out I loved animals, a loser maintenance man who thought he was going get in my G-string bought me a Himalayan kitten I called Trinity. Lori dug animals, too, so Trinity became our third roommate. He was a grouch most of the time, griping constantly in a shrill, nasal whine, but Trinity was beautiful, and his sour little face cracked me up.

Everything was cool. The only wildcard was Heather. She'd become so volatile that it was impossible to predict what she was going to do.

I went on about 12:30 one morning, did my preliminary work and stepped aside as Heather squeezed the crowd. Some drunk Frat Twerp and a bunch of his buddies came in. That dickhead ripped a $100 bill in two and handed Heather half. He took the other half, creased it and put it over his nose, grinning, like, 'Sit on my face if you want the other half, bitch.' I'd had idiots jump on stage with me, paw me like I was an animal in a petting zoo and try to grab my tips and run. Heather and the bouncers handled them easily. Something about the Frat Twerp hit me wrong, though.

He was sitting at a table right against the stage; Heather towered over him, smiling. All his little frat buddies were going, 'Tee, hee, hee.' Heather bent down, aimed her fist at that half a hundred and power-drove him out of his seat. She left him unconscious on the floor and went to the dressing room.

The bouncers threw that bunch out and brought me the other half of the bill and a bag of ice for my hand. They were laughing and calling me "Rocky." I had my hundred bucks, but as usual, I'd screwed myself. I hurt my hand so bad that I cooked the rest of that shift and a couple nights afterward. Angela doesn't know why it happened, and Heather's not talking, but punching the Frat Twerp cost me a bundle.

CHAPTER EIGHT

Heather Captured

One night, six or seven new guys came into Showgirls, flashing a lot of cash. They were all dressed in standard-issue *Scarface* uniforms: shiny suits, silk shirts with open collars and a bunch of gold. The main guy was named Melvin. He even looked like Tony Montana – nasty, dark and short. He wasn't loud, but he acted like he was always ready to make some moves. Melvin ignored every dancer except Heather. He sat in front of her and stared up with little, mean, black eyes, peeling big tips off a fat roll. Of course, Heather played to the money.

Over that weekend, he kept coming back with his crew and sitting right in front of her. Everybody in the club was making fun of me – "Oh, oh, Melvin's back to see Heather."

I smiled and counted my growing wad.

The third or fourth night he was there, I was walking out to my car after work. For some reason, the bouncer didn't accompany me, like he usually did. I didn't mind, because I'd parked close to the door. I got in, but before I could pull the door closed, a limousine pulled behind me, blocking me.

Someone called, "Hey, remember us? Come on over here, doll."

I saw it was Melvin and his crew.

You have to respond to the cash, so I said, very cheerfully,

"Hey, dudes, what's up?"

I left my car door open and my purse and keys on the seat and walked to the limo. I could make out the dark forms of several guys sitting in the back. The door swung open. 'Damn, it smells like someone's burning rubber in there,' I thought, and then hands reached out and grabbed my arms and pulled me into the limo. They held me down and hit me with a hypodermic. Whatever that shot was, it knocked me right out.

It seemed like I was comatose for hours. When I came to, there were guys sitting across from me on those backwards limo bucket seats. One of them was holding a little glass pipe coated with something that looked like tar. He was grinning like a hyena. His teeth were stained a nasty brown-black; his eyes were looking right through me.

'Holy shit, Ang!' I thought. 'These motherfuckers are smoking crank. You're in deep shit!'

I'd done more than my share of drugs, but I wouldn't go near meth. I watched it transform humans into drooling beasts within weeks, if not days. Melvin was holding me across his lap. I was crunched between him and another guy. I was pretty sure we were headed west, through endless, flat, dark fields.

When the sun rose, I was woozy. We climbed a long gravel driveway and stopped on a plateau in front of a metal warehouse that looked bigger than an airplane hanger. I got out of the car, stumbled and fell. Melvin and another guy carry-dragged me toward a door.

Whatever was going on in that warehouse was a big operation. There was a helicopter sitting on a pad to my right and lots of cars and trucks, all high-end stuff – Hummers and Mercedes and Jags – parked around the mouth of the driveway, like a luxury car dealership. There were dozens of workers coming and going. They weren't talking. They weren't asking questions. Everyone seemed to know his purpose.

Some guy charged out of the door, straight at Melvin. He was tall and skinny with light brown hair and had on a wife beater and a thick gold necklace and bracelet – a semi-badass Mafia Pledge Boy talking a lot of junk. Two guys with pistols in shoulder holsters followed him.

"Who the hell is *she*?" he screamed at Melvin. "What the fuck do you think you're doing?"

"Nah, nah, it's cool,' Melvin told him. "That's Heather. She's my girlfriend."

Meanwhile, I'd never said more than hello to him.

They dragged me into the warehouse. In the front part, freezer strips covered all the doorways. It looked like an auto body shop. Another room was filled with expensive-looking furniture. As Melvin and Pledge Boy bickered, things became tense.

"I'm just here to change out cars," Melvin finally said. "I'm not staying."

"Get the fuck out!" Pledge Boy said.

We got into a brand-new Lincoln. Two of the crew stayed

behind, but the other two went with us. They sat up front. Melvin and I were in the back. They kept me pretty doped. I went in and out of consciousness. Almost every time I woke up, they were holding a lighter to that glass pipe and passing it over the seats and babbling about the women they fucked or the dudes they fucked up. The chemical fumes made my eyes water. I tasted sulphur.

We stopped in Niagara Falls. It was dark and rainy and foggy. We parked in front of a bar with a shamrock on a sign over the door.

We went upstairs into an office, where a fat guy was sitting at a desk, like a toad on a rock. He had muttonchops and wore a white, short-sleeved, button-up shirt with two black stripes on the front, a gold watch as thick as a waffle and a heavy gold necklace, like all of those guys did. The Toad treated Melvin just like Pledge Boy had – like he was a fuck-up who needed to get his act together. Melvin kept apologizing and stroking him and assuring him everything would be fine. Then Melvin said he had to go somewhere and walked to the door. As he left, he looked at me over his shoulder like, 'Brace yourself, bitch.'

I remember The Toad's fat hand on the knob, pulling the door shut. I started to say something threatening like, 'You better keep your hands off me, asshole,' but before I could put my thoughts together, he was on me. He backhanded me so hard that snot and spit flew and then punched me in the stomach. I doubled over and retched. I didn't have anything in me to throw up except greenish, yellowish slime. I couldn't catch my breath.

He slapped me around without making a sound, but his face looked like he was conversing with himself or turning himself on somehow. He tore the button from my jeans and pulled them off, bent me over his desk, held me down by my hair and raped me, still mumbling to himself.

The Toad finished with a grunt, said, "Clean yourself up and sit there on that chair" and left.

My whole face throbbed. My lips were swollen. I felt my left eye puffing up and getting warm. I was pissed because I'd let myself get trapped in a box and handed off to a fat dirtbag like a party favor.

The door was right across from me. There was a phone on the desk and a letter opener next to it. It's easy to say: 'Oh, I'd just grab the phone and dial 911'; or, 'I'd stab him with the letter opener'; or, 'I'd kick him in the balls and run.' Run where? I was a kid. I was uncertain. I was stoned and sick. I'd been raped and beaten. Even if that door wasn't locked and I made it out of the office, then what? If I picked up that phone, and he came in or someone else was on an extension, then what? If I tried to stab him and didn't bring it off, then what?

'I might not make it out of this alive,' I thought, my insides turning cold. 'This isn't any fucking television show. I've seen these guys' faces. Why would they let me live?'

The kidnapping, the beating, the rape, the drugs, the exhaustion, the fear, the pain – I no longer felt like I was on earth in a living reality. I sat there terrified that whatever opened the door next might be even worse than what I'd already been through. Thank goodness, nothing did.

The bar was within walking distance of Rainbow Mall. Since I had only the clothes on my back, Melvin's guys took me shopping. I was under heavy guard, and those dudes were not nice. Any time I opened my mouth, someone said, "Shut the fuck up, bitch." If I pissed anyone off, I got smacked or punched.

In the midst of the nastiness, Melvin would creep up on me and tell me how much he loved me, how much he needed me, how much he wanted to marry me. The first time, I yelled, "Fuck you, you piece of shit!" Then he beat me and raped me. After that, I refused to say anything.

We finally left Niagara Falls. We went south with the two other thugs. As we stopped along the way, the cast of characters changed. Dirtbags disappeared, new ones replaced them. Obviously, some business stream connected them, but I didn't know what it was – chop shops, human trafficking, running crystal?

Melvin kept me jacked out of my mind. Whenever we stopped at a motel and he left me alone, he handcuffed me to the toilet or sink. I was constantly terrified, high and confused.

That sicko had a thing about cords. He smashed lamps and used the cords to whip me and then choked me out while he screwed me. Afterward, he'd calm down, run his hands over my face and say, "I really do love you." I thought I could play into that, but a couple of hours later, he'd tear a hair dryer out of the bathroom wall and strangle me with the cord while he fucked me.

At every turn, I was looking for a way to jump. They knew it. They watched me carefully. They had no gaps. The only potential gaps were the people, but I couldn't get close to anyone.

Melvin drank and sucked on the glass pipe all the time. I waited for him to fall asleep or get sloppy, but he never did. It was like booze and meth were his regular diet. He barely slept, and even when he did, I could feel his eyes on me.

One night, he went berserk in a shitty motel in Mississippi or Missouri. He beat me from one room to the next. I couldn't get away from him. He chased me and punched me and choked me and kicked me for at least 15 minutes. I tried to fight back, but he was much bigger and cranked out of his skull. It was futile. When it was finally over, I lay on the floor between a bed and a wall, where I'd rolled to get away from him.

I was hypnotized by the sight of my blood on the flat white institutional paint. I kept touching it and smearing it around like a finger-painting, amazed I could lose so much and still be alive. I wondered what would happen when the poor maid came in the next morning and found a psychotic child's artwork on the wall.

I went into the bathroom, wiped the blood from my face with a damp towel and looked in the mirror. My eyes were swollen and bruised. He'd split my upper lip so bad that I could see my teeth through the tear. I was sure Melvin was going to kill me. I would never see Granny or Grandpa or Johnny or grumpass

Trinity or anything else that I'd taken for granted for so long again.

CHAPTER NINE

The Bald Guy in The Ball Gag

After dropping the last of the other guys off along the way, Melvin drove to a private home in suburban Houston. It was late. A woman opened the door, and as soon as she did, I could tell there was bad history between them. She was older, with blond, butchy hair. She was in shorts and a shirt, very casual, like Ellen DeGeneres on steroids with a dash of sinister thrown in.

Melvin gave her instructions: "Hey, I've got to go take care of some things. I want you to hold on to her. I'll be back. Let her sleep and get her something to eat."

The woman didn't know what was going on, but she knew who she was dealing with, so she said I could stay. We walked through the fancy, hand-carved front door and came off the landing into a huge sunken living room. There was a long bar and a big winding couch set in the middle of the room. Everything was gorgeous.

Ellen stopped, looked at me and said, "Honey, tell me what's going on."

I was still so befuddled that I couldn't piece it all together. I wasn't sure what to make of her, either. I wanted to trust her, but I had no idea what that woman's world was. 'Play the game and buy time,' I thought. 'At this point, what do you have to lose?'

As I followed her through the house, she was laying down lines of coke, and we were snorting them. She led me into a big kitchen, brought me a drink and said, "Now, tell me how you got here. How did you meet Melvin?"

Now, the blow was talking. Before I could stop myself, I spilled the whole story. When I was done, she said, "Let me tell you, honey, that is a dangerous man."

I already knew that, of course, yet hearing her say it scared me even worse.

She told me to follow her again while she went around to different rooms in the house. She kept asking me questions and answering the phone, which rang every few minutes. She was obviously preparing for something big. I finally figured out she was a madam. She had a Heidi Fleiss thing going on, placing girls out on calls, but she also had a side hustle at the house. That woman had probably seen hundreds of girls like me – young, scattered, in deep shit. She was getting ballsy, too. I could see plans for me forming in her eyes.

"I've got company coming, so I have to leave for a little while," she said. "Why don't you go to work for me? You'll make good money, and I'll take care of you. When Melvin shows up, I'll tell him you ran away. I'll take that bite on the ass, and you can stay here. Think about it."

By then, I was on a go-fast cocaine thrill ride that was making my heart race and my head swim. I just needed a minute away from her to compute what was happening. She took me into a dark room and laid me on a bed.

"You just nap in here while I take care of my appointment," she said, "and then we can talk and figure this out."

I lay down. She sat next to me.

"I'll be done with my company in a little while. We're going to work this out," she said.

She started stroking my hair. I'd been picking up on vibes that this woman was going to try to make it with me, and I was not digging it. I closed my eyes and pretended to sleep; she kept petting me.

She finally gave up and went to meet her "company." About a half an hour later, I got up. I'm guessing it was half an hour. I was so groggy I couldn't keep track of time. I wandered out of the bedroom and turned off of a hall into the pit of that place.

I'd seen more action in my life than I wanted to remember, but I had no reference point for the kind of sick stuff that woman had going on. She was in a studded, leathery, feathery, freaky costume, with an old bald guy who looked like Alfred Hitchcock. He was about 70, naked, on his hands and knees, all tied up with a leather cord and a ball gag in his mouth. She was behind him, holding a big dildo in one studded leather hand and the end of the leather cord in the other. It was like a mediaeval torture scene.

The freak show added to the madness. I turned around and scurried back down the hallway and lay on the bed in the dark, trying to figure out my next move.

A little while later, the door opened. I was on my side, fully dressed, and she came in wearing that freaky costume and tried to talk to me. Again, I pretended to be asleep, but I was completely tripping. No thought, no vision, nothing around me made any sense, but it was all too real. Ellen sat on the bed again; now, I had to talk to her.

She told me Hitchcock was one of her long-standing clients. Obviously, he had money. Coming to her house for that kind of special party wasn't any 500 bucks, that's for sure. I didn't know exactly what kind of conversation they'd had about me, but she must've bullshitted him.

She gave me a little card and said, "He saw you, and he liked you. He wanted me to give you his card. If you ever get to Florida, this guy will hook you up, and you can make some serious money."

I didn't want anything to do with that weirdness, but I shoved the card in my back pocket.

CHAPTER TEN

Tex

When Melvin came back, I was in a bedroom right off the front door and down the hall with Ellen, who was still trying to talk me into going to work for her. We were not ready for him, but he pounded on the door until she had to open it. He was furious about something.

"Leave her here," Ellen said. "She's not in good shape. Go do what you have to do and come back in a few days."

Melvin either knew she was going to try to pull something with me, or whatever he'd been doing had gone sour, because he got even angrier. Real quick, both of them were yelling, "Fuck you! Fuck you!"

Melvin grabbed me, and we left. We ended up at a Howard Johnson's right off the freeway not far from that woman's house. When we got there, he opened the connecting door to the next room. Two younger guys Melvin knew were staying there. Those dudes weren't Mafia. They were white, rough-looking, countrified guys in their 30s. The taller one reminded me of a something out of Urban Cowboy: pointy boots, bowlegged, tightass jeans, big belt buckle, wide-brimmed hat. His name even turned out to be "Tex," and both of them really were from Texas.

Tex's partner was short and scrawny and agreed with

everything Tex said. I don't know if they were dealing drugs or what. Nobody told me anything. Melvin handcuffed me to the bed and went to their room. I heard him repeat pretty much what he said to the Ellen woman: "Don't let her out of your sight. Don't lay a finger on her. I'll be back."

The Texans weren't very bright, but they tried to be sweet. Tex was cute and, right away, got all flirty and touchy. They brought me snacks and a can of soda. They played cards and kept the door between the rooms open so they could watch me and talk.

Melvin came back a couple hours later and told them he was going to be gone overnight.

"Look, dude," Tex said, "it's really messed up you got her handcuffed. We'll vouch for her. We'll take care of her. We'll make sure that she's not going anywhere. Just keep the handcuffs off."

Before he left, Melvin surprised me by removing the cuffs. It was dark, and the boys took me out to the swimming pool. We had our elbows up on the side and were getting friendly. I was coming down off the drugs, relaxing and starting to think semi-rationally. They said they had "some stuff going on with Mel." They weren't really in with him full-time, though. They knew he was a dick and were clearly scared of him.

When I told them what'd happened, Tex said, "You've got to be kidding me. That's really messed up. We can get you out of this."

I thought they might be my chance to escape, then trouble started again. I was getting dressed, my hair still damp from the pool, and Melvin came back. He was irritated, pacing, not talking to the boys. The connecting door was closed. He finally went over there, and right at dawn, he rushed back into the room. He had his gun out. He snatched me up and dragged me to the car. He didn't even pay the bill. He was scrambling, like something he hadn't anticipated had happened, and he needed to get out of there immediately.

CHAPTER ELEVEN

Rough Landing in Miami

Melvin drove to the airport, left the Lincoln in the parking lot and hauled me onto a flight for Miami. He thought he had me under control, but I wasn't handcuffed anymore, and the plane was full. By that time, my head was pretty clear, and I'd had enough of that psycho.

As soon as the plane lifted off, I shouted, "This guy kidnapped me and raped me! He's an asshole!"

Everybody flipped.

He tried to calm things down: "No. She's on drugs. I'm trying to help her get clean. She's my girlfriend."

The flight crew led me up to the concession area, pulled out a little jump seat, put me in it and kept an eye on Melvin. I tried to tell the attendants who I was, who he was and what was going on. They weren't digging him, but they weren't believing me, either. They didn't know what to do other than keep us separated until we landed.

As he got off the plane, he tried to take me with him. He was still acting like he was the sane one and I was a crazy troublemaker. An attendant stood between us and said, "No, no, no. We're going to keep her here. We're calling airport security. You get off first."

He walked very slowly down the ramp, arguing, until he got

onto the concourse. As the flight crew walked me out, he was still running his mouth, trying to convince them that he was responsible for me.

Security didn't come running like they would now. Finally, a pair of rent-a-cops moseyed up. They didn't know who Melvin was, so they walked right past him. When he saw them, he shut up, murked into the crowd and started making his way out of the airport. I tried to explain to the security guards what was going on, but I didn't know who he was other than his first name, and I probably seemed pretty frazzled.

The last I saw of Melvin, I was standing near the door to the taxi line. He was in the back seat of a cab, four or five cars ahead, glowering at me like he wanted to drag me back into that motel room in Mississippi or Missouri to finish what he'd started. Before I could say anything, the cab pulled away.

CHAPTER TWELVE

Black Sky, Black Water

Since I didn't have any money or even any ID, I couldn't leave Miami. I was so wigged out the airport people didn't know what to do with me. I had no idea even who to call. I certainly didn't want Granny to know what had gone down. But I was in Florida, and what was in my back pocket? I pulled out Hitchcock's business card. I looked at a wall map, and according to the address, he lived in that area. I didn't know exactly who he was, but he was totally cool when I called. He came to the airport and picked me up in his rich old man car – a silver, two-door Cadillac with white walls and spoked rims.

He took me to a penthouse on the 15th floor of an exclusive complex, across the street from the beach. There were brass mailboxes in a brass lobby and a private elevator for residents. There was nothing comforting in his condo. It was a cold, shiny, sterile environment – marble and glass and brass, no plants, no drop pillows, no family pictures, no magnets on the fridge. I guessed it was his fuck pad, if you want to call what that dude was into "fucking."

Hitchcock's bald head reflected the light, as he told me that I looked like I could use a shower. He was right. I was freezing when I came out into the air conditioning, so I put on a pair of his satin pajamas. They were cold and shiny, too. The only warm thing I felt in there was a fluffy white robe he gave me.

Once again, I didn't know who I was trapped with, so I was jumpy. Since the Ellen woman had probably lied like hell to him about me, he didn't know what I'd been through. He thought I was working girl connected to that woman and knew the drill.

He poured me a drink and apologized that there was nothing to eat in the condo. He offered to order takeout for me. I didn't want to wait around for food and then have to eat in front of him. I wanted gone and on my way home. I tried to put out an edgy vibe, like I was seconds away from snapping, and he didn't want to be holding the bag when I went off. That wasn't far from the truth.

"This isn't my thing," I told him. "I have no way to get home. I'm stranded."

"Oh, why don't you stay?" he said. "I'll give you $15000 cash and all the shopping you can handle to stay here for one month."

We were at checkmate. The money was more than right; I wasn't going into any bedroom with that man, though. I'd seen his idea of fun, and I wasn't that advanced. He didn't get aggressive or anything, but he kept trying to touch me. I cinched the robe tight around me and stayed on the move.

I said, "Oh, I've never seen the ocean. Can we go look at it?"

He said we could see it from the roof. While we climbed some stairs, I kept Hitchcock in my peripheral vision, which is hard to do with one eye. I never turned and faced him, because that would've been a signal to start something. There was a private pool area on the roof, with lounge chairs and palm trees and tropical flowers.

The ocean was no big yip – no horizon, just sky on water, black on black, with a glimmer of silent lightening way off somewhere and bobbing lights from a few boats and the sound of the waves whomping and hissing on the sand. I was weak from the drugs, drained, trying to find an angle. I pretended to be interested in the people strolling along the beach. I was ready to bolt at any second, but I had nowhere to go. I seriously considered jumping off that roof. I looked at the black sea again and thought about sharks hunting the dark water around shipwrecks with crews of drowned sailors.

Finally facing Hitchcock, I said, "Dude, I just want to go home."

He wasn't pleased, but the next day, he put me on a plane for Ohio. When I got to Columbus, I gave Granny a PG overview of what happened, and she took me to the hospital. They put me in detox. They drew blood, examined the needle marks on my arms and butt, ran a rape kit, tested me for venereal disease and pregnancy. My eye was purple, I had bite marks on my legs, torn lips, a necklace of bruises, welts on my back, abrasions around my wrists. I was wired. If you were a guy, you couldn't flinch or talk too loud around me, because I'd react instantly, and you'd better duck, because I was coming right at you.

Some federal agents showed up, flipping badges, to debrief me. They came around every day, asking follow-up questions or getting the timeline straight. As they brought up new stuff, they asked more questions, not that I could tell them a whole hell of a lot.

Melvin turned out to be a long-standing badass. They told me he was from Battle Creek, Michigan, and he was on some Top 10 list or something. They said he was into distributing porn in addition to lots of other uncool stuff. The feds wanted me to keep playing with him. They wanted to use me as bait, see if he showed up, wear a wire and all that shit. As soon as she heard just how much of a creep he was, Granny wasn't having it.

"No, we're done. We're done. We're going home," she said.

I don't know if they ever caught Melvin; I was never called to testify. I don't know what happened to Tex and his little buddy, either. Sometimes when I try to remember that night, I'm sure I hear gunshots; other times, I'm equally sure I don't hear anything. I'm absolutely certain, however, that I don't ever want to catch up with Melvin again. He was one very nasty guy.

I didn't have any way of talking to that Ellen lady in Texas, either, not that I really wanted to. I never got a phone number, I didn't know the address and she had no way to get hold of me. She was a screwball, too, but she was running some serious action. She catered to high-end, specialty stuff and from what I know now, was making heavy money. I'm sure if I'd been more mature, we could've worked something out. That would've been a trip, but I wasn't there yet.

CHAPTER THIRTEEN

Cyrus

I must've had PTSD, because I tried to go back to Showgirls. They wanted nothing to do with me. Strip clubs get jerked around by so many girls that they don't fuck with anyone. The manager flat out told me that if I was dumb enough to get kidnapped, I shouldn't be working there. They wouldn't even give me my last paycheck. At least the cops still had the z28 and purse.

I packed up Trinity and what little else I owned from Lori's apartment and went back to my grandparents' house. Granny and Grandpa were overjoyed to have me home. Granny bustled around, getting my room ready, cooking mountains of food, insisting that I eat and rest. I was happy to be back, but Granny could tell something wasn't right. She hugged me, held my hand and talked softly to me. She didn't ask many questions, and I couldn't let her know the whole truth.

I smoked reefer and drank Little Kings while I tried to figure out my next move. I finally settled down enough to call Arletta. When we met, she was so happy that she asked me to move into the townhouse that she, Luke and Johnny were renting in Reynoldsburg. I went home with her, eager to see the boys.

They were all beautiful people. Arletta was the most ethereal woman I've ever seen face-to-face – a 6-foot Amazon with long brown hair parted in the middle and brown eyes flecked with amber and a perpetually bronzed complexion. Johnny had grown up to be tall, dark and muscular, with black hair and long lashes and thick black brows. He was funny and daring and immature. Luke was just as handsome and charismatic and just as much of a delinquent. They'd started out by siphoning gas from cars and selling it to older guys and moved on to breaking into houses and dealing pot.

I promised my grandparents I would visit often and moved with Trin to Reynoldsburg. Things worked out perfectly. We four were thicker than thieves. The arrangement didn't last long, though. I suck at cooking, and there were stupid little lacy curtains hanging right beside the stove. I caught them on fire. We were all really high, so the blaze quickly got out of control. Poof – I did $15000 damage. We moved into a nice two-bedroom place on the west side.

Of course, money was an issue. One day, I bumped into my half-sister Patty. She told me some old black chick named Mona, who was kind of like a madam, was taking calls from men and passing them on to her for a percentage. I listened to her, thinking, 'Ang, you're 18 and have nothing to show for it except a cranky cat and two lifetimes worth of grief. Men have been dogging your tail your whole life. All you've ever gotten out of it are bruises and nightmares. For once, why not use what you have to your advantage and make some real money?'

The irony of my going into hooking is that I've never had any interest in sex except as a tool; I absolutely don't want to screw anyone. I don't like to be touched, and I've never allowed anyone to kiss me. A kiss is too familiar, too personal. For normal people, I think, the word "sex" connotes love, commitment, loyalty, children, family. Not for me. Sex, for me, has never been sacred, beautiful or intimate. It never had a chance to be.

My childhood was strange and disturbing in more ways than I've admitted. The summer I turned 12, my best friend was Audra Jackson*. She lived down the street from The Hag. I slept at her house all the time. She had lots of brothers and sisters who were all very nice. I loved the girls and felt like part of their family. Their house was a free-fire zone. There were huge wild parties that went on for days, cases of Little Kings on ice, lots of weed, Skynyrd or Credence blasting. We kids were right in the middle of it. No one cared if we drank or smoked pot.

Audra's parents were divorced, but her dad, whose street name was Cyrus*, was in and out of the house all the time. He was a tough guy who hung around with other tough guys and had tough kids. Hip and fading handsome, he had a long mullet and a beard and wore a jean jacket cut off at the sleeves, ripped and faded Levi's, wraparound shades and a big leather wallet on a chain. He was forever working on his Harley.

A set of rickety steps led down into the full basement of the Jacksons' long shotgun house. There were several "showers" down there – really just sprinkler heads above drainpipes, all wide open, without walls or curtains. I'd go down to shower with Audra and a few of her sisters, some older, some younger. While we splashed and soaped and giggled and rinsed and toweled, Cyrus sat on the steps and chitchatted with us. Since the girls acted like it was perfectly normal, I did, too. It wasn't. My best friend's father did everything short of fuck me.

Cyrus would wait until everyone else was stoned around the fire or passed out and then slip up behind me, like he didn't want me to see his face. He'd reach under my top and feel me up or put his hands down my pants and finger me. When he thought it was safe, he pulled my clothes off and kissed my neck, pinched my nipples, nuzzled my hair, stroked my ass and rubbed between my legs with his calloused hands, telling me how hot I was and how much I turned him on. He hugged me and ground against me, making a contented burbling sound in his throat, like he was swallowing a big gulp of the powerful moonshine he cooked in a secret still. His hard dick poked at my back.

Cyrus's beard was as scratchy as wire. His fingernails were crescents of grease. His hot breath was the worst, though. It smelled like adult – curdled milk in cold coffee, booze, cigarettes, rotting food stuck between teeth. It turned my stomach. I don't know why he didn't try to go all the way with me. To be honest, I don't know what I would've done if he had. I never tried to stop Cyrus. I knew I couldn't stop him. If I'd learned nothing else by then, it was that I had no power, no control over my own life.

The first few times, he handed me a couple 20s or a bag of weed when he was done and whispered, "Don't tell anyone about this. This is our secret."

The next day, Cyrus always went back to being Cool

Daddy/Buddy, passing around fat bomber joints or mason jars of his latest batch of kickass shine.

I felt sick, scared and guilty, but, really, who would I tell? What would telling get me? The truth is I was terrified that someone would catch us. I had too much at stake – friends, a home where I was accepted, the basics that normal people take for granted. When I wasn't at the Jacksons', the moment I woke up every morning, the tape loop of questions began playing in my head: 'Where are you going to sleep tonight? What will you do for food? How can you stay safe?' Nothing was certain.

Sex was the only commodity I had to trade for the necessities of life: a warm place to sleep, clean clothes, a little bit of fucking toothpaste and a brush to squirt it on. What I was doing had nothing to do with right, wrong, sin, virtue, morality; it was about survival. Cyrus knew I was vulnerable, and he exploited that weakness, drawing me into in a conspiracy of deceit and denial against friends who really cared for me.

Those trysts with Cyrus were the first time I was actually cognizant of what was happening; however, I can't say I lost my innocence that summer. How can you lose what you never had? That's when I took to the streets totally. I began trading myself for some Thai stick, a couple lines of blow, a handful of 'shrooms, a hit or two of acid – analgesics all. After a while, it became what was expected of me; worse, it's what I expected of myself. I was a helpless kid who couldn't provide for herself, while the grownups around me were opportunists who used me however they could. I learned to fake it and detach myself from what was happening, while I skipped off to play in magic gardens with bronze unicorns and funny stone dogs and romp the narrow, quiet hallways of an enchanted castle, alone and content.

That fall, I entered the seventh grade.

CHAPTER FOURTEEN

Beach Babes

After I talked to Patty that day, I decided to go into hooking fulltime – as an entrepreneur. I wasn't about to work for anyone. That decision probably sounds extreme for someone so young – and so damaged – to make. It didn't seem that way to me. Years of molestation and my natural hatred of authority prevented me from developing the inhibitions and controls that Sheep People have. To me, laws and rules and organized religion were meant to turn me into a good little obedient girl – "angelic," like my name. Rebelliousness was always in me, though, and I never learned to say "no" to it. Sexual abuse only heightened it. I easily jumped over boundaries that Sheep People wouldn't dare cross.

Arletta always wanted to know about anything I got into, so I turned her on to escorting. She acted snooty and above it all, but she was actually a cheerleader gone rouge – a perfect escort, in other words. She was the only person who knew that Angela Harter and Heather Smith were one in the same.

Arletta became Candy, and we took out an ad in the classified section of the *Columbus Dispatch*, just a phone number and "Beach Babes, Escorts," even though neither of us had ever set foot on an actual beach. We paid 10 bucks a week and sat back and took the calls. Since the boys sold reefer, there was plenty of cash around.

I immediately saw that escorting is a lot like stripping, so I just applied The Stage Witches' lessons to my new job. Once again, it was all about creating illusions. If you're not ahead of the game and controlling it, what're you going to do, tell the client "No"? That's going to go south real quick. The men have the money, and girls who aren't hip to the game end up whoring for 50 bucks a trick: 'Your time's up. Who's next?' That's all wrong. First, like The Stage Witches said, you have to consider your clientele. You're looking for the most vulnerable men – older, lonely, square, with money. Then you have to figure out what they're really looking for. Of course, everybody wants to get off, but The Stage Witches taught me that every dude is seeking something else, too: attention, praise, affection, admiration, dominance, submission, fear? And lies, they all want lies, lots of lies. Find a guy's vulnerability, and you can tailor your lies to it. If you massage that weakness just the right way, it'll lead you directly to his heart. From there, it's an easy drive to his hip pocket.

Sex, The Stage Witches said, is more addictive than any drug, and that's how you handle it. Give a guy a free taste and then back away and wait. Eventually, he'll be happy to show you exactly how to fuck up his life. He'll tell you his wildest wishes, while you tell him – or suggest strongly – that you'll hand all those fantasies back to him, erotic increment by erotic increment, if only he'll pay you enough to do it.

Say you're a customer at a club where I'm dancing, a well-off seminerd whose wife treats him like shit. Some of your buddies have dragged you into the place to watch the premier performer, whose name happens to be Heather Smith. You've already had a couple too many gin and tonics, when Heather, the hottest babe in the club, makes eye contact with you during her routine. She dances down the stage past a line of guys eagerly waving bills. She stops right in front of you and shimmies there like you're the main stud in the club. You gulp your drink and hand her your cash, promising yourself that you're going to find her after the show and ask her for a date. That night, you confess your deepest desires to her, and just like that, you're hooked. Over and over, Heather hanged dudes with a rope they helped her weave out of their own wet dreams and fragile egos.

Thanks to The Stage Witches, I came to every gig with plans A through F chambered: 'Tick tock. You got an hour. What're you going to do?' I'm in control, but the client doesn't realize it, because I'm being super nice: "Three hundred. That's fine. Lie down here. Get comfortable. Oh, you're really cute. I'll bet you work out. Did you play football or something?"

The client thinks, 'Ooo, my wife never makes me feel this good. She treats me like an idiot. I knew I was smart. I knew I was sexy.' As he inches toward, 'I want more. I want more,' I'm working to get deeper into his head and his wallet, so I say: "Oh, you know what? We only have 20 minutes left. How much are you willing to go?"

They say animals don't choose, they do; that's a perfect description of a man's dick, as well, so no matter what he offers, you raise the bar. You have to make it sound attainable, though. All the while, you're beating the clock. You want to make them feel like, 'Oh, I hope I didn't waste her time. I want to see her again. I need to have more money next time.' They never get the clue: 'I'm not going to fuck you, jackass, until you walk in with an ATM strapped to your back and give me the code.' Once things get to that point, the client's greatest fear is that Heather will disappear, taking with her that sweet, magic tickle he felt one adolescent midnight in his dark bedroom 30 years ago. He's bewitched. He'll give her his car keys, his bankroll, his eyeteeth – anything for just one more hit.

You have to be taught those things, like I was, so when you find the Big Fish with major money, they're not controlling the situation. Most amateurs never know what I know, and there's no one left to teach them. The old pros who believed in a fair price for specialized services are a dying breed, if not already extinct. It's not something I'd be willing to pass on to younger girls. It doesn't happen overnight, it's not easy, it's not safe. Once you take someone's money, you invite him into your life. Then things can become complicated. I had an advantage over most girls, though: When it came time for the heavy lifting, Angela went out for coffee and let Heather handle it. Angela is a Virgo, after all.

That might sound callous, but we weren't bad people. I've always been willing to help anybody, even when it hurts me. Johnny was the class clown who kept everyone entertained. Luke was so nice he put on a suit and took my mentally retarded half-sister to her senior prom when she didn't have a date. Arletta is the kindest person I've ever known. We weren't trying to hurt anyone or get rich. We just liked to get high and didn't have any legitimate way of making decent money.

Man, we had some fun. We were kids, barely legal age, and it was an active environment. There were wild characters coming in and out of our lives day and night. We had money, so we got wasted every night and giggled our way through the three-ring circus.

CHAPTER FIFTEEN

You'll Go Straight to Hell!

The party rolled on right up until Arletta and I got pregnant at the same time. We shouldn't have let it happen, but we did, and we were in a serious mess. The thought of abortion sickened both of us. The last thing I wanted was to hurt any of God's creatures, least of all one growing inside me. However, we were in no position to take care of babies and weren't even sure who the fathers were.

As lovely and compassionate as she was, Arletta was also a pure badass. One night at a crowded house party, some guy wouldn't stop bugging me. He was grabbing at me and getting nasty. Arletta snuck up on him, punched him behind the ear, knocked him senseless and walked away without saying a word. People moved out of her way like she was a lioness who'd shown up to party. She went to pieces, though, over the predicament we were in. She sobbed all the time and didn't want to get out of bed.

I was freaking, too, but we had few options. I needed Heather, not as a disguise but as a surrogate who would take over and do what had to be done, no matter the cost or stress or pain. Heather told Johnny and Luke exactly what was going to happen and ordered them to stay out of it.

She told Arletta, "We've got to move forward and get beyond

this."

We had to hustle hard to pay our regular bills and make $350 each extra for the abortions. Once we rounded up the cash, I drove us to a parking lot across from the clinic and we got out. Protesters were four-deep in front of the door, shouting and waving handmade signs and Bibles. Arletta hesitated, tears streaming down her face. I grabbed her hand. We crossed the street and shoved through the crowd. People screamed at us, pushed us, tried to break our hands apart.

"Get the fuck off us!" Heather snarled. "Don't you dare touch us!"

She only made the protesters more aggressive. For some reason, they assumed that I was Arletta's escort, not another patient, so they left me alone as they ringed her and shoved pamphlets at her.

A blousy, middle-aged woman and a priest grabbed her arm and jumped in her face, shouting, "If you murder a baby, you'll go straight to Hell!"

Arletta was hysterical. I looked up at some windows on the second floor for help, but the whitecoats lined up there seemed amused by the show. I dragged Arletta through the door, and we battled up a flight of stairs jammed with protesters. It was chaos; however, when we finally made it into the clinic, the nurse who greeted us was so nonchalant I felt like I was ordering coffee.

"Okay, you're on the schedule," she said. "We're overbooked today, but we'll handle all of you."

She gave us each a pill, told us to take it and directed us to different rooms. Heather wouldn't do it. She had to help Arletta.

"No, I'll go first," she told the nurse, "and then I'll come back and go in with her."

The procedure was painful and terrifying. I took the pill and then there were lights in my face, and they were stabbing me with needles, and I could smell blood and hear stainless steel snicking between my legs. I knew this was something that smoking another joint wouldn't fix.

When they finished, Heather sat up and said, "Okay, are we done? Where the hell are my clothes? I need to help my friend."

Heather dressed and went with Arletta into her room. When it was done, Arletta could barely walk, and I felt too awful to worry about anyone yelling at me. I had to half-carry Arletta to my car. A Beach Babes client had bought me a little Pontiac Fierro. It was a rough rider, with a four-speed transmission and no power steering. On the way home, every time I shifted gears or turned the wheel or hit a bump, pain tore through me.

I got Arletta into the apartment and went to my bedroom and closed the door. In an aquarium on my dresser, I kept two chameleons a client bought for me at a circus. I also had Joshua, another kitty. I found Joshua in a shabby little pet store owned by an Asian woman, when I was looking for crickets to feed the chameleons. I heard faint whimpering coming from the back of the store and walked around looking for the source. The woman followed me, jabbering. I didn't understand anything she said, but I could tell she didn't want me in the back of that store. I found out why – stacks of tiny wire cages all holding kittens and bunnies that I'm pretty sure were meant to become food for pet boa constrictors and rattlesnakes.

I located the cage the crying was coming from. When I opened it, something jumped on my shoulder and stopped screaming. It had clumps of gunky filth all over it and was so tiny it fit in my palm. The name "Joshua" popped into my head.

"I don't know what this is, but it's mine," I told the woman. "How much?"

I gave her $20 and took him to a veterinary clinic. They kept him for two or three days. When I got him back, he was a smell-good, fuzzy ball with green eyes.

The vet said, "He looks like a Maine coon cat," and that's what he turned out to be. He was as loving as Trinity was crabby.

That day, after the "procedure," I lay on the bed, sick, hugging myself. My insides were cramping and squirming like a bunch of eels. I concentrated on the chameleons, wishing they would change colors. Joshie jumped up and curled by my side, purring, and I petted him. As usual, Trinity was hiding somewhere, moping.

CHAPTER Sixteen

The Cougar on Flamingo Beach, The Three-Legged Black Lab in The Villa Next Door and A Visit With Jesus

While I was still trying to come to terms with what happened, the horny maintenance man from Showgirls – the one who bought Trinity for me – somehow tracked me down and started stalking me. That obsessed jerkoff drove up and down our street day and night and followed me everywhere, even if I was with one of the boys.

The stalker knew the Fierro was mine. When I wouldn't give him the time of day, he started shooting my car windows with a BB gun. Johnny and Luke ran him down in the parking lot of the church next door one night and were kicking his ass. He pulled a box cutter and ripped Luke open from his navel to his collar bone and ran.

Luke was in the hospital for a long time. He came home, and we settled him in to finish healing. I was starting to think that life had become way too crazy and something had to change.

One day, I ran into my creepy step uncle Bo*, who owned a strip club called Urban Thrill*. He was a tall, pimpy, widow's peak, dumbass who wore silk shirts unbuttoned to his navel, a cascade of gold chains and stacked disco boots 20 years after they went out of style. I didn't like Uncle Bo, so I never went into Urban Thrill*. Although he wasn't aware of all the details about Beach Babes and Heather, he knew that I was lost and looking for something.

"Angie, listen," he said. "I have this friend who's got a lot of money. He'll be really nice to you. He's harmless."

Since Uncle Bo was a schemer and had never cared about me before, I was suspicious. I had no idea how he could possibly know anyone rich. His club was a dump where guys could get a $5 handjob under the table or a $20 quickie in the backseat of a car in the parking lot. However, Uncle Bo said he would make it worth my while to go out with the guy. Money was a hassle; I knew I couldn't smoke weed and con lonely old men forever. 'Hmmm, let's take a look and see what we've got,' I thought.

I gave him my number and agreed to go to dinner with a wealthy businessman named Grant Campbell*. I couldn't stand him. He was 15 years my senior and wore thick glasses. He dressed like a dorky Jim Morrison impersonator – collarless white linen shirt, strings of Indian beads, skintight leather trousers with lace-up fly – and gave everyone a lot of attitude, like he really was a rock star. He made me so nervous that I poured a drink into my lap at dinner and told him to take me home.

Uncle Bo wouldn't let it go. He spotted me across the street a few days later and hurried over and said, "Just give it one more try. Let him at least call you."

To get away from him, I said I'd think about it. Grant called again and told me how beautiful I was and insisted we immediately go clothes shopping. He'd made arrangements to have an upscale boutique open after business hours. A "personal fashion consultant" met us there – a miserable prune who obviously resented coordinating expensive outfits for a piece of Lockbourne streetmeat. She never said a word to me, only to Grant, as she measured and pulled and pinched and *tsk-tsked*, sniffing like I'd stepped in dog turds. As she and Grant stood outside the fitting room discussing the appropriate wardrobe for my new life, I stayed inside, naked and apparently to them, brainless, until they had me appropriately attired.

This time, he took me to The Refectory, a gorgeous old church that had been turned into a French restaurant. They served food I'd never heard of, which didn't matter since I've always felt uncomfortable eating around people. Grant dressed in a normal suit, but he still swaggered around and treated everyone like peasants. I made it through that date and thought, 'Never again, never, never, never.'

Damned if Uncle Bo didn't track me down again. I kept saying, "No, no, no," so he bribed me. I got a hundred bucks to go to dinner again. I took his money and said, "Five minutes, but I'm not guaranteeing you anything."

Soon after, Grant appeared, gave me one red rose and asked for one more chance. We went to a normal place, and he dressed casually and dialed his ego down. In fact, he was being pretty cool. Although he still looked nerdy, he seemed harmless, just like Uncle Bo had first described him.

After dinner, he said, "If there's one place in the world you could go, where would it be? I'll take you anywhere in the world you want."

I hadn't touched my food, so I was drunk on my ass. I sipped my wine, thinking, 'What else do you have going on? Why not?'

"Costa Rica," I said – I think I actually pronounced it "Costo Rico." I still don't know why I picked that place. I must have seen it on TV or something. Just like that, we were on a plane. I didn't tell anyone where I was going, just left a message asking Arletta and the boys to take care of Trin and Joshie.

I didn't even know if Costa Rica was an island or a country, but it was cool – all superheated colors and supernice people who kept saying *"pura vida,"* not that I knew what that meant. It was beautiful, with ominous gray volcanoes that rose into the clouds, manicured white beaches and dense, towering rain forests daubed with phosphorescent flowers. The whole country smelled like it had been spritzed with expensive frangipani perfume.

We stayed in a villa on the ocean with a private pool. A manservant named Victor* never left our side. He laid out my clothes, made our dinner reservations and chauffeured us anywhere we wanted to go.

A three-legged black Lab lived next door. That guy's name was Tarzan. I talked to him every morning and fed him treats through the wrought iron gate. He was a cutie-pie. I loved him to pieces. There were animals everywhere: overdressed birds showing off all kinds of neon finery; geckos that skittered around like tiny, spray-painted windup toys; prehistoric iguanas napping in the sun, as motionless as rocks; wiseass monkeys flirting from the treetops, like randy construction workers catcalling a businesswoman on her way to the office. If I didn't know what a bird or animal or plant's right name was, I asked Victor. He was happy to help, but he warned me never to set foot in the jungle, where some of the most venomous snakes in the world live.

I could sit for hours in the shade of palm trees, watching iridescent butterflies search beds of belladonna lilies and *labios de puta*, as if they'd misplaced something important. Hummingbirds sipped from magenta bougainvillea and flaming *passiflora*. One morning, a scarlet macaw sat on a limb and squawked at me, tilting his head over and over, as if his right eye mistrusted what his left claimed to see. He was hilarious. Down on the beach, troupes of noisy sandpipers chased fiddler crabs and silvery minnows marooned by receding waves. Frigate birds hung like kites in the cloudless sky.

Victor's main duty was to keep me happy, which meant making sure I was busy. He booked lots of sightseeing trips. One day, we rented dirt bikes to ride to a site that Victor guaranteed me would be incredible. He wouldn't be any more specific.

When I sat on the bike, my feet didn't touch the ground, so Victor and Grant had to hold me up and help me start it. Grant was normally gawky, but he handled his dirt bike like a professional – fast, agile and confident. The bike's engine throbbing between my legs, I watched him speed away. The streetrat came out in me. I slammed the bike into gear and shot up the highway after him like I was Evel Knievel. Unfortunately, the four-lane gradually turned into a narrow, steep, winding dirt road, and I crashed the damn bike. Somehow, Grant knew I'd wrecked. He spun around in a cloud of dust and sand, sped back down the hill, jumped off his bike and helped me up. I had just some bruises and scrapes. The motorcycle wouldn't run, though. Grant put me behind him on his bike and drove me the rest of the way. He seemed quite *gallant*.

Victor was right. We went to *Cristo de la Misercordia*, a statue of Jesus that stands on a cliff overlooking lovely San Juan Bay. From the bottom of the hill on which it was built, it looked as tall as Lady Liberty. We had to climb a brick road and a lot of steps to reach the top. When we got there, I saw Christ's white arm was outstretched and his hand raised, like he was blessing the whole world. I read the legend at the base of his feet: *Jesus en ti Confio*. Victor said it meant "Trust in Jesus."

There was a little stone chapel below the statue, where people had written their names on the walls. I borrowed a pen from Victor and wrote, "Angela was Here!"

A low cement wall surrounded the statue. I sat on it, legs hanging over the cliff, and looked out across the bay and watched the sunset. It was spectacular: pink and orange pastel light streaked purple thunderheads as the dying sun rippled in the darkening water. That sunset stole my breath and for the first time, made me contemplate God's wonders. There was no doubt in my mind that I was beside the Creator, who knew exactly how dumbfounded I was to be soaring over a bay at the same time I was sitting on a wall in Central America. Grant and Victor kept calling for me to come before it got dark or I fell off the cliff, but I would not be interrupted until everything turned black and constellations were wheeling above Jesus and me.

We went to a resort for rich foreigners one day. There were buffets that looked like still-life paintings in a museum, top-shelf booze, impeccably uniformed and mannered waitstaff. A halfmoon of charming bungalows lined the quarter mile of walled-off beach. Almost everyone was sunbathing nude. It didn't take long to figure out that the place was actually a private club for the invisible, global, perverted elite. I was creeped way the hell out.

Except for putting his arm around me and holding my hand while we walked on the beach, Grant hadn't made a move on me during the whole trip. We even slept in separate rooms. I assumed that seeing all those naked people would fire up his hormones, so I prepared myself to start paying to play. It never happened. He bought me stuff, indulged me in any way I wanted, hugged me, tried to kiss me; that's as far as it went. I was confused.

One afternoon, we walked to a rundown village called Flamingo Beach. A shrunken, sun-darkened little man had a cougar chained to a plywood box, just above the high-tide line. As I approached her, the cougar's ears twitched; her green eyes never left my face. The guy said her name was Cricket. You could give him money to have your picture taken with her. Grant tried to stop me. He said she was so filthy that I had no idea what diseases she carried, and she might be dangerous. I ignored him, of course. When I stroked her head, Cricket closed her eyes and rubbed her cheeks on my hand and purred.

After that, Victor was off the hook for entertaining me. I spent most of my time in Costa Rica hanging out with a captive cougar and a special-needs dog.

When I look at pictures from Costa Rica, I see a skinny, sad, sun-burned blond kid with a shag haircut, wearing a floral sarong. Dwarfed by emerald jungle, she looks bewildered, like someone had scooped her up in a helicopter and dropped her off in an alien world, which is basically what happened. I hardly know that girl.

We stayed there for a month. On the flight back, Grant asked me to come live with him at his house in Dublin, an exclusive suburb of executives and celebrity's north of Columbus.

I paused to assess my situation. Certainly, Beach Babes wasn't a sustainable career option, but it had been pretty good to me in some ways. Through it, I'd met Fred*, a retired architect who owned a construction company. He was extremely well off and incredibly kind.

Fred would buy me anything to make me happy or protect me. He paid $40,000 for a burgundy Mitsubishi 3000 GT and handed me the keys and title right on the showroom floor – a nice step up from the crummy Fierro. Just before Uncle Bo badgered me into going out with Grant, Fred also bought me a condo in a gated community on Lake Shore Drive, between the Scioto River and Quarry Lake on the west side of Columbus. I'd only had it for a couple months before the Cost Rica trip.

In fact, Fred bought me my chameleons, which I'd released outside his condo on Sanibel Island. Fred wanted me to marry him to ensure my future. I should've been smart enough to do it, but I was embarrassed because he was almost 65 years older than I was.

Looking over at Grant in the seat next to me, I thought, 'I'm only 19 years old, for God's sake, and I hardly even know this guy. Enough already.'

I used every excuse I could think of to turn him down: 'I have to go home and take care of my cats. I don't have any clothes.'

He said I should spend the weekend at his house. He would buy all the clothes I wanted, he said. We would talk and then he would help me do whatever I decided to do.

Whatever else, Grant was very rich. I mean, like $60 million rich. I was a kid with no future and a God-awful past. I went. I mean, what would you do?

CHAPTER SEVENTEEN

My Fair Lady

Grant's home sat on a wooded lot in a fabulous, upscale neighborhood. It was a *nuevo riche* American version of a French *chateau*: imported yellow stone, dark wood floors, massive fireplaces, sunlight reflecting through bay windows, polished silverware set on long tables, 17th-Century antiques shipped in from Sotheby's and William Doyle, a curved white-marble staircase that looked as wide as an off-ramp on I-70. Grant said that a craftsman had spent weeks on scaffolding, like Michelangelo in the Sistine Chapel, covering the crown moldings around the 30-foot vaulted ceilings with 24-carat gold leaf.

He showed me upstairs to my private bedroom, just down the hall from the master suite. I was FOA. When that weekend was over, I picked up Trinity and Joshua and moved to Dublin. Once again, I didn't even tell anyone I was leaving.

I had lucked into a Big Fish who was being kind and supportive and not asking for anything in return. There were maids and gardeners. College was going to be taken care of. I zipped around Dublin in a red Ferrari Grant bought me as a surprise. During the holidays, we hosted parties that were right out of *The Great Gatsby*, with landscapers and interior decorators and florists and musicians and premier chefs who were flown in.

'Man, I won the life-lotto,' I thought. 'I have the ticket in my hand. All I have to do is cash it in.' That was easier said than done. Before I went to Dublin, Grant had acted carefree and chipper. As soon as I moved in, all that immediately disappeared. I wanted to make him happy, but it was almost impossible for him to enjoy himself. He never touched the golf clubs in the hall closet. All week long, he hid in his study, muttering as he reviewed his investments, checked his accounts, filled notebooks with his meticulous printing. He'd come out to eat, but then it was right back to the study and the computer screen. Anytime he wasn't around that laptop, he was straining.

Grant saw no profit in the things other people do for "fun." I tried to get him to go for walks along the golf course, take me to a movie or just sit on the couch and talk. I suggested concerts, but he didn't like any of the bands. Any time I said I wanted to do something, he assigned me a self-improvement task, mostly working on my grammar, vocabulary, diction and enunciation. I had plenty of time to work on those things, because Grant didn't allow me to go anywhere by myself. If he even caught me in a back room playing with Josh and Trin, he broke the game up. It was like *My Fair Lady*, with a harsher edge.

His only hobby was business. We went to lots of dinner parties with his big-noise pals and business connections. Every dinner was Russian roulette. When the rich, important people were nice to me, I felt like Cinderella at the ball; however, when the smug, paunchy, gray-haired men and the battle-scarred veterans of the Cosmetic Surgery Wars they were married to were nasty, it was like The Night of a Thousand Knives. The more Glenlivet and Grey Goose the men drank, the more they sidled around, sniffing, and the snootier their wives became. I never knew which kind of night was coming, so I was always on edge.

During my first year in Dublin, Grant told me we'd been invited to a dinner at the home of some guy whose family had made a fortune manufacturing steel and selling it to build skyscrapers all over the world. Super-amped, he paced around like a coach before a big game.

He went on about how this family had been wealthy and powerful for generations. He said I had to be on my best behavior and remember all the social graces we'd been going over – my posture, what subjects are appropriate for conversation, when to pause, when to smile, when to keep quiet and look good. He said I had to pay attention to the way I stood up from the table and excused myself and to never, ever use the word 'toilet.'

I sat there listening carefully, trying to keep all the P's and Q's straight, particularly how to properly use the utensils, which always freaked me out: start at the outside and work in toward the plate; dessert spoon and fork parallel to the plate at the top; soup spoon and oyster fork at the far right of the place setting.

'Fuck that,' I thought, 'I'm not about to slurp any soup in front of these people, and I've never eaten an oyster in my life, and I'm not about to start now.'

Wine and water glasses form a triangle on the upper right side of your plate, red on the outside, white near the desert utensils. Holy *fuck!*

This dinner was so important that Grant developed a system of hand signals and voice cues for me to follow. Most important, I was never to speak first, only to follow his lead with any comment I made, and to immediately do exactly what he said. He instructed me to always keep one eye on him – which, depending upon the seating arrangement, could be hard as hell for me. If he scratched his nose, I was to 'shut up'; if he rubbed his right thumb over the knuckle on the middle finger of his left hand, I was to 'stop slouching and sit up straight.' If he said, 'Angela made a good point about that subject the other day,' I was to repeat, verbatim, a conversation we'd rehearsed. It went like that, on and on, until I expected him to start tossing me treats across the table whenever I got a command right, like a trainer lobbing frozen fish to a barking seal at an amusement park.

After he finished, I was so nerved up that I couldn't stop grinding my teeth, but I was determined to please him by looking like a proper lady. I took so much time getting ready it was like I was preparing for an audience with the Queen Fucking Mum. I tipped and teased and tucked and sprayed my hair into a swirling updo that looked like spun chiffon and squeezed into a floor-length, off-the-shoulder, sequined dress that zipped almost all the way down to my ass crack. The dress looked gorgeous when I bought it and seemed to fit just fine when I'd tried it on, but I didn't feel right in it that night for some reason. I kept squirming around like I'd been swallowed by a silver lizard. By then, it was too late to do anything about it; all I knew is that Grant was so worried that messing up this gig would probably earn me a blindfold and a cigarette or, worse, a one-way ticket back to Lockbourne.

We drove way up north of Dublin to this unbelievably gorgeous home somewhere out in the True Big Bucks Wilderness. The White House didn't have shit on this place. Inside, it was like a jaw-dropping gilded museum. For all his millions, Grant would've been nothing but a houseboy there.

Around the long dinner table sat a dogpile of upper crust society – bankers and real estate moguls and attorneys and their sons fresh out of college, "just getting a start in the family business." Everyone was ass kissing and deal making; all of them were glancing sidelong for the approval of a stocky Holy Honcho in his later 60s with dyed hair, who sat at the head of the table, nodding, shaking his gell-slicked head, harumphing, frowning, smiling ever so slightly, sipping his Scotch rocks, subtly directing the conversation, always at the top of the heap. Grant was puckering.

The wives, rude as fuck, amused themselves by scrutinizing me. I felt like I was taking some kind of ominous test or job interview, or like I was expected to perform for a crowd of extraordinarily privileged strangers like a mechanical doll, and not just to make clever remarks, but to handle myself properly while everyone studied every move and every word. Terrified, I kept going over the correct order and uses of silver utensils and crystal goblets. Eventually, I became so flustered I couldn't remember if I was supposed to use the cutlery from the outside in or the inside out.

Oblivious to my presence at the same table, the Sisterhood of Wrinkled Crones whispered about my "rough edges" and my "raw beauty" and my "untapped potential." If this was supposed to be my audition in front of the super-rich, I was sinking hopelessly in the realization that I could never meet these people's expectations because they would just keep moving the goal posts. Choking on the fear of a fatal mistake, I couldn't eat, so I drowned the urge to scream with lots of wine – whatever color, from whatever damn goblet I pleased.

When it came time for the fucking oysters, the Sisterhood grew very excited. They said the only way to eat oysters properly, dear, is alive in their own liquor. These specimens had been chosen exclusively by their personal captain, bagged, iced and flown in immediately, they said. The Sisterhood said the oysters had to be shucked carefully and served while still living. 'These are the tenderest, most precious specimens you'll ever taste, dear,' they said happily. 'Enjoy.'

A server set three of the little guys in front of me, pulsing, waiting to be stabbed with the tiny devil's pitchfork, bathed and gulped. By that point, I was totally on the side of the mollusks. I wanted to lean over and whisper, 'Don't worry, guys, I'll get you off that plate and out of this torture chamber,' but I was as trapped by that crew of meanass aging sorority girls as they were. 'Well,' I thought, 'at least your hell is about to end.'

The dress was driving me out of my mind, too, so at a certain point, I just had to excuse myself to use the "powder room." When we first came in, I'd noticed a staircase that led up from the foyer, which was in a part of the house far from the dining room. I found it, slipped upstairs and located a 'toilet' where I could fiddle with the lizard skin in private, take a few deep breaths and decompress. I did the best I could with both problems and then started back down the staircase. Since I was about three quarters loaded, I had to hold the railing and tiptoe carefully on the steps, which were lit only by feeble electric candles winking in fancy wall sconces. I was afraid I was going to trip and break my neck.

When I was about halfway, Holy Honcho himself slithered out of the darkness, around the corner, into the foyer and started up toward me, all bogus charm and graciousness.

"Oh, hello, there you are, my dear," he said, in an oily voice. "With all the chatter at the table, I haven't had the chance to tell you how lovely you look and how much I appreciate your coming this evening."

I stopped and watched him rising. To be honest, I wasn't one bit surprised to find him there. I saw it in his piggy eyes the moment I was introduced to him, and he'd been shooting me quick looks all night, his nostrils flaring like he was trying to catch my scent, the peeks lingering as everyone drank more. I somehow knew this man, who was obviously used to getting whatever he pleased, would follow me.

He kept climbing and cooing, casting his poisonous bread over the water – my fabulous dress perfectly complimented my supple young body, my vivacious personality enlivened his table as never before, my relationship with Grant couldn't be that serious. I felt like the whole point of the evening, for him, had been to trap me, if not on these stairs, then somewhere else in that massive house, all alone.

Then he was standing right next to me. With no more attempt at seduction, he pinned me against the railing, jammed his stubby body against mine and started chewing on my bare shoulder. He had me trapped and was nipping and licking at me like an eager puppy, pawing that awful dress, sprinkling sequins over the stairs. He treated me like a dessert he'd ordered up.

I froze. I was in a bad place, and there was nothing I could do about it. If I smacked Holy Honcho or screamed or kneed him in the groin or raked my French nails over his cheeks, he would run straight to Grant and say, 'Your rabid beast got off the leash and attacked me. Obviously, you don't belong here. You'd best run along now, fella' and my ass would be back in Lockbourne by dawn.

Just as his gross tongue started oozing up my neck, I saw Grant in the foyer, a cigar clamped between his teeth. I could tell by his expression that he knew exactly what had been going on – no explanation required.

'Thank goodness,' I thought. 'He'll stop this sick prick.'

Except my heroic rescuer didn't do shit except clap his hand on Holy Honcho's shoulder, expel a plume of blue smoke, chuckle and say, "I could use another drink. How 'bout you, sir?"

In a split second, Holy Honcho went from full-on humpfiend to hale fellow well met.

He grinned and bellowed, "I can *always* use another drink, old boy!"

Ignoring me, they wove off, arm in arm.

By the time I reached the foyer I was sober and shaking with the cold knowledge that that bastard would've fucked me right there if he wouldn't have been interrupted.

I thought, 'These rich cocksuckers would chase us on horseback in packs like foxes in Merry Old England, or form lines of drunkass Good Ole Boys and drive us like tigers across country clubs and jogging trails and hang us from poles by our ankles and wrists – a bunch of fat Frank Fucks bringing us back alive for some special fun and games – rape as a group sport, if you have the pedigree for the group, of course. God damn them all!'

My dress was ripped and missing some scales and my face was flushed when I rejoined the party, but no one seemed to notice. In fact, neither Grant nor His Holy Honchoness so much as glanced at me. A dead fly in the salad dressing would've drawn way more attention.

I kept my mouth shut for the sake of whatever business Grant had going on with those scumbags. I didn't even bother mentioning the incident to him on the ride home. There was no point. I knew that he'd just turn it into a lecture on everything I'd done wrong that night. I took comfort in picturing the extravagant gift he would buy me to make up for it.

CHAPTER EIGHTEEN

How We Live

On weekends, Grant pulled himself away from his laptop and emerged from the study. I learned to be packed and ready on Friday afternoons for a dash to the airport and a flight to someplace I'd never heard of. At first, those trips were exciting – shopping for jewelry by appointment at Cartier's in Quebec, touring auction houses in New York, skiing in Aspen, looking at *chateaux* in France. Gradually, though, everywhere we went became for 'educational purposes' – my education. Our trips turned into lectures, not holidays.

He told me early one week that we would be making a vitally important trip that weekend. He handed me a detailed packing list, even though he didn't bother to reveal our destination. On Friday, he ordered me to unzip the leather time capsules sitting on my bed so he could inspect them to see "how invested you are in this trip." He made certain that I had the proper creature embroidered on the proper white or pastel polo shirts, that my cocktail dresses were the proper length, that my slacks were properly beige or white, that my linen pantsuits and lace silk blouses were properly muted, that I wasn't attempting to smuggle any lowcut tops or short shorts.

As he sifted through my bags, he recited the rules of attire and accessorizing: no shorts unless they are culottes that fall below the knee; no flashy jewelry; no sandals unless they are espadrilles; no shoes without socks during the day; no t-shirts with pictures of animals or big lettering; no loud colors at any time; dresses-only for dinner, no flamboyant patterns; hair worn up at all times, never blowing naturally. He checked my nails to see that they were properly done, smelled my perfume to make sure that it wasn't "whorish."

"This place we are visiting is all about protocol," he said. "Everything here is classically refined. Nothing is cheap, nothing is uncouth."

'Oh, fuck!' I thought.

We went to Newport, Rhode Island, a collection of splendorous "summer homes" of the unimaginably wealthy – the Vanderbilts, the Astors, the famous artists, architects, writers, politicians and other denizens of cliffsides overlooking the sea. We visited Newport Country Club, where, he said, the first US Open Golf tournament was held and the court where the first US Open Tennis Championship was played.

'Whatever,' I thought.

I dug moseying along Thames Street, the charming waterfront of taverns and boutiques, thrilled to be so close to the ocean again. My favorite spot was the Green Animal Topiary Garden, which Grant didn't care about because the house in the midst of the garden was just a white clapboard cottage. He was really juiced about The Breakers, the sprawling 70-room castle that Cornelius Vanderbilt had constructed on the same site where a previous mansion had burned down. Grant was practically salivating as we toured it.

Finally, he took me to St. Mary's Church. In the courtyard, for reasons I didn't understand, he took me by my shoulders and maneuvered me onto a specific spot. Once he had me situated, he looked me in the eyes and said, reverently, "This is a very important place. This is where Jack and Jackie Kennedy stood when they were married. This is the exact spot."

I didn't tell him how I felt to be standing there: weird.

Later, he quizzed me about the houses – the names of the families who owned them, the addresses, the dates they were constructed, the numbers of rooms, their price tags, how the families became wealthy and famous. He said it was crucial for me to familiarize myself with the titans who founded exclusive, traditional places like Newport.

"This is who we are," he said. "This is what we do. This is how we live."

'*We?*' I said to myself. 'Apparently, you musn't be familiar with the Harters of Lockbourne, fella. We're famous for taking our liquor without raw oysters and not bothering much about marriage ceremonies.'

CHAPTER NINETEEN

The Fat Girl in The Mirror

His good mood lasted until we got back to Dublin, and then he disappeared into the study with his beloved laptop, leaving me on house arrest again. I didn't know what to do with myself, not that it really mattered. He was as regimented as a drill sergeant about his own life, and he scheduled everything I did, too: awake at 6, jog, come in, dress, have expresso and light conversation, prepare for the day. There was no watching TV. I got a half hour of CNN in the morning while I was waking up over cappuccino or expresso, and in the evening, CNN for another half an hour downstairs in the great room with cocktails.

After a couple years of adjusting to being rich, I enrolled at Ohio Dominican to major in psychology and minor in philosophy. Grant picked those subjects, not that I was opposed to them. He pulled strings and had me admitted. I didn't even have a GED, but when I went to orientation, they handed me a bunch of papers, and just like that, I was a college student.

Back in the day, Ohio Dominican had been an all-women's school. One of the women who helped start it was a nun called Mother Angela. That coincidence didn't make me any more comfortable there. They emphasized prayer and reflection – stuff I had almost no experience with. I always felt like the preppy boys were leering at me, the prissy chicks resented my existence and the priests could see my many sins written all over me.

I also didn't realize how unprepared I was for higher education. I had none of the skills that most kids develop in high school. I had to ease into it, signing up for a class or two at a time. I took my hits the hard way, met my demons in the dark and found solutions. I studied my ass off, because I believed my new life depended on earning good grades. Grant didn't understand why I wasn't ready for school. He'd never gone to college. He's a genius who started speculating in commodities when he was young and made a fortune on his own. He demanded that I excel.

He hired a tutor named Henri* who met me at the house several days a week. We studied French and went over etiquette while he burned time and kept an eye on me. Henri became more like a babysitter, there more or less to keep me under control until Grant got back from the office. Henri kept track of my every move, including all my academic work, and fed intelligence to Grant. If I had a quiz coming up, Grant drilled me at the dining room table until I knew every answer. He edited and re-edited my papers before I turned them in. When he couldn't work with me, Henri did.

I can't say that I enjoyed college, because it was so difficult. However, I took surprising satisfaction in knowing I could do the work. I do have to admit that looking good helped – too much, sometimes. During my freshman year, one of my professors started stalking me. He put notes on my car window, conveniently bumped into me in the snack bar, asked me to come to private tutoring sessions in his office, invited me to his apartment, guaranteed me A's without even showing up in any course he taught. Unless I was home in Dublin, it was open season on Angela. He knew my entire schedule. It was super-creepy and uncomfortable, and it pissed Grant off. I finally had to tell the guy to leave me alone, or I'd report him. He was so infuriated that I ducked him for then on.

Grant said he was showing me how civilized people behave. Maybe, but I can tell you for sure what *rich* people do: They drink. Dinner started out with aperitifs. The Kir Royale was my favorite – champagne and Chambord with a raspberry. A progression of wines accompanied dinner, which ended with cordials. Grant liked to drink Drambuie; I became a connoisseur of fine port. When we went out, I couldn't wait for the wine flight after dinner. All I was interested in was the most expensive, rarest, oldest port. I loved that thick, oaky taste. Port is nefarious shit, though; it will knock you on your ass. It didn't take me long, however, to figure out that because of the "civilized" way they drink, rich people are never "drunks."

Grant said comportment was everything, and my mistakes came with repercussions. If I committed some kind of *faux pas*, the pleasant evening was abruptly taken away. The music went off; the candles went out.

"You've just spoiled a fine evening," Grant would say. "You're worthless. You don't deserve this. Damn you, I knew not to invest in you. Don't you have some homework to do? Oh, and you will not be driving the Ferrari this weekend."

He'd retire to his study, open his laptop, and I wouldn't see him again until morning.

After he let that soak in, he'd give me another shot, and I'd better have it down this time. If I got it right, I received the benefits. If I didn't, he punished me by continuing to withhold the keys to the Ferrari or by shunning me for a few more days.

"This is how we learn," he'd say. "I'm preparing you for life."

When we'd checked into our hotel in Newport, the place smelled wonderful, like I'd walked into an old-fashioned bakery. The woman behind the front desk gave us our keys and then offered us scrumptious-looking chocolate chip cookies bigger than my palms.

"Would you like one?" she said, taking two from a wicker basket and holding them out. "They are homemade. Delicious."

I reached for one, but Grant said, brusquely, "We won't be having any cookies, thank you."

The woman arched her brows at my hand hanging in the air between us, then shrugged and placed the cookies back into the wicker basket. From that moment on, whenever we went to restaurants, Grant made cutting remarks about anything I ordered. At home, I was not permitted to snack. He organized the pantry and labelled everything with what I could eat at what times. I felt like I was back in Lockbourne with The Hag.

"We don't want to get fat now, do we?" he'd say. "We're looking a little heavy lately."

One morning, I asked a waitress for some dry wheat toast to go with my oatmeal, and he said, "Are we sure we need both? We should be careful."

The strain of living up to Grant's expectations wore on me until I felt trapped in a dead zone, amped up, cornered. I knew I was stupid and ugly. I weighed myself obsessively; no matter what the scale said, I studied mirrors, looking for the fat girl I knew was in there somewhere. I ran mile after mile on the hottest days and then went straight to the gym and worked out until I could barely stand.

I'd feel myself losing control, but I could never stop what was coming. I'd eventually hit the pressure-release valve and eat a week's worth of food in a couple hours. It was like I was trying to smother the stress and depression under shovelfuls of pizza, ice cream and candy bars. Then I did as Silky taught me, puking until my brain pounded against my eyeballs and tears soaked my cheeks. Afterward, exhausted and lifeless, I slept entire days away.

Inevitably, Grant figured out what I was doing. He made me go to a therapist. Jerry told me that what The Stage Witches referred to as managing my pain was actually bulimia, a potentially fatal eating disorder that is very difficult to overcome. He said I should be able keep the problem in remission with regular, reasonable exercise and a healthy diet.

"Unfortunately," he said, "bulimia is merciless and unrelenting. It will always be there inside you. It might go away for years and then suddenly return with no warning."

Only I could tame it, Jerry said. No one could do it for me.

CHAPTER TWENTY

Princesses

I never knew the exact nature of his business, but Grant was obsessed with secrecy and avoiding taxes. He was what's called a Perpetual Traveler. Periodically, he received red and blue, leather-bound volumes that had just the gold-embossed letters "PT" on the cover in parentheses. They were guidebooks for an uber-wealthy boys' club with dual passports and citizenships and secret accounts in Luxemburg, the Isle of Man and the Caribbean.

Grant was most comfortable conducting his affairs in Luxemburg because it's a duchy that carefully guards financial records. We went there often so he could meet with lawyers and bankers.

Luxembourg City looks like Euro Disney plagiarized it out of an illustrated volume of Grimm folk stories, prefabbed it and moved it onto the most scenic countryside they could buy. The narrow cobblestone main street winds like the Yellow Brick Road through closely-packed wine shops and cute family-owned eateries. Everything is pristine: people dressed to the nines, luxury sedans whispering slowly past, each blade of grass curry-combed. The shops sell nothing but top-of-the-line stuff: Louis Vuitton, Gucci, Tiffany, Chanel. Strangely, though, lots of banks are shoved in among the quaint businesses. Every major bank in the world must have a branch there. Walking around

Luxembourg City was like wandering through a lair of super-wealthy globalists. I always felt uncomfortable there.

In fact, I could never enjoy any of the beauty or culture of Europe. I'd wake up in the morning and say, 'I'd like to go here. I want to see this.' I was not allowed, because Grant was intent on shoving history and art and architecture down my throat. I still have copies of the unbelievably-detailed, down-to-the-minute itineraries he handed me every morning: how I was to dress, when and where we were to eat, what sites we would visit, how long we would spend at each one. He even calculated the precise distances and travel times between locations.

Grant expected me to study and learn, not have fun. During the day, I took notes for the exams that I submitted to him every night to be graded. At dinner, I was to make intelligent, informative, sparkling conversation about what I learned that day. I quickly came to resent his controlling me and ruining every experience. Maybe that's why I always ended up getting into trouble in Europe.

One year, he took me to Paris for my birthday. We arrived in France about a week beforehand and toured the countryside, meeting with realtors who showed us genuine *chateaus*, and then traveled to Germany.

We had reservations for one night in a bed and breakfast that turned out to be an ancient castle in the middle of the Black Forest. A tallow-complexioned old dude whose lank, greasy hair fell over the shoulders of his canvas farmer coat met us at an iron gate, unlocked it and led us inside. The castle had no electricity, just candles. In every corner, spooky shadows drifted and leaned.

We followed the caretaker to where his witchy wife was preparing dinner on a huge wood-burning stove. The door to the iron oven was so big that she could've shoved me inside and baked me. The stink of porky, fatty, gravied noddle slop made me sick, so I brewed a Kir Royale and asked the caretaker where the other guests were.

"You are *zee* only *vuns, Fraulein*," he said, like a character from a Dracula movie.

When he added that he and his wife were leaving and would lock the gates and wouldn't be back until morning, I started slamming the drinks as fast as I could pour them, hoping the champagne and Chambord would settle my nerves.

Needing some time without Grant breathing down my neck, I grabbed a candle wobbling in a heavy pewter stick, carried my overnight bag to the second floor and found an empty suite at the end of the hall. As soon as I closed the door, I was sorry to be alone. The suite was pitch black, except for a silvery sliver of full moon spilling through the French patio doors. I put on my nightie. The bedroom seemed spotless. The canopy bed and heavy linens swallowed me. I was drunk enough that the bed felt like it was drifting. The candle's yellow light was feeble, but I left it burning on a nightstand.

I lay there listening to the ancient castle creak and moan. Most of the noise was coming from downstairs. Kir Royale and curiosity eventually got the better of my uneasiness. I climbed out of bed, put on my slippers, grabbed the candle and tiptoed down the stone staircase, past the ghostly, wavering portraits of snobby, overdressed rich people.

I followed the noise through the kitchen and pantry to the basement steps. They were cordoned off by a thick rope. I climbed over it and crept down narrow dirt stairs into a freezing root cellar that smelled like moldy stones and dusty spiderwebs. I held the candle up and looked around. Two huge, luminous eyes suddenly flared in front of me. A high-voltage surge of fear slammed me back. Prepared to defend my blood, I gripped the candlestick with both hands and cocked it over my shoulder, thinking, 'Werewolf! Vampire!'

When nothing happened, I lowered the candle and slowly raised it again. My good eye adjusted to the faint light. I saw what was making all the noise: For reasons I didn't even want to try to guess, there was a fucking ostrich caged up in that basement. He stared down at me with a witless expression. His neck swelled, and he made a weird sound – a cross between a burp and a chirp – like he was telling me I had no business being in the basement of a medieval castle, in the middle of a deep, dark forest. Neither did he, but I wasn't about to stick around down there and argue with a goofy bird.

I hurried back upstairs and spent the rest of the night packing and dressing and sobering up. At the crack of dawn, I knocked on Grant's bedroom door and told him I was ready to leave. We were waiting at the iron gate when the caretaker and his wife showed up. I didn't want to hear anything about breakfast, and I didn't say a word to anyone about the prisoner in the dungeon. We booked out of the Black Fucking Forest.

On the night of my birthday, we went to dinner at an exclusive restaurant in Paris. I'm calling it a restaurant, but that's not right. It was more a private estate, a haunt of celebrities and the purposely-invisible elite. They served dinners only by invitations that were sent out a year in advance.

The *chateau* sat almost obscured by acres of grape arbors, like something out of a fairy tale. A long walkway snaked through the vines and ended at a Magic Door flanked by guards and valets. It was incredible. The problem was that Europeans don't eat dinner until 10 o'clock, so I had ample of opportunity to sample the local vintages before we ate. By the time I staggered through the Magic Door, I was well on my way to being smashed.

A *maître d* seated us. Candelabras that looked as if they'd been lighted in a ritual order meant to evoke the past flickered over invaluable antiques and works of art. In the murky dining room, pools of ochre candlelight painted the tables. It was like sitting in one of the Rembrandts I'd seen in the Louvre. It was very quiet. The only sounds were muffled conversation and silverware tinkling against fine china.

I thought, 'These people can buy and sell any of those assholes who think they're such hot shit back in Ohio.'

Off the main serving area, there were smaller private dining rooms. A gauzy curtain, like a big veil, hung over the entrance to the one nearest us. The nook was as dim as a peepshow. The people eating in there all had big linen napkins draped over their heads, like they were trying to hide their faces. They were hunched over their plates, wolfing their food, saying nothing. It was freaky.

Everyone there had obviously been bred to luxury and power and idle superiority. Grant looked around happily, basking in the presence of bluebloods, probably because he'd been brought up in a middleclass home in rural Ohio. He was still a climber who was using this lavish dinner as an opportunity to impress and, if possible, make contacts.

Since Henri and I were barely past *merci*, *bonjour* and *au revoir* at the time, Grant said he would order for me. While I waited, a tall, slender woman with an exotic, high-cheekboned face came in, wearing a chiffon and satin Cinderella skirt and a see-through top that left nothing to the imagination. Two older men dressed in immaculately-tailored tuxedos accompanied her.

The woman was willowy and graceful, long-necked and long-limbed, floating among the tables like a swan, her chin up, her head perfectly still, like she was balancing a champagne flute on it. She seemed serenely confident that everyone had come there not to dine but to see her, and, indeed, all the elegant people in that opulent place stopped and stared.

As she glided past our table, I could feel my jaw dropping and my eyes widening. She looked at me for a split second. Her disdainful expression said, 'Yes, these are my tits, little American twit. Lovely, are they not?' Then she and her escorts drifted away.

I drank *vin rouge* until a waiter finally placed my food in front of me. He stood back proudly, hands clasped at the small of his back, waiting for me to *ooh* and *ahh*. I looked down at a little plucked bird with its feet tied together, lying on its back in a pool of blood. I asked Grant what the hell it was.

He looked at me over his thick glasses like I was an idiot and said, "Squab. It's called *pegeonnmeau*. It's a delicacy in France."

"Delicacy, my ass!" I said, flaming loud. "It's a goddamned pigeon! Get this fucking thing away from me!"

I grabbed the plate, turned it over and slammed it on the tablecloth. I jumped up, crying, kicked my chair away and threw my silverware. Grant was trapped on the other side of the table, horrified. He lunged but couldn't reach me. Three more waiters scurried up. They surrounded me and backed me into a corner. They tried to push another menu into my hands, bleating, "*Madame! Madame! S'il vous plait! Arrete! Arrete!*"

The stiff-necked, aristocratic pricks who'd been admiring Cinderella's boobs were gaping at me like I was rabid zoo creature who'd crept in through the Magic Door. One of the waiters desperately shoved a dessert cart in front of me and waved his hand over it, like I should pick whatever I wanted. Another cried, "*Que diriez-vous d'une salade?*"

I understood *salade,* so I said, "Salad, okay, but don't you bring me anything with a fucking bird or a frog or a snail on it!"

I went back to my chair, downed more *vin rouge*. Grant was fidgeting and sweating and looking like he wanted to hide under his napkin. I composed myself . . . until they brought me a bowl with a couple shreds of lettuce in it. I went sideways again.

"Get this shit out of here!" I shouted.

A waiter grabbed the bowl before I could fling it.

Nervously, he said, *"Voudriez-vous des truffes blanches?"*

We'd studied truffles on one of our excursions. I knew that *truffes blanches* – white truffles – were the rarest and most expensive kind. I regally nodded permission for him to put truffles on the sorry bowl of lettuce. He took it away. When he came back, he placed it warily in front of me, like I was going to bite him, and darted off.

He'd shaved smidgens of white truffle onto the lettuce. They didn't look appetizing, and they smelled funny, but the truffles tasted okay, like cheesy mushrooms lightly spiced with potting soil. There sure weren't very many of them, though. That dinky *salade* cost Grant $400. I know the waiter did that just to get back at us. I tried to hide my grin as I watched Grant fume over the check.

'That's what you get for ordering me a dead pigeon, fucker,' I thought.

The next day, we were walking around, deciding where to have lunch. The sun was intensely bright, and I was sick with a brutal hangover. After a block or so, I noticed that the streets were almost empty, except for a lot of guys in black suits and wrap-around sunglasses. Earpieces hung over their collars. Gendarmes carrying automatic weapons stood on every corner.

It was weird.

"I wonder what the heck's going on?" I asked Grant.

A Parisian dude walking past overheard me.

"Americans?" he asked.

I nodded.

"You have not heard?"

When I shook my head, he told us that Princess Diana had been killed in a car wreck the night before in a tunnel not far away. We got directions and walked down the street. We found where everyone was – gathered around the crash site, weeping, praying, taking pictures. A lot of them were carrying lovely bouquets. Flowers filled almost the entire tunnel. Princess Diana had died, it turned out, at the same time I was throwing a hissy on my birthday. I felt even sicker.

CHAPTER TWENTY-ONE

Roman Holiday

It doesn't take an eating disorder to know that baby pigeon backstroking in its own blood is gross, but how do Italians, of all people, fuck up pizza? We were in Roma on another holiday, going from *trattoria* to *osteria* to *enoteca*. None of what they served appealed to me; too much octopus and squid drenched in garlic and butter kept appearing on my plates. One of the few foods I enjoy is pizza. I bugged Grant about it, but he said we could get all the pizza we wanted in Columbus. I insisted. He warned me that the pizza in Roma was much different from what I was used to. When we finally went to a *pizzeria*, I was hot pissed. I was expecting a deep-dish pie stacked with double peperoni; I got $20 worth of hand-tossed, hammered shit. The crust was charred and as thin as notebook paper. I don't even want to say what the white sauce looked like. This time, Grant was ready. He grabbed my elbow and led me out of there.

Food was actually the least of my difficulties in Roma, however. The city turned my stomach so bad that I barely ate the whole time we were there.

The Coliseum was disgusting and depressing. We saw cages where they kept big cats, bears, elephants, rhinos and monkeys that died in an orgy of gore so that the Emperors of Horror could demonstrate how wonderful they were. I felt those animals' pain and fear. I have a picture of me outside of that foul building. I'm wrapped in a toga and wearing a costume jewelry tiara. My mouth is pinched, and my complexion looks greyish-green, like I'm sick. I was.

The catacombs didn't make me feel any better. For centuries, persecuted Jews and Christians illegally buried their dead in crypts that line the gloomy passageways. I hated rubbing shoulders with the dead. I have no idea why anyone would want to go down there, let alone pay to do it.

Gladiators, chariot races, human sacrifice, crucifixion, rape, slavery, massacres, psychotic dictators – I smelled the tragedy that still permeates that city today. Romans preserve and worship blood-soaked ancient times as if the conquering legions are coming back next week to rule the world again.

That's why I've never felt bad about what I did in Caesar's Palace. One day, I escaped to do some exploring on my own. I found the palace of Caesar Augustus, which I'd seen in a guidebook. They were doing some work on it, so it was supposed to be off-limits. Maybe it was siesta time or something, because there was no one around. I snuck in. It looked just like all the other decaying ruins I'd seen, but I decided I might as well take home a keepsake. I pried up two little mosaic tiles – one from the floor and one from the wall – and slipped them into my pocket.

Grant was burning to get to the Vatican, which made no sense since he openly professed his atheism to anyone who would listen. We went anyway, and the Vatican dropped me into a whole new level of shit.

I'd already bought several pieces of handmade jewelry for Granny, but I still had my eye open for souvenirs. She was very religious, reading her Bible all the time at the kitchen table. I thought she would appreciate something from the Vatican. Even though she wasn't Catholic, holy water seemed perfect.

They sold holy water in the gift shop, but I suspected it came from a faucet in the bathroom. To verify that I had the genuine article, I wanted to fill my own bottle. I knew there were a lot of fountains around, and I assumed they were all blessed. I found a tiny plastic Virgin Mary bottle and stood in line to buy it. When I finally made it to the check-out, I got into a dispute with the nun behind the register. I couldn't understand how much the Virgin Mary bottle cost or how much my fistful of Monopoly money was worth.

The nun and I both got loud. She kept calling me *pazza*. I won't repeat what I called her. The gift shop was packed. Other people jumped in. A full-scale, round-robin argument broke out in half a dozen languages. I threw all my bills at the nun and left with the bottle. When I went through the door, people were still yelling at each other.

We were in St. Peter's, which is basically a three-story hole in the ground with a big umbrella over it. I didn't see what all the fuss was about. I snuck away from Grant and found a little fountain in a musty alcove off the main room. I was alone, so I took out the Virgin Mary bottle and dipped it in.

"*Signora*, you cannot do that!" someone shouted. "No, *signora*!"

Startled, I looked up. A furious Nosferatu dwarf wearing a black undertaker's suit was charging at me. He had dark circles under his eyes and a black widow's peak and was very pale. I didn't understand where he could've come from. He grabbed my wrist and twisted it, trying to take the Virgin Mary bottle. When he saw my shocked and angry expression, he backed off. I wrenched the Virgin Mary away and gripped her with both hands.

"You cannot do this!" he said, his breath reeking of garlic.

"I just wanted a little bit of holy water for my grandmother," I said. "What's the big deal?"

He held out his hand and said, '*Scusami, scusami*, so sorry, I will get you some, *signora*.'

Remembering the Swiss Guards with their swords and axes standing beside the entrance, I gave the bottle to him. He took it and disappeared through a concealed door in the wooden wall.

'All this over a couple drops of water?' I thought.

I didn't expect to see the dwarf again, but he popped out of the wall, handed me the Virgin Mary and popped back in. I figured he'd filled it with tap water, but I didn't care. I was so unnerved that I just wanted out of there.

I was too late. I felt that little alcove fill with an invisible but palpable energy. It was powerful and malevolent. It engulfed me like a mist seeping out of the catacombs. It expanded, pressing against the walls and against me, until I thought that alcove would explode. The miasma swirled into a face that glared ferociously at me. Terrified, I hurried back into St. Peters to find Grant and get the hell out of the Vatican.

No matter how I implored him, he wouldn't leave. It was like being back at The Breakers, times 100 or 1000. Saucer-eyed, he skipped along the halls, clapping. He had to see every chapel and museum and basilica in that enormous place – all the paintings and statues and jewels in glass cases.

Right then, I saw Grant's true nature. He acted like all the other Sheep People who paid the price of a circus ticket to wander through wall-to-wall decadence. The Vatican is a shrine to greed and deceit, overseen by shadowy figures in cassocks and cowls and habits. Any square foot could feed the beggars and panhandlers who crowd the streets around it for the rest of their lives, but the incredible wealth stays locked inside and grows. The Sheep People think they're witnessing evidence of God's glory, when they're actually bearing false witness to Mammon. It is idolatry. The difference was that Grant was not fooled for a second and didn't give a shit. He was no atheist. He was ecstatically worshipping his true deity – one of silver and gold and gems – in all its divine glory.

As he rushed from room to room, I sensed that dark force following me, staring down. It wanted me to feel it, but it wouldn't fully reveal itself. I couldn't say anything to Grant. He'd just start yelling at me for being stupid and crazy, and, later, find some way to punish me. I couldn't cry for help, and I couldn't run.

That trapped feeling didn't pass until we made our way out

into the sunshine through the hordes of Asian tourists snapping pictures, watched the Pope do his thing and were drinking wine at a *trattoria* near the Piazza del Popolo. I was terrified that whatever it was would come back for me that night, but I didn't feel it again. At least not for a long time.

One of Grant's business associates accompanied us on that trip. The flight home was endless. When I got bored, I pulled out the two little tiles I'd lifted from Caesar's Palace and showed them to him. He went ballistic. He said I was risking an international incident and could go to prison for desecrating history. He also ratted me out to Grant, who stopped speaking to me.

I still have those tiles. The only thing that separates them from brown rocks is the note that I wrote on a torn sheet of notebook paper and Scotch-taped to them: "Piece of mosaic wall & floor from Caesar's house in Roma."

CHAPTER TWENTY-TWO

Mitzi

Very late on the night we came back from Roma, Grant and I were walking through the airport. I was jetlagged, barely able to keep my eyes open, dragging my luggage like a ball and chain but glad as hell to have the Atlantic Ocean between me and whatever had pursued me through the Vatican. I'd left Mitzi at the airport when we flew out, so I had to pick her up in long-term parking. Grant drove home in his own car, thank goodness. I was eager to get away from his sulking over my attempt to destroy Western Civilization.

By the time I found the car and started for Dublin, it was after midnight. I pulled out of the lot and got on 670. I felt like I was fighting myself for control of Mitzi. I could turn the wheel and step on the brakes and flip the lights and turn signal, but I couldn't choose where she was going. At the Harrisburg Pike exit, Mitzi turned south and headed straight for Central Point, my grandparents' neighborhood. I surrendered.

"Okay, go wherever you want," I told her.

When we reached Ransburg Avenue, Mitzi turned again.

'What am I even doing here?' I thought. 'It's one o'clock in the morning, and I haven't seen them in months. If I show up pounding on their door, I'll scare them to death.'

Mitzi stopped in front of the house, next to an ambulance.

Blue and white roof lights swept over the house and the little front yard. Two EMTs were wheeling a gurney through the door. I jumped out. In the porchlight, Grandpa's face was as white as the sheet covering him. His eyes were closed. Uncle Pete was standing there, staring at me.

"What the hell are you doing here?" he said.

"I have no idea," I said.

Granny came through the door, and I said, "Granny, come on. I'll take you to the hospital."

We followed the ambulance to the ER. As we sat in the waiting room, I remembered Grandpa talking about Pearl Harbor. He'd shown me a few pictures and his Purple Heart and some letters he and Granny had written to each other. He also told me a little about the bombing and a friend who was killed that day. Later, Granny filled in the blanks. When the sneak attack started, Grandpa was with his buddy. His ship took a direct hit. His buddy was so badly wounded that Grandpa had to stuff his guts back into him. Grandpa was wounded, too, and so traumatized that he was catatonic. He was still in his 20s, but his hair turned completely white. He stopped talking and barely ate.

The navy kept him in a hospital for a couple of months, then discharged him and sent him home, saying maybe he'd snap out of it. Granny said he was a complete mess. He stayed in one bedroom of the house and stared out the window silently, like a dog waiting for his master to come home from work.

Grandpa's family was from Florida; his mom was the daughter

of a Seminole chief. She scared Granny to death. Granny didn't tell her what happened to Grandpa. Nonetheless, the woman showed up out of nowhere.

"No matter what," my great grandmother said, "don't open this door" and went into the bedroom with Grandpa.

Granny said that for three days and nights, she smelled smoke and saw shadows and lights flickering under the door, like that bedroom was on fire. My great grandmother was chanting and singing, and Grandpa was screaming like he was being flayed. Granny was afraid the house was going to burn down or the neighbors would call the cops.

She said on the fourth morning, everything became quiet. A few minutes later, my great grandmother unlocked the door and walked out with Grandpa at her side, right as rain. His hair was still white; otherwise, he was just like before the war. The woman immediately returned to Florida and never came back to Columbus. Granny was pissed because she'd burned a hole in the carpet, but there was no other damage to that bedroom. Grandpa worked for Swan Cleaners for 40 years. When he retired, they gave him a gold Rolex. I don't know if my great grandmother was a witch or a shaman or whatever, but I do know that Granny never lied in her life, and that's the story she told me.

I sat in the waiting room that night, holding Granny's hand and praying for another miracle, but about an hour after we got to the hospital, Grandpa died. His military funeral was lovely and touching – the three rifle volleys, "Taps," the body bearers who carefully folded the flag and presented it to Granny. I was at her side throughout, but to my everlasting shame, I immediately fell back under Grant's thumb and wasn't around to help her grieve.

CHAPTER TWENTY-THREE

Diamond Leash, Gilded Cage

Grant took me places and bought me things that were beyond my dreams, but he also cut me off from everyone in my previous life, and not just my grandparents. He said they were all no-good hillbillies. With Arletta, it didn't matter. I heard she'd had a baby, so I tried to reconnect with her. She made it clear that she would never forgive me for abandoning her and our friendship was over. All I got out of that brief conversation was a warning that Johnny and Luke were getting into more trouble all the time.

Even Heather wasn't around much. When Angela stopped needing money, she more or less disappeared. Every three months or so, I got so lonely that I snuck away to spend the day with Granny. When she saw me, she hugged me almost me to death.

During every visit, she'd say, "Do you want to sleep here tonight?"

When I told her I couldn't, she insisted that I go up and nap in my old bedroom until she called me for dinner. The bedroom was exactly as I left it when I ran away. My Sean Cassidy and Joan Jett posters were still on the walls. A fresh towel and washcloth were folded at the foot of the hundred-year-old, queen-sized, four-poster bed. I was the 11th kid to sleep in that bed; I inherited it from Uncle Pete. Granny still dusted and vacuumed the bedroom every week, like she was preserving it for the day I came home to stay.

The broken-down delivery van was still parked right under the window, too. When I was a kid, that van was my escape route. I waited until my grandparents were asleep, then jumped out the window onto its roof and took off into the night. Granny knew what I was doing, but she never said anything. She just tried her best to make home more attractive than the streets. She never had a chance of taming me; I was already too wild.

Although Granny sensed that I was in a bad place with Grant, she didn't pressure me to leave him, just clung to my hand like she wanted to keep me in that little house forever.

If I'd just paid closer attention to how Trinity and Josh acted around Grant, I would've seen things clearly for myself. The cats sensed his insecurities, and he knew that. Grant hated those guys, and they hated him. Josh hid from him, but he made Trinity red-eyed with fury.

Grant had carpet slippers that he loved, super-fancy things with gold thread and tassels that had belonged to some Grand Poohbah jerkoff. He bought them at Sotheby's or Christie's. Trin crapped in them every chance he got. Grant tried to keep him out of the bedroom, but Trinity yowled and beat on the door until he opened it, then he snuck around and waited for his chance to squat in the slippers. It was hilarious. Cleaning those slippers was on the daily schedule for the maids.

Since we traveled all the time, Grant kept saying it was a shame the cats had to be alone while we were gone. He nagged me into finding a new home for them. I put them with some very nice people who lived nearby, but I drew up a contract that said if I didn't feel right about the arrangement, I could come get them.

Trinity and Joshie had been trying to tell me something to protect me, but I didn't listen. Instead, I sent them away. When they were gone, I was completely alone, on a diamond leash, in a gilded cage.

CHAPTER TWENTY-FOUR

Hustlers in Paradise

Periodically, I became so frustrated and angry that I bolted from Dublin. One morning, I pretended to be sleeping, until Grant left for the office. I packed a bag and drove to the airport, determined to jump on the first available international flight, no matter where it was going. There was a seat on a plane to Jamaica, so I bought it. First class, of course.

The cab from the airport to the resort passed hillsides of vivid pastel mansions lording over sun-blasted wooden shacks with rusted metal roofs, tar-paper sides and blue plastic tarps for doors and windows. Scrawny goats and cows nibbled crabgrass yards just a few feet from the sapphire ocean. Battered fishing dinghies that seemed about to sink bobbed beside catamarans as big as football fields and yachts with two or three masts.

I stayed at a first-rate resort named for a former sugar plantation that had been worked by hundreds of slaves. The concierge said that the plantation's three-story great house was haunted by a "white witch" who murdered a bunch of her husbands and lovers. 'Hmm, that sounds a little harsh,' I thought, 'but it's definitely something to consider.'

On the way in, I'd noticed a little marketplace almost directly across the street from the resort entrance. A knee-high limestone wall surrounded a cluster of tiny stalls made from gaily-painted lumber and tarps. Shoppers were carrying bamboo baskets on their heads or shoulders or bunches of plastic bags wrapped in their fingers. I'd caught a passing look at bins of fruit, t-shirts, beach towels and cover-ups. I'd been in such a hurry to escape that I hadn't packed the right clothes or even any suntan lotion. I thought I might pick up a few necessaries on the cheap.

As soon as I walked into the plaza, a Jamaican woman who was at least twice my size grabbed my arm, dragged me backward into a stall and shoved me down on a chair. Another woman – even bigger than the first one – started braiding my hair. I was bugging so bad that I went stiff, too scared to scream.

Then the biggest woman of all came at me with a machete. Standing over my chair, she swung it. I closed my eyes, flinched, heard the blade chop into something that wasn't me. When I opened my eyes, the woman was holding a long green stalk of some plant over my head. She sliced it and ripped the innards out and started smearing white goo all over my face, arms and shoulders. As she rubbed it in, I just knew that this was a voodoo blood sacrifice that would end with my head shrinking on a bamboo pole in the center of that shopping plaza.

"*Yuh a too fair, m'lady,*" she said. "*Aloe will protect yo.*"

When they finished braising, braiding and beading me, I fished some bills out of my purse, gave them to the biggest lady and got the hell out of there.

"*Respect, m'lady,*" she called as I hurried out of the shack.

I went to my room and looked in a mirror; the dreadlocked

Predator monster from that series of movies was peering back at me, trying to figure out exactly what I was. It took me hours to pluck out those tight braids, and I never did figure out how three women bigger than sumo wrestlers fit in that cramped stall. For everything I needed in the tropics, I paid exorbitant resort prices, even for aloe, which did keep my sunburn under control.

During the days, I lounged in the pool or walked the hot, sun-kissed beach for hours, trying to worry my way out of the cage I'd willingly stepped into. Back at the resort, I prowled for an earl or duke or viscount who would set me up in Paradise forever. There was no Prince Charming to whisk me off to his castle, however, just a lot of bloated Europeans smelling of coconut oil and armpit sweat. The men's beet-red bellies flopped over teeny-weeny Speedos that were just short of pornographic. Their sullen bovine wives waddled along next to them.

I thought I'd bumped into to something promising one afternoon while I was drifting in the ocean on a blow-up raft. An extremely hot Latin dude paddled up to me on a colorful plastic innertube and started talking. He had black hair and dark bedroom eyes and was as lithe as a bullfighter. He was dashing – well, as dashing as anyone can be folded up into a little kid's flowery donut thingy. He immediately began bragging about how beautiful his family's huge *finca* back in Columbia was and how high up in the government they were and how much money they made from coffee.

I caught a whiff that this guy was trying to con me, but with pickings so slim, I agreed to meet him for a drink later so I could do some research. Things went sideways when he walked me to my room and tried to force his way inside. I slapped some sense into him, and he apologized and left. He didn't realize that if he'd gotten into the room and closed the door, he was going to dance the *cha cha cha* with the stun gun I'd smuggled through customs in a big box of tampons and stashed in the nightstand next to the bed.

He kept pestering me, turning up in the pool bar, the lobby lounge, the restaurants. I'd be half-asleep on a beach chair in my cabana, and his face would loom over me like a bad mirage. He was clearly just another hustler in Paradise, trying to latch onto an American woman, but no matter how rude I was to him, he kept coming back. I avoided him as much as I could.

On my daily walks, I dodged little kids frolicking in the surf, reggae troubadours recycling a handful of Bob Marley songs and Freelance Beach Hustlers hawking junk necklaces and bracelets, hats and baskets woven from palm fronds, parasailing and snorkeling excursions, bandanas, polished conch shells and, on the sly, little baggies of pre-rolled joints. I dug that they were just trying to earn a living, but the Beach Hustlers were relentlessly daring, coming too close, talking too fast, probing for signs of weakness. They made me jumpy; however, I couldn't very well conceal an illegal stun gun in my bikini.

When the Jamaicans talked, I had a hard time following them. Their rapid speech seemed to be *frapped* out of four or five languages, like the ingredients in a daiquiri. I thought I heard the rhythms of French in it, but their sing-songy words muddled into each other and then pulled apart like taffy. It was lyrical and confusing and punctuated by the kind of genuine laughter I'd never heard in Lockbourne or Dublin. I had to grab the few words I understood and try to glue them together into a comprehensible idea.

Evenings, I sat on the veranda, sipped strong, expensive port, and took a few surreptitious tokes of harsh, overpriced Jamaican skunk weed. I smelled the salty air, listened to palm fronds rustle in the breeze, fed my dinner to the shorebirds and stray cats and watched the white sun dissolve into the pewter sea and burnish the horizon. I remembered that soul-stunning, technicolor sunset in Costa Rica and shook my head at the nasty joke I'd played on myself by calling my first escort business Beach Babes. I felt like one of those lonely single women who vacations by herself and makes all the lovey-dovies uncomfortable.

I got up at dawn one morning and walked shin-deep into the gorgeous aquamarine sea. The water was glass-flat and clearer than a swimming pool. The only sound was the soft lap of ripples on wet sand. I waded along the shoreline, completely alone.

I caught a fluttery movement out of the corner of my good eye. It was a stingray about the circumference of a frying pan, gliding over the ocean floor with effortless flips of her wings. She almost bumped into my ankle. I followed her. Another one appeared from nowhere and, like magic, another. Then there were a dozen rays swirling all around me like a squadron of little jet fighters, pin wheeling and soaring and snuffling for their breakfast of shellfish and crabs and minnows. I don't know why, but in an instant, they were gone. They didn't dart into deeper water; they vanished down into the sand, all of them, in a blink and a brief cloud.

I waded to shore. A Beach Hustler holding a white net bag filled with lumpy boxes was watching me.

"D ray ow yuh kno Jamaica is a waah great country," he said.

I waved at him, and he said, *"Respect, m'lady,"* and slung his bag over his shoulder and strolled away, calling out to no one I could see, *"Cigars, cigarettes! Ita guh be a hut, hut day!"*

A day or so later, a Beach Hustler who smelled like he bathed in *ganja* smoke and Hugo Boss cologne told me that the color of my hair proved that God loved me. I said I hoped so. Eager to do anything different, I let him talk me into purchasing a horseback excursion into the jungle. He said I would see wild dogs, big cats and lots of beautiful parrots. I saw one yellow and black snake and a couple nervous lizards. As the underfed, dispirited horses plodded along a sand path deeper into the broiling jungle, mockingbirds jeered us.

When we finally got back to the resort, the guide looked at me and, his merry, bloodshot eyes crinkling, and said, *"M'lady, mi cudda rapt you wheneva mi wan, mi."*

Any woman anywhere would know exactly what that meant,

in any language.

I thought, 'You cudda tried, asshole, you,' but I kept my mouth shut and went to my room.

The concierge hooked me up with a bodyguard. Javier was a super-cool, buffed-up Mexican dude who spoke precise, accented English. He wore polished loafers, pressed khakis, polo shirts and summer-weight sport coats to hide the pistol and extra ammo clips he carried on his belt. His eyes were never still behind his Oakleys; his body never uncoiled. He reminded me of leopards and cougars I'd seen on nature shows. His first assignment was to get rid of the aspiring gigolo from Columbia, which took him all of 10 minutes.

Javier didn't talk a lot, but he did tell me that hiring him had been smart. Going off into the jungle alone with a stranger who had no affiliation with the resort, on the other hand, had been foolish. He said Jamaican cops were completely corrupt, and drug posses were the only real government on the island. Kidnapping and human trafficking were big business there, he said. To certain people, I was a very marketable commodity.

Javier accompanied me everywhere. He must've had a heavy rep, because wherever we went, people stepped aside, even on the crowded streets of downtown Kingston, which he said was a one of the most dangerous cities in the world, for Jamaicans and foreigners alike.

I felt safe with Javier, but, eventually, I had to face the realization that if Grant cancelled my credit cards, I'd be stuck a very long way from home, in a strange land where nobody knew who I was. As always, I followed the trail of apologies, promises and expensive gifts back to Dublin. First class, of course.

Javier was at my side all the way to my gate at the airport. I settled my bill, tipped him $150 and handed him the stun gun to give to his wife. He'd told me that he feared for her safety when he wasn't around. Any woman anywhere would understand exactly what he meant.

CHAPTER TWENTY-FIVE

Alley Cats of The Eternal City

Grant repeatedly asked me to marry him, but a voice in my head warned not to take that step. I kept saying, "Oh, I'm not ready. Just wait."

Being legally tied to someone when I wasn't head-over-heels, *Gone with the Wind* in love didn't make sense. Grant used to call me "Love Puppy," but I'd never loved anybody except Granny and Grandpa and Johnny. I grew up watching people abuse other people. I was abused. Love was never part of the arithmetic.

Because of my childhood, I was never able to tell when a guy was sincerely interested in me. The summer when I was 15, Teddy* started hanging around my crowd. He was a couple years older, a dark-haired Italian who rolled his Marlboro reds in the sleeve of his t-shirt and drove a tricked-out '72 Nova. He took me out all the time and brought me little presents. I sat on his lap and rocked on the porch swing, while he put his arm around my waist and told me how crazy he was about me. Teddy was handsome and had steady access to very good weed, but I figured he was just another asshole laying down another line of jive to lease a parking spot in my panties. That's how I treated the relationship. However, at the end of that summer, when I started running around with another guy, who had more money and a cooler car and even better pot, Teddy flipped. He stopped me one day, grabbed my arms and shook me, crying.

"I loved you," he blubbered. "You crushed me. My heart is broken. I can't believe you did this to me."

I had absolutely no frame of reference that would allow me to understand his feelings. I completely missed all the signals. After that, I started telling dudes up front, "Look, we can go out. Maybe we'll even fuck. It might happen again; it might not. But that's all it's ever going to be. If you understand that and agree to it, then we're good to go, man."

Grant had been the exception to that rule. Sixty million bucks makes a difference. I don't remember having sex with him at all for the first year or so. Eventually, though, he asked me to sleep in the master bedroom, with its big fireplace and canopy bed surrounded by floor-length sheers. At first, he was gentle and considerate, but over time, he became less and less thoughtful. Every Thursday evening at 7 o'clock, in that *faux* romantic room, we had sex by the numbers. There was no foreplay, no soft seduction, no tenderness, not one bit of thought for me. Instead, he took my clothes off, went into his pre-flight checklist and got things over with. I wanted to ask the flight attendant for a drink and some peanuts.

For years, Grant also badgered me about having kids. "I'm wasting my prime years with you," he'd say. "I have to have an heir. Time is running out."

Whenever he brought it up, I flashed back to the sidewalk

outside the abortion clinic. People are screaming and aiming Bibles at us; Arletta is sobbing and trying to pull her arm away from the priest and the angry woman. Then I'm lying on my bed, in pain, hoping the chameleons will change colors. I just couldn't go back there.

I wanted to get a boob job, but he forbade it, because he said it would stop me from breastfeeding. I told him that was ridiculous, but he was adamant. I began secretly taking Depo-Provera shots to keep from becoming pregnant. He couldn't figure out what was wrong.

Grant always said he was guiding me to where I needed to be in life. In a way, that's exactly what happened. As smart as he was, however, he didn't anticipate how I would change with that learning curve. The new woman standing in front of him didn't appreciate someone dictating every second of her life. I was no longer a flighty, wild-ass kid. I became educated, confident, assertive, engaging, and I finally saw clearly what had been going on: He knew that I would feel out of place in Dublin and grateful for being rescued from poverty and insanity. I think the current term for it is "coercive control"; basically, Grant held all the cards, I had nothing, so he felt he could treat me however he wanted.

I slowly assembled bits and pieces of information into a jigsaw puzzle that – as close as I could figure it – explained why Uncle Bo had been so eager to put Grant and me together. Given how I was hustling money at the time and how scummy Uncle Bo was, I should've seen the backdoor play, but I missed it. Grant, I figured, was a daytime businessman and a smooth operator who cruised through the downtown clubs at night. Urban Thrill had been one of his regular stops to check out the girls. If he'd seen Grant throwing money around, Uncle Bo would've been drawn to him like a fly to a turd. That would've led to, 'I need to borrow 2000 or 5000 or 10000,' and ended up with Uncle Bo owing Grant a bundle. Uncle Bo wanted to settle his tab, but he didn't have the cash, which really didn't matter to Grant. He was interested in something else – the girls. Uncle Bo must've run through his stable of chicks, so he tracked me down. I was just another installment on his payment plan.

That insight led me to another one: The kidnapping in Ft. Wayne hadn't been just a vicious coincidence. There was a reason the bouncer didn't walk me out to my car that morning, as he did every other morning. Either he or the club manager – or both of them – had sold my ass to a meth-head maniac gangster for who knows what – cash, drugs, to pay off another debt? It wasn't that they didn't want me back at Showgirls; they never expected to see me again, and they sure didn't want me asking questions about that night. They wouldn't give me my last paycheck because there wasn't one. If I'd never pick it up, why would they bother cutting it?

The thought that I'd been tipping that Neanderthal bouncer to nearly get me killed made a black storm churn up inside me. I'd walked right into it, just like I'd walked right into Grant's bullshit. Because of sick, devious men, I'd been stripped of my innocence, abducted, savagely beaten, repeatedly raped, deprived of my true nature, damaged for life. I hated anything with a dick.

A woman whose name I never knew crystalized things for me. I woke up very early every morning to jog and get away from Grant for an hour or so. Almost every day, I saw another woman kind of speed-walking along. Dublin is a small place, but I didn't know her name. She was maybe 50 or 60; I couldn't tell because she was very dressed up even though it was so early. It must've taken hours for her to apply her makeup. She had on rouge. Her hair was sprayed. She wore stylish sunglasses and jewelry that matched her jogging suits. I didn't understand why someone would get so dolled up just to jog.

One night, I saw her having dinner with her husband at the country club. They were sitting close to Grant and me. Right in front of her, this ugly old man was blatantly eye-fucking me. His wrinkled lizard face was bug-eyed rapey, his tongue running over his thick lips. He kept it up the whole time we were there. I was so disgusted that I couldn't look at food. Meanwhile, she sat with her head down, quietly humiliated, drinking martini after martini.

'Clearly, you're drunk,' I thought, feeling sorry for her. 'Your life is over.'

She looked up; our eyes locked. For a time warp moment, we were *doppelgangers* – I was her past; she was my future. The truth flashed on me: 'Holy shit! That's me! If I go ahead and lie down and take this from Grant and stay here, I'm going to end up like her!'

Grant, I realized, saw me as another investment – an arm piece that had to be perfect in every way or face the consequences. So far, my looks and compliance between the sheets had overshadowed everything else; however, the moment I allowed myself to get fat and ugly, he'd dump me like an underperforming stock. To Grant, everything was about profit and loss.

I finally understood what Silky the Stage Witch meant by balancing your pain. No matter how beautiful you are or how much money you make or how wild you drive men, once you market your body, you become a commodity for sale to the highest bidder. You are not really human; you are never safe; you can trust no one. To me, even the smiling stranger who opens a door for me has a secret motive behind the gesture.

The streets – and Heather – flared up. I became defiant and argumentative. This new woman scared Grant, and that fear infuriated him. Things quickly escalated into combat. He never punched me, but there was a lot of shouting and constant belittling. I didn't leave, though. I'd let the silver and the silk and the crystal and the social-circle two-facers who pretended to be my friends seduce me. I'd broken The Stage Witches' first rule – I'd lost control. Now, every time Grant said he loved me, it felt like a threat. The isolation and depression and utter dependence gnawed at me until the rebellious 10-year-old wildling reappeared and opened a guerilla war against him, using food as her weapon. Gorging on something fun and forbidden buried my pain; throwing up purged it. Those episodes only made matters worse, but I couldn't stop them from happening.

Grant and I went back to Europe, and tensions rose. He'd read my mail and found out about the Depo-Provera, which added to the animosity. The trip degenerated into a series of screaming clashes. To make things bearable, I went missing at every opportunity, looking for animals. If I found a little zoo or someone on the street with a parrot or a monkey, I stayed with them for hours, no matter how angry Grant got over not knowing where I was.

My attraction to animals explains the fiasco in Roma – well, at least part of it. We were drunk over dinner at an outdoor *trattoria*. My anger and resentment were like open wounds. I glared over the table at him, thinking, 'You kept telling me I was worthless and brought nothing to the relationship, and for a long time I believed you. No more. I will not allow you to obliterate me, motherfucker.'

"I'm not going to be having children with you," I said. "This isn't going to be wrapped up with a marriage. I'm done. I want to go into my own life. I can see everything you've been about, and I can't stand you."

Before he could speak, I stormed away. I staggered around Roma, completely drunk. There are a lot of stray cats in Roma. I was following one, talking to her and trying to pet her. She led me through a maze of narrow streets and down a dark alley. Before I realized it, I was at a brick wall dead end.

I was bombed and lost and mad as hell, but I still had my street instincts. A few blocks earlier, I'd noticed two local jerkoffs behind me, trying to be inconspicuous. I turned around, and they were coming toward me, one on each side of the alley.

'Holy crap! These assholes are up to something. This is interesting,' I thought.

They figured they'd found a dumb American girl to pounce on. I was wearing a dress and a shawl and lots of expensive jewelry and was so drunk that I was tottering on high heels and talking to an alley cat. I didn't know if they were muggers or rapists or what, but those assholes offended me. I walked straight at them, snarling and screaming, "What the fuck do *you* want? Bring it, dirtbags!"

They must've thought they'd cornered the devil herself, because they sprinted out of that alley. Just as I was congratulating myself on being such a badass, I remembered Grant had my passport and purse and plane tickets back in our suite at the Hotel Columbus, right down from the Vatican and that dark entity.

They call Roma "The Eternal City," right? Well, that night, I thought I was going to be stranded there forever. I was on the streets – alone, with nothing – again.

CHAPTER TWENTY-SIX

Carnal Geometry

Grant tried to be nice during the long flight home. But as soon as we got to Dublin, I told him, "I want out. You've done this whole number on me, and I'm finished with you."

"You realize if you leave, you take nothing, right?" he said. "We're not married. You have no legal claim."

For weeks, he searched for the combination that would make me circuit the way he wanted. I saw what he was up to. He couldn't make me bend; he wasn't about to surrender his power, though.

I knew that leaving him would be jumping from one ledge to another. I'd gone from poverty and abuse and running the streets to unlimited spending money and platinum credit cards. I was just a few credits short of my degree, and classes were starting up soon. I was even thinking about going on to graduate school. However, I looked at the hard work I'd put into the relationship, the concessions and adjustments I'd made trying to get it right. I'd pushed so hard and put up with so much shit that I just didn't give a fuck anymore. I was at the door to the cell, and they were about to slam it shut and swallow the key in front of me if I didn't bolt right now.

For several weeks, we lived in ice-cold silence. I was leaving the house one night, as I often did just to get away. I'd kept in touch with the family who took Joshie and Trinity, which really made Grant angry. I was on my way to visit them. He demanded to know where I was going. I wouldn't tell him. He tried to grab me to stop me.

"Fuck off!" I screamed, pulling away from him.

I ran around the house, scooping up everything I could, jumped in my Mitsubishi and tore out of Dublin. I came back later to collect the rest of my stuff, while a cop watched me. I didn't even try to take the Ferrari. It was a piece of over-priced junk, anyway. I managed to escape with a lot of jewelry and clothing and some cash, but Grant was exactly right about the rest of it.

I'd hung on in Dublin for almost 10 years; now, that life was over. I was on the run again. I swung by to take Joshua and Trinity out of foster care and went to the condo on Lake Shore Drive. Fred had died shortly after I moved in with Grant, whom he despised. Grant kept bugging me to sell the condo. Guilty as shit over Fred's death, I'd adamantly refused, paid the taxes and fees and otherwise pretended the condo didn't exist. Being there creeped me out, but I had to go somewhere.

It's not like I didn't have my chances to go back to Easy Street. Grant wouldn't accept what happened. He sent flowers and candy. He continually got inside the condo gate and left syrupy post-it notes stuck to my door. They weren't signed, but they were printed in black marker on yellow paper, just like he always did.

I didn't want to hear his shit. I even scheduled the boob job he wouldn't let me have. I thought, 'You'll get that signal, buddy. You'll be flaming pissed. You won't want anything more to do with me once you see I got my boobs done.' It didn't work. In fact, he commended me about it in a note. I'd gone to the Cleveland Clinic, and his note said, "At least you were smart enough to go to the best." I ignored it and him.

Unprepared for the instantaneous devastation of the breakup, I was shattered and lost. I had a place to live and the start-up capital I grabbed on the way out of Dublin, but as close as I could figure, I had to bring in three grand a month just to stay in the condo. That seemed like a hefty nut for someone with no marketable skills and no understanding of how to be an adult in Sheep World.

Fred had talked about leaving me everything, but his kids made sure that didn't happen. He did create a trust fund for me, though. It was somewhere around $200,000. The money was invested in stocks and bonds and stuff, so I'm not sure exactly how much was there. It's not like I could put my hands on it in a lump sum, so it wouldn't do me any good with regular expenses.

That was the flashpoint. I looked around at the possibilities. I remembered the stripper pole, the stage, the crowds of adoring men elbowing each other for the privilege of giving me their cash. I remembered the easy money and carefree fun of Beach Babes. I fell back on my looks and escorting. Sex sells, doesn't it? It pays, too, if you know what you're doing. Heather knew what she was doing.

I was 28, free, and in hell. I started running with girls I knew from the streets. Dancers, sex workers, whores – whatever you want to call them, they were half-dressed and completely wild. That worked out fine, since Heather was a viciously self-destructive maniac who was determined to implode with drugs and alcohol, instead of food. I wandered around, perpetually buzzed, in a fog that was so thick that I couldn't tell anymore where Angela stopped and Heather began. Sometimes, I felt like Heather had imagined Angela, instead of the reverse.

My street girlfriends and I ripped people off with every conceivable hustle, from outright theft to credit card scams. I wasn't planning on staying in this world for long, anyway, so I didn't care what I did to myself or to anyone else.

For a while, it was a mattress-to-mouth existence, a serious daily hassle to find money. Relief arrived in the form of Grant's Dublin pals. These old dinner-party dudes were very rich international players, some of the most influential people in the state. When I lived in Dublin, they'd hounded me – always flirting, suggesting, touching. Now that they knew Grant and I were quits, they no longer had to be satisfied with creeping up on me and rubbing the crotches of their ugly double-knit golf slacks against my ass at cocktail parties.

Like Holy Honcho, those guys were all money on the hoof, so Grant either ignored their advances or turned them into a joke, saying he could make a fortune by leasing me out. Now, I took that statement as a business tip; I just cut out the middleman. The old dudes were rutty enough to track me down and proposition me. I was smart enough to take advantage of the opportunities.

Grant had drilled two pieces of advice into me: "Take notes on everything"; and, sounding a lot like The Stage Witches, "When you leave home for work, pick up your keys and hang up your heart." I decided to apply both to my new career. His harping about comportment and etiquette combined with Heather's instincts and my internship with The Stage Witches to perfectly prepare me for my start-up enterprise.

To be honest, though, I've never had sex that didn't benefit me after an up-front agreement, either directly stated or strongly implied. Well, that's not exactly accurate. Years before, I tried to have a funfuck, with Luke. He was handsome enough to be a double for Thor in those Marvel movies, and we were both high and drunk. It was late, so I decided to let him stay the night, like normal people do. I figured everyone else seemed to enjoy sex, so this might be a little bonus for me

We graduated into the bedroom and took our clothes off. I started whispering some single-X dirty talk in his ear to turn myself on and get him revved up. He giggled like a nervous schoolboy. I was still technically a minor, but I instantly realized that I was the only adult in that bed.

I rolled out with the blanket around me and said, "Get the fuck out!"

He jumped up and backed into the doorway, naked and confused.

"What don't you understand?" I yelled. "Get the fuck out!"

When I wasn't working, I occasionally found myself around an interesting, attractive guy. Trying to act normal, I went with the flow. In guys' minds, though, the flow always leads into the bedroom, and that's where I – and the guy – would inevitably confront the damage that had been done to me so long ago, damage that made it much simpler to treat sex as a business transaction than as a personal interaction.

Some of my new clients wanted an attractive, poised escort to a dinner or concert or the theater; some wanted a little dessert afterward. It was all negotiable, and those old dudes certainly understood how to conduct business deals. Some called so often that I gave them a frequent flyer discount. My most profitable customers – call them the Tiffany Preferred Level – received a rewards package tailored to their special perversions. I thought it would be funny to pass out punch cards, like Starbucks, but I figured the clients wouldn't be amused. Men always want to maintain the illusion of romance – or at least to have plausible deniability for their lechery.

Those wealthy, powerful businessmen were paying for sex, but they were also buying confidentiality. Secrecy was as important to them as any private, physical act. Obviously, most of them knew my real name. However, they weren't about to ignite a scandal that would blow their corporations, their families and their reputations to bits. A reliable, lucrative revenue stream in exchange for a little effort and a lot of silence? At the time, it was the best arrangement a broken girl like me could expect. I spent a lot of time riding in the backs of limousines, smiling and listening. When I make an agreement, it's for life, so I won't name the limo owners.

Everything comes with its own price, though. Just like Grant, my clients kept reminding me how lucky I was to have them, how much they were doing for me, how lost I would be without them. They pissed me off, but I was making so much money that I was like a drug dealer who doesn't know what to do with all the cash. I had wads of bills stuffed into my glove box and under the seats and in Mitzi's trunk. For a while, I worried what I'd say if a cop pulled me over, spotted all the money and asked where it came from. That problem soon solved itself, as good word of mouth, so to speak, expanded my client roster. I had cops, their bosses and their bosses' bosses as clients, up to and including a state senator. I had clients from Ohio and from other states. At least once a month, I saw an FBI agent who ran names for me and gave me the heads-up on raids, stings and campaigns by bluenoses looking for votes. Everyone on my roster wanted to keep Angela – or Heather, depending – happy.

Not to be petty, but the job also came with a couple other very satisfying perqs. While Angela had been figuring the math on the burndown with Grant, Heather was working carnal geometry. She saw doing Grant's buddies as a way to stick it to a bunch of charity-ball, lacquer-haired snoots at the same time their husbands were sticking it to her, by whatever name. Better yet, it was a covert means of lashing out at Grant. He'd assume that financial necessity would eventually drive Angela back to

Dublin, Heather reasoned. When it didn't, he'd know something was up. Plus, men can't help whispering about their sexual adventures. Eventually, she said, Grant would figure out what was going on. Picturing his reaction made her gleeful.

The Stage Witches would've kicked Heather's ass for allowing anger to drive her; they said never to become emotionally involved. She didn't care. Now, Heather the Avenging Angel was on a scorched-earth crusade against every entitled douchebag who crossed her path.

CHAPTER TWENTY-SEVEN

Lot 302

Burning time one day, I ran into my married friends Jerry and Terry. They knew how much I liked animals.

"You want to go to Mt. Hope and see some exotic animals?" Jerry asked. "I think you'll have lots of fun."

I told him I had no idea what he was talking about. Jerry said that they'd bred several bear cubs and were going to something called the Mid-Ohio Alternative Animal and Bird Sale to sell them on consignment. 'I have nothing to do,' I thought. 'I'll get to see some cool animals, and Mt. Hope is a nice name for a place. This'll be a hoot.'

I met Jerry and Terry in a huge parking lot that was packed with every vehicle from three-seater Mercedes convertibles to pick-ups held together with putty and duct tape. There were license plates from lots of states on huge horse trailers and trucks stacked with wire cages; there were hundreds of people: farmers with sunburned necks and cracked hands, bikers in patched cut vests and black stomper boots, drunk frat-boys, families carrying balloons and stuffed animals and fat-cats in Oxford shirts, pressed jeans and expensive jogging shoes.

I paid my admission and followed Jerry and Terry into a vast barn. The place smelled like overflowing Porta Johns, boiled hot dogs, fried grease, B.O. and another foul odor – one I couldn't place.

We walked around pens holding zebras and donkeys, camels and weird, hairy cattle and skittish little deer and rooms filled with massive constrictors and slit-eyed venomous snakes that Jerry said could kill a person with a scratch of a fang. There were strange rodents bigger than cats, prehistoric-looking lizards, tortoises as round as manhole covers and birds wearing electrified plumage – all kinds of striped and spotted and feathered and furry and scaly things I'd never seen before and didn't know the names of. In the maze of corrals and cages and pet carriers, animals howled, whinnied, screeched, bleated. Jerry said they were all legally for sale. It was very freaky, and to add to the freakiness, I was smashed and stoned. I felt like Alice after she nibbled the magic mushroom.

Jerry got some ping-pong paddle thingy, and we went into the room where they auctioned off the animals. It was like a lighted loading corral facing concrete stairs that rose almost straight up. We found space on the uncomfortable bleachers to watch the auction. It was bizarre. Amish dudes wearing suspenders and straw hats and funky chin whiskers, their denim shirtsleeves rolled to their elbows, lifted plastic pet kennels from stacks loaded on wheeled carts and set them on the floor. One would reach into a kennel and pull out an animal so young its eyes were barely open. He'd hold the tiny creature over his head and carry it around, turning to give everyone in the bleachers a clear look. There were baby monkeys and wolf and bear and leopard and bobcat and tiger cubs.

People around us shouted; the Amish guys yelled back. The ones who were showing the babies nodded, pointed, arched eyebrows. Over a PA system, a disembodied voice chanted rapid-fire numbers and information about the kids' species and blood lines and friendly dispositions and outstanding breeding potentials. The patter was hypnotic.

For some reason, Jerry's paddle ended up in my hand. Everyone kept raising and lowering their paddles like they were doing the wave at a football game. I figured it was some kind of hillbilly ritual, so I started throwing my paddle up and down, too.

An Amish dude carrying a kitten of some kind bellowed a number; the voice stopped. The Amishman pointed at me and said something that sounded like, "Heeyah!"

Now, the whole crowd was staring at me. I looked at the number on the paddle I was holding. It took me a few heartbeats to realize that I'd been bidding on the kitten every time I waved that paddle and had bought an "alternative animal" without even knowing what it was. I glanced sideways at Jerry. He was red-faced with fury and shaking his lowered head. I didn't want the guy to stroke out or flip on me, so I acted like nothing was happening. 'Okay, be cool,' I thought. 'No matter what this is, you can deal with it.'

"Where's the office?" I asked, casually. "I need to pay for my purchase."

Jerry frowned and directed me to a room that was disgustingly dirty and chaotic. A woman there acted like I knew what I was doing. Of course, I pretended that I did; meanwhile, I was clueless about what I'd just bought. Whatever it was, it cost 450 bucks, cash only, all sales final. Thank God, I had the money in my purse. The woman took it without asking a single question or even saying what species of animal I now owned. She just called it "Lot 302."

She gave me a receipt and told me to go to Building 2. I walked there and handed it to an Amish guy. He left, and I looked around the room. There were three or four little tigers and some bear cubs jammed into cages. They were all terrified – hunkered down, bawling. It was hard to make myself accept that what I was seeing was real. 'I can't believe I have clearance to walk around in here. I can't believe there are baby tigers in this awful room. I can't believe they're actually treating these little animals like this,' I thought.

The Amish guy came back with a small, flimsy wire cage marked "302; *Binomen felis concolor*." Despite three and a half years of college, I didn't know what one word of the scientific language meant, but whatever was in that cage was only a few days old and was crying in a pathetic, squealy voice. The Amish dude handed it to me like, 'Okay, there you go. You're out of here.' He didn't say a word to me about how I was supposed care for whatever I'd bought.

I was sobering up, I'd just laid down significant cash and I wanted to know what was happening. I peered into the cage; two tiny eyes were shining up at me. I knew the creature was a kitten, but it was obviously no Himalayan or Maine Coon.

'Damn, now I'm stuck with this animal,' I thought.

When I got to the car, I took a closer look at this 302 thingy. As she cried, her carmine mouth gaped between the drooping ends of a tiny handlebar mustache of black fur, and her blue eyes narrowed under tilted black exclamation points. By God, I knew it was a baby cougar, a tiny girl who'd been taken from her mommy. She was frightened, probably starving, absolutely helpless.

"No one wanted you, did they?" I whispered. "They're just getting rid of you, aren't they? They don't care what happens to you. They just care about the money. No one wanted me, either. We're both rejects, little girl."

The reality of Mt. Hope washed over me in a nauseating tidal wave: it was a fucking Kids-for-Cash Supermarket. To the cold-hearted, matter-of-fact, Benjamin-chasing dirtbags who bred and sold her and the rest of the animals at that despicable place, the precious little cat in front of me was nothing but a commodity. That stench I couldn't identify earlier was the evil perfume of greed and cruelty. It overpowered the human and animal stink. Mt. Hope proved that Mammon truly has dominion over the earth and all its creatures.

I looked into the kitten's sparkling eyes again, and, right then, I named her Jewels and started wondering what I was going to do with her. I carried her to the car, trying to imagine how Joshua and Trinity would react when they saw a cougar cub on their turf; then I realized that whatever issues any of us had didn't matter. Wild, domesticated or somewhere in between, we four were going to have to learn to get along, at least for the time being.

CHAPTER TWENTY-EIGHT

Against Veterinary Advice

On the way home, I called everyone who might have any idea how to care for a cougar cub. It was getting late on a Saturday, and no one I called had a clue what I should do. By the way she was whining, I could tell Jewels was hungry, but I couldn't stroll into PetSmart and ask for the cougar aisle. I did the only thing I could think of – I called the Columbus Zoo. They immediately put Jack Hanna on the phone. I introduced myself and told him what had just happened at Mt. Hope and what was riding on the passenger seat next to me.

"I know I have to feed her, but I don't know what or how," I said.

Jack started explaining the techniques for feeding a cougar kitten. He stopped and said, "Wait a minute." He put me on hold. As I waited, I became more upset at myself for being so stupid.

Jack came back on and said, "Listen, I can fix this right now. I know the man who can help you tonight. Tell him I sent you his way."

He gave me the number for a Dr. Don Burton. I called Dr. Burton, and even though his clinic, Animal Care Unlimited, was closed, he gave me the address and told me to meet him there.

Dr. Burton was as stiff and authoritative and dignified as an admiral. He had short, receding, salt-and-pepper hair and a neat beard flecked with gray and wore wire-rimmed glasses. Several staff members had Kitten Milk Replacement formula and baby bottles ready for me. He gave me a primer on how to feed Jewels. He examined her and said she wasn't old enough for shots. Then he warned me that for my sake and the cat's sake, I should surrender her.

"Let me take her off your hands right now," he said, dourly. "You have no idea what you're getting into."

I was already feeling sympathetic toward this frightened kitty. Besides, after the auction and vet bill and all the stuff Jewels needed, I was a thousand bucks in the hole.

"Okay, listen," I said, "I'm putting out money here. You know what? We're going to go home now. I'll schedule an appointment for her shots. Let me decide what I'm going to do from here."

That first night, I watched the adorable little ragdoll as she staggered and stumbled and fell down on the carpet. She mewled and batted at a string of pearls I dangled in front of her.

"I cannot believe you're in my bedroom, so helpless, and you don't have a life, either," I said. "I just came out of another life, and I don't have anything to do. I'm thinking about driving off a cliff. This might be what I'm supposed to do now. I can handle this."

First thing Monday morning, I called Dr. Burton and told him I was keeping Jewels.

CHAPTER TWENTY-NINE

Arms of The Mummy

Jewels was trouble from jump. She didn't come with an owner's manual, so I sought information everywhere about what to feed her, caging, veterinary needs. There was nothing available. Period. Dr. Burton was the only one I could turn to.

The problems started with feeding. It wasn't like leaving some Fancy Feast in a bowl for Josh and Trinity. Dr. Burton told me she'd been weaned way too soon. Since she hadn't been drinking mother's milk, her stomach would be sensitive. She could have only KMR, which I bought it in big cans of powder. Jewels was so young I had to bottle-feed her.

"Bottle-feeding a kitten is not like bottle-feeding a baby," Dr. Burton told me. "Never forget this, Angela: Feed with all fours on the floor."

Jewels was finicky, and KMR is fickle stuff. I tried to get the consistency perfect by timing how long I shook the bottles. I'd put a few drops on my wrist to test the temperature, hoping it was okay for her. If I made the formula too thin, she got diarrhea. If I made it too thick, it clogged and wouldn't come out of the nipple, so she shredded it.

Dr. Burton said to put Jewels on my lap, belly down, never on her back. I'd lay her on the pink blanket I used for feeding. She squirmed and complained until I held her head still with one hand and wriggled the middle finger of the other hand into a corner of her mouth. When she started sucking my finger, I quickly replaced it with the nipple. I held her head back as she drank and purred and kneaded the blanket, her eyes tightly shut.

My routine was to wake up, feed Joshua and Trinity and pour my coffee. Before I was fully awake, Jewels wanted breakfast. As soon as she smelled formula, she climbed my pajamas and latched onto the nipple, screaming, as ferocious as a famished vampire. If I wasn't ready, Jewels ripped the bottle out of my hands and tore around the condo, spraying KMR. I chased her down and refilled the bottle while she wailed and clawed my legs. Of course, Trin and Joshie wanted to know what was going on, so they complicated matters even more.

I tried to make Jewels understand: 'You can have the bottle, but I have to hold it.' She didn't, of course. She already had her baby teeth, and her claws were razor sharp. From lick one, she taught me: 'Yeah, I'm cute and helpless, but guess what? I scratch, and I bite.' She sank her claws into my hands until she drew blood. She put a deep gash almost two inches long between my right thumb and forefinger. I had it stitched, but Jewels tore it open again the very next morning.

Before every meal, I had to work up the nerve to feed her. When she finally drank her fill, she collapsed and passed out, her belly swollen, wheezing like an old wino. I sanitized the bottles by boiling them in bleach water and swabbed my wounds and wrapped my arms with gauze until they looked mummified.

CHAPTER THIRTY

Mutilations

When I took Jewels back to Animal Care Unlimited for her vaccinations, Dr. Burton saw my wounded arms and thumb, which looked like someone had tried to saw it off with a steak knife.

"Angela, are you crazy?" he asked. "We have to take her claws off."

I figured he knew best and left her there to have her front claws removed, since those were the ones that did all the damage. I drove back the next day on pins and needles. Traffic was being rerouted for a big golf tournament that was going on at Muirfield Country Club. Despite the mess, I managed to get there early. The staff told me to hang out in the waiting room until Jewels woke up from the anesthetic. As soon as I sat down, I heard her squalling. I went up to the desk and asked what was going on. They were all like, 'Oh, Miss Harter, we assure you blah, blah.'

I sat down, heard her again, jumped up and blasted right past the desk, through a set of swinging doors into the lab and operating area. Jewels had a surgical cone on her head. She was in a cage, fighting and squealing in a way that set my blood on fire. I barged past Dr. Burton and ran to her. I immediately saw that he'd removed her front *and* back claws. My little girl was a bloody mess, she was woozy, she was whimpering.

I snatched the gate open. Jewels jumped on me and draped her front legs around my neck. I held her on my hip like a toddler. She was crying. Blood splattered my white jersey, white jogging pants and white shoes. I went sideways.

"Burton, you motherfucker, how dare you?" I yelled. "I'm going to sue your ass. Go to hell!"

Everyone went silent. Dr. Burton froze and gaped at me.

"If I didn't have to hold her, I'd kick your fucking ass!" I shouted.

I ripped up the check I'd written for the surgery and dropped the pieces. I carried Jewels out to the Toyota Land Cruiser I'd bought specifically for her. Kathy, Dr. Burton's lead person, followed us and stood nervously outside my window. When I rolled it down, she flinched like I was going to punch her, handed me a bag by her fingertips and said, "Here's Jewels' prescriptions, Ms. Harter. Here's Dr. Burton's cell number. He said to call him if you need him."

I screeched out of the parking lot with blood all over me. I got Jewels home and gave her the meds, bedded her down and tried to adjust to the fact that Dr. Burton had mutilated my little girl.

CHAPTER THIRTY-ONE

The Vanishing of Heather

I'm still not sure if that surgery was a mistake or if Dr. Burton was trying to protect me from myself, but after a while, I forgave him. At least he cared and was willing to help. He must've forgiven my tantrum, too, because he advised me as I tried to get Jewels to start eating meat. At first, I whipped up this awful goop of ground turkey, KMR and vitamins in a blender. She was okay with that, but then I had to wean her off the KMR completely and get some straight meat into her. She did *not* want to shift; she wanted her bottle. Dr. Burton and I tried all kinds of stuff: little shrimps, lobster shreds, teeny pieces of bloody meat that I tenderized with a wooden mallet like a blacksmith forging horseshoes. She didn't want any of it.

"You're going to have to make her go with no bottle," Dr. Burton said. "Offer her fresh meat, but when it gets warm, you have to take it away because bacteria will grow on raw meat."

I'd prepare her dinner; she'd turn her nose up at it, offended. A couple of hours later, I'd throw the food out. She did that for days. She wanted that bottle.

"No bottle," Dr. Burton insisted. "You've got to make her hungry enough to eat solids."

Even after she finally started to nibble sliced turkey, I had to get the calcium and vitamin supplements right; however, she grew so fast that every two weeks or so, the formula changed. A baby cougar in the wild spends her first two years with her mother; Mom's going to naturally do things right. I was responsible for Jewels' development, and there wasn't going to be any do-over. An adult cougar can jump 25 feet in the air. If she doesn't receive the proper nutrition as a cub, her bones will shatter. You can't cast a big cat, so a broken leg is a death sentence. Even though I tried to understand her needs and follow Dr. Burton's suggestions, every day was an experiment. I could only pray that I was getting it right.

My life wasn't my own anymore. Jewels dictated every move I made. Cold-turkey, I stopped drinking and doing drugs. Heather disappeared off the streets. I cut my whoring calendar way back, as well, booking just enough gigs to keep us in the condo. My girlfriends thought I'd lost my mind, but I had to be there for that kid. I was all she had.

I'd been very worried about how my domestic cats would react to Jewels. Joshua was always a lover. He treated Jewels like he was her surrogate parent. He shared his food and his sleeping basket and licked her all the time. Trinity, as usual, acted like a dickhead. I'd see his blazing yellow eyes under the bed and know that he and Jewels had been scrapping. She loved aggravating him, chasing him until he got pissed and rolled her down the hallway. He never hurt her, though. Just between us, I think he had a secret crush on her.

CHAPTER THIRTY-TWO

The Phantom Ocelot of Hidden Lake

My condominium development was called Hidden Lake, but Jewels didn't stay hidden for long. No one ever said anything about the drunken, stoned-out, adults-only antics of my rowdy girlfriends; however, they sure started complaining when they saw Jewels. I lived on the second floor. My balcony ran the entire length of the condo. I paid a maintenance man to install a kennel cage that was nearly as long as the balcony so Jewels could lie in the sun and fresh air. To keep her from jumping out, he made a roof out of chain link.

She still wasn't completely secure, though. An older couple lived on the third floor. They were nice, but they knew Jewels was obviously not a tabby kitten and shouldn't be living in a gated community five minutes from downtown Columbus. They called the authorities.

A buffoon from the state showed up with a deputy sheriff, pounding on my door. I spied them through the peephole, but I had no choice except to let them in. That pompous jackass rambled on about how wonderful he was and how he'd been doing this for 30 years and how powerful he was and how much he knew about animals and how much Jack Hanna respected him. I batted my eyes and pretended to be impressed.

Then he said, "I hear you have a wild animal here."

"I don't know about that," I said. "I went to an auction and bought a little kitten."

As I tried to be flirty and cute and explain everything away, Jewels strolled around the corner into the living room, right up between my feet, curious about the visitors. We all stood there, silently looking at each other. I could see the jackass's dim brain spinning in overdrive.

I finally broke the silence: "Well, there she is. You can see for yourself."

"Ha!" he cried, triumphantly. "That's a juvenile ocelot!"

"Oh, seriously?" I said, setting a finger against my cheek and cocking one hip in a surprised and alluring pose. "Is that a bad thing?"

"Yes, it can't be here," he said.

With that, he and the cop left. A couple days later, I got a registered letter informing me that I was violating City of Columbus Health Code Chapter 241.05. Ohio had no state laws about private ownership of exotics, but a local ordinance, which I didn't know anything about, banned them.

The letter accused me of keeping an ocelot in my residence. That's how much the jackass knew about animals. Baby cougars do have spots, but anybody who knows anything would never mistake one for an ocelot cub. Jewels' species didn't matter, though. Ocelot, cougar, whatever – she was considered a dangerous wild animal. I could either give her up or move out of Hidden Lake.

Just like that, I was out and on the run again, but this time, wherever I went, I'd have a very serious alternative animal along for the ride.

CHAPTER THIRTY-THREE

Busted

Phil*, an older Beach Babes client, invited us to stay at his ranch south of Columbus, where he bred and trained thoroughbred racehorses. He said Jewels could have a bedroom on the second floor of his farmhouse. Pretty soon, Phil and I started screwing around. He's another one who said, "I love you. I want to marry you. I can take care of you."

He had money, and I'm into older men. I thought, 'Oh, maybe,' then that goat started playing games. He swore he wasn't seeing anyone else, but when he wasn't around one night, I pushed redial on his phone and got the Regal 6 movie theatre in Grove City. I went over and slipped inside. He was sitting there with some woman, watching *Double Jeopardy*. It was so dark they couldn't see me creeping up on them. I smacked Phil right in the mouth; the sound was as loud as a firecracker. As I strolled out, with Tommy Lee Jones' huge head looming behind me, the woman was screaming, and the audience applauded.

Obviously, it was time for Jewels and me to move on. I looked at million-dollar estates and rundown dumps until I finally found a house not too far from Phil's farm for $250,000. The realtor said there were no laws against cougars there, my financing was approved and I took the keys. We were scheduled to close in the morning.

On the way to the new house, I stopped at the farm to pick up Jewels. Phil knew I was leaving, and he didn't like it. He wouldn't let me in the house.

"My kid is in there, fucker! You can kiss my ass!" I said. "Get the hell out of my way!"

The grooms and stable hands who were bedding down the horses heard me yelling. They stopped what they were doing to watch us argue. When Phil tried to block me from entering the house, I grabbed an ice pick that was sitting there and chased him. He slipped and fell and scrambled up and ran away with me right behind him. The hands were standing in the barn door, whooping and laughing as if they were betting on whether their boss would make it out alive.

Phil was surprisingly quick and nimble for an old dude, so he managed to get away. I wasn't really going to kill him anyway – or maybe I was; I was so furious I didn't know what I would do if I caught him.

I kept a ladder right under the window to Jewels' room, because she was good at locking the door from the inside by pushing the little button, and I had to have a way to get in. I laid the ladder up against the house, climbed it, opened the window, went in, clipped Jewels to a leash and took her out to the Land Cruiser. I planned to fetch Josh and Trin from Hidden Lake the next day.

When we pulled in at the new house, heavy snow was falling. I took Jewels inside, closed the door and immediately saw bar lights flashing. I looked out the window, wondering what was going on. A fleet of prowl cars jammed my driveway and the road in front of my house. I thought, 'Man, there must be some serious shit going down for so many cops to be out on such a nasty night.' Just as I stuck Jewels in the bathroom, cops burst through the front door and cuffed me, hands behind my back.

Before I could ask what was up, one of them said they were going to have to shoot the mountain lion. I went batshit, screaming and swearing and struggling. They dragged me toward a cruiser. I cursed and fought until we all fell into a snowbank and wrestled there. They lifted me and tried to calm me down. Uncertain what to do, those big snowy cops stood around me in the flickering light like a ring of flocked Christmas trees decorated with badges and medals.

They rushed me, carried me to the car and shoved me in, covered with melting snow and shouting. They tried to talk to me through the cage. I didn't want to hear it. My hands were still cuffed, so I kicked the windows and seats and tried to bite the cops. That cruiser was rocking like a t-rex had hold of it.

"I have that cougar legally, you assholes!" I shouted. "I have money! I know people! I own that fucking house. That's the Land Cruiser I bought specifically for that cat. I'm somebody, damn you!"

I was rolling: "That cat's a Colorado red. She's an endangered species. You shoot her, and you're in big trouble. I will sue the hell out of every one of you! I'll sue this whole city. Your fucking kids will be paying me until they die. Get your boss here now!"

The cops closest to me lowered their heads and whispered to each other. They got on the radio and summoned a supervisor.

Even more cruisers arrived; John Dillinger wouldn't have attracted so many fucking cops. The window finally rolled down, and a face that was as pale and shapeless as a bowl of tapioca appeared. A short, fat man whose collar was cinched deep into his chins by his tie identified himself as the officer in charge.

"Just give me my phone," I growled at him. "Let me call my vet and get my cat out of here. I'll sit here until Dr. Burton comes, and then I'll go downtown peacefully. We'll deal with the rest of it later."

They wouldn't unlock the cuffs, but they dialed Dr. Burton and listened in on the call. He answered, and I said, "Something went down, and these cops are threatening to shoot Jewels. You have my American Express on file. There's no limit on it. I'll give you a thousand bucks to come down here to Grove City and pick her up."

The snow had gotten heavier, but he said, "All right, Angie. Done. I'll be right there."

The supervisor was stupefied.

"Ah, Miss Harter, Dr. Burton is on the way?" he asked.

Now, he realized that I had enough juice to turn all their lives into a shitstorm. I sat there, scowling. An hour or so later, Dr. Burton walked up to the window.

"Go get Jewels out of the house and take her to your place," I said.

Jewels and I both spent that night in jail. The cops hauled me off, and Jewels was darted and taken to Animal Care Unlimited. In the morning, the cops wouldn't release me out of the front door. They shoved me out the back into an alley, like they were glad to be rid of me. My lawyer picked me up. It'd taken him hours to find me because I'd supposedly been "lost in the system."

When I got to Animal Care Unlimited, Jewels was stoned over from the meds and so pissed that Dr. Burton and his staff wouldn't go near the kennel she'd been kept in overnight. She growled and hissed at them worse than I had at those cops the night before. I guess being busted for the first time upset her.

I put the leash on her and walked her out to the Land Cruiser. As I passed the clinic windows, Dr. Burton held up a hand-lettered piece of paper that said, "CALL ME!"

Jewels sat shotgun, like she always did, and glared over at me like, 'C'mon, bitch. What's up? Let's roll.'

We rolled.

CHAPTER THIRTY-FOUR

Hi, Mom!

As I was being hustled out of the police station that morning, a cop yelled, "We'll be back." I thought the *Terminator* bullshit was way over the top, just as the all-out blitz on my house had been. Then my lawyer filled me in on what had gone down. Phil called the sheriff's office and told them I tried to kill him. He'd made it sound like I was a maniac on the lam with a dangerous, illegal wild animal. He left out the part about keeping Jewels away from me, of course.

The real estate agent had either been dishonest or incompetent, because there was a local ordinance against keeping exotic animals in my new neighborhood. I cancelled the deal; we had only a couple days to move out. I had to find somewhere I could live with Jewels without being harassed by neighbors and the law.

My friend Marsha was a real estate agent. She'd just stumbled across a place a few miles outside of Lancaster. A lady bought it and died of cancer three days later; the house wasn't even on the market yet. Marsha said it was seven or eight acres out in the country. The woman owed 130,000 on it. That's all I knew – that, and Lancaster didn't have any ordinance about keeping exotics. I saw the place only once, at night, then went to the signing and picked up the keys. When I finally saw it in the daylight, I was like, 'Holy crap! There's a graveyard right there, and I'm afraid of the dark.'

The house was a cute, one-story log home with a loft, next to a church with a high white steeple and that graveyard. It was secluded in the woods, at the top of a long gravel driveway, invisible from the road. I was a domestically challenged city girl who didn't cook or clean. I can't stand weeds or grass or bugs. This place was way out in Yahooland with spiders as big as baseballs and weeds 10 feet tall. It was perfect.

'I hate the sex industry,' I thought. 'I hate men. I'm sick of this aggravation. I'm going to stop the running, grab some normal and live here forever, just me and Jewels and Trinity and Joshua. This is my shot.'

I dumped the condo cheap just to get out of the taxes and monthly fees, but now I had a fat mortgage on the log house. I didn't have a job. I didn't know what I was going to do with myself. I was living in the midst of hillbillies. My roommates were two domestic cats and a mountain lion. We had a coffee pot and a little TV with no cable. At night, Jewels and I shared our only recliner. For that summer, she was just another housecat romping around while I tried to figure things out.

My yard was a jungle. I didn't own a lawnmower and wouldn't know what to do with one anyway. I stopped one morning at a farmhouse that had a row of reconditioned mowers lined up in the yard for sale. A guy in his 70s came out and introduced himself as Don Nugent. I bought the mower he recommended. It obviously wouldn't fit in the Mitsubishi, so Don said he would deliver it.

When he brought the mower to the house, I let him in without thinking and offered him coffee. Don sat on the recliner; Jewels sauntered down the hallway and plopped on her butt in front of him. 'Uh oh, this is where it all goes south again,' I thought.

Cool as could be, Don reached over, patted her head and said, "And who do we have here?"

Jewels craned her neck and purred as Don stroked her.

When I admitted that I didn't even know how to start the mower, Don cut my grass. All I had in the house was coffee, Diet Mountain Dew, a bag of pretzels, cans of cat food and a cooler full of raw meat on ice. Don must've noticed, because the next day, his wife, Marge, showed up with a huge picnic basket of food and household stuff and set about helping me put the house in order. I didn't know what to make of these *Green Acres* characters, and I'm sure they wondered about me and my cougar and my Prada sunglasses and spike heels and satin jeans and makeup and jewelry. Nonetheless, Don and Marge soon became my surrogate grandparents and guides to Wild America.

Through them, I hired a boy to mow the lawn. I only allowed him in the front because I didn't want a stranger to upset Jewels. Whenever he came, I made sure she was somewhere in a back room, with the door shut and the blinds down.

When Jewels wanted to go outside, I put her on a long leather dog leash and walked her around. We didn't take any 15-minute doggie constitutionals around the cul-de-sac. I had to schedule my whole afternoon for her. I hate the country, but because I cared for that girl so much and because I knew she loved it so much, we walked the entire property. I didn't exactly walk her; I was just on the other end of the leash. We'd go out the back door, and she'd sniff, sniff, sniff. She made me stand in the hot sun, while bugs swarmed me, as she rolled around on her back or swatted at dandelions for 20 minutes or tried to catch a butterfly. When we finally came back in, she catnapped. She woke up, ate, then was all over the house again, investigating.

Taking care of her was difficult, but my life became more meaningful. I started to believe I was receiving subtle mental imprints from Jewels, like I could feel what she was feeling. 'We're building mutual respect and trust,' I thought. I was thrilled.

Thanks to Don and Marge, I gradually became more comfortable with the area and the people. I hired a contractor to build an enclosure for Jewels behind the house. We planned it and engineered it, and they sent a crew to work on it. When they showed up, I told them not to worry – Jewels was there legally and wasn't any threat to them. They were fine with it. It took a while to build, because I had them put up a jungle gym of old tires and wooden beams at the same time.

Three or four of them were finishing the project one afternoon, as I was scooping poop at the back of the enclosure. Jewels was playing on the jungle gym. At some point, I felt her behind me. When I turned around, she was crouching, her belly on the grass, the black tip of her tail snapping, her ears flattened against her skull. She glowered at me. She took two or three quick, low steps, snarled and exploded into me. I braced my legs and held my forearm up to try to absorb the shock and fend her off.

Although Jewels was still young, she was unbelievably powerful. She staggered me, but I managed to push her away. She pounced right back, snarling, biting my forearms and raking at my stomach with her back paws. It felt like she was punching me in the gut over and over again.

"No, Jewels! You'll hurt Mommy!" I screamed.

At first, I thought she was playing, but she meant business. Every time I shoved her away, she rebounded and attacked again. She ripped the buttons off my shirt, scratched me all over. My arms were bleeding. To escape, I had to make it to the back porch, 15 or 20 feet away. Instinctively, I knew that if I went down, I'd be in even bigger trouble. I couldn't do anything but let her rip my arms and pummel me, keep shoving her off and stumble a few more steps toward the porch, praying that I didn't fall. She kept pouncing, snarling, slamming into me, biting and scratching. I pushed her as hard as I could. The more I fought, the more aggressive she became, like she was playing some kind of deadly game.

I was trapped with a creature that was no longer Jewels – my best friend, my kid, someone I loved more than life itself. This was a wild animal in full-on killing mode. She even looked different. Her face was hard, angular and menacing instead of round and soft and loving. Her eyes were burning; her muscles were coiled under her coat. I thought I was going to die right there, in an animal cage in Hillbilly Land.

With my last bit of strength, I fought my way out of the enclosure and shut the gate. Crying, bleeding, I steadied myself against the porch and tried to catch my breath. 'Holy shit! What the hell just happened?' I thought. I almost slumped to my knees, but I couldn't let the guys working on the cage see me drop. I was afraid one of them would wake up to what had happened and call 911, and Jewels would end up shot or confiscated. I turned around to reassure them that all was well. They were all staring at me, bug-eyed, their mouths hanging open. I realized my shirt was completely gone.

Shocked and bare-breasted, I tried to sound blasé as I sputtered, "Oh, it's all good, guys."

I hurried inside and threw on a long-sleeved sweatshirt to hide my wounds, not to mention my tits. I dashed back out and said, "Oh, she was just playing. I'm sorry if she scared you. We do it all the time. She's really not dangerous at all."

When I looked in the cage, the wild cougar had vanished; Jewels was back. She rubbed her cheeks against the fence and looked up at me. She opened and closed her eyes very slowly, like she was saying, 'Hi, Mom!"

I still believed I was empathetic with Jewels, but only with Jewels, not with the wild animal that lurked inside her. Even if that part of her was hidden most of the time and she didn't have her claws, that girl was a for-real mountain lion – almost a hundred pounds of teeth and muscle and impulses I'd never understand. I'd been treating her like she was my daughter. If Dr. Burton hadn't removed her claws – by accident or whatever – she would've disemboweled me.

When that dog mauled me, I'm pretty sure it was about food. Melvin, of course, was a psychotic icehead rapist. However, I never did know if the homeless nut who kidnapped me out of the yard was planning to kill me or molest me or sell me to the highest bidder or what. Likewise, the reason Jewels attacked me was a mystery. Was she still mad about being declawed? Did the builders aggravate her? Was my perfume different? Was it something I was wearing? Did she blame me for getting busted? I'll never know.

I did know that I couldn't go to the emergency room and tell them my mountain lion had attacked me. If that got reported to the wrong people, the authorities would be all over me, and Jewels would be seized or killed. I call it "the 10-cent solution" – a cop's bullet to the animal's brainpan.

I poured alcohol on my wounds, bandaged myself the best I could and hoped a killer infection didn't set in. All the bites and scratches and bruises hurt like hell, but what stung even worse was the realization that as much as I loved her and as much as I thought she loved me, Jewels just might kill me someday.

CHAPTER THIRTY-FIVE

Close Encounters at The Siberian Tiger Foundation

I couldn't be mad at a cougar for following her nature, but after Jewels gave me my baptism in blood, I was more careful around her. I paid close attention to the signals she was giving off, trying to read her moods. Like most big cats, Jewels was mouthy, but whenever she growled or purred or chirped or whistled or cried or screamed, it was hard to figure if she was saying something specific or was just generally happy or mad or hungry. Big Cat was much harder to learn than French, and I didn't have a tutor like Henri to help me translate. No matter what, she was still my little girl. The problem was I didn't know anything at all except for what Dr. Burton said, and even his knowledge was limited, since exotics were a small part of his practice. It was all home-study and on-the-job training, like trying to teach yourself to play the oboe, that is, if the oboe could rear up and rip your hands off.

I needed a crash course on caring for a kid. A place called the Siberian Tiger Foundation, in Gambier, had started to get some media attention because they took "trainees" for internships with exotic animals. A married couple, David and Diana Cziraky, ran it. The Czirakys seemed to be exactly what I was looking for, but when I mentioned them to Dr. Burton, he turned out to have been their vet at one time. He knew them all too well.

"Listen, Angela, I can place this cougar somewhere else," he said. "Please don't do this. This is a bad way to deal with things. Don't go near the Czirakys."

I knew I should listen to him. I'm like Alice in Wonderland, though: I generally give myself good advice, but I seldom follow it. I went to the Siberian Tiger Foundation and met David and Diana. They were eccentric. He was short and dark and very hardworking and backward. She was about 5-9 and beady-eyed. She had long chestnut hair, wide hips and almost no chest, and she obsessed about her white teeth. She called herself "The Tiger Lady."

The course was $2500. Thanks to my trust fund and the sale of the condo, I could afford it. I'd earned almost a hundred college credits. I figured the internship would be just another class; when it was over, I would be able to deal with Jewels.

The Czirakys said they were all about public education and raising awareness of the plight of exotic cats in the wild and in captivity. They owned a bunch of healthy-looking tigers and lions, and their enclosures were clean. They said they would teach me about the cats and allow me to get a little bit of hands-on experience. More than a little bit, actually. I had to do 500 hours on-site before I earned a certificate that said I was a trained volunteer and 1000 hours before I was "fully trained in animal behavior and control."

I had to sign a liability waiver that said, "Trainee assumes full responsibility for any accidents, injuries or related incidents that may occur to themselves, the cats, or others while training with the exotic cats."

The Czirakys operated a big-cat petting zoo. Walkup visitors to the Siberian Tiger Foundation paid $35 to have a "close encounter" with a tiger or lion, and by "close," the Czirakys meant actually free-petting a massive carnivore. That seemed dangerous, but I assumed they knew more about cats than I did.

People came in droves for "pet and play time," and not just a bunch of yahoos. There was a judge, some college professors, businesspeople, nurses, college students, lots of school kids and their parents. Just before a group was to arrive, we interns and volunteers went into the cats' enclosures and hooked them to the fence or a big wire spool with a two- or three-foot length of heavy logging chain. Then, wearing a little khaki romper to make herself look official, Diana paraded everyone from toddlers to disabled senior citizens in to see the cats. She'd take a group of customers into an enclosure, stop them near a cat and let them approach it one at a time. She encouraged people to kiss the cats, sit on their backs, even to put their hands and arms in the cats' mouths. Diana said it was all good, because she could tell by looking at them which cats wanted to be handled that day and which guests were suited for an encounter.

Guests had to sign a waiver that was even scarier than ours: "I understand that entering into the compound with Lions and Tigers is VERY dangerous and that I can be injured in many different ways by the lions or tigers themselves or just by falling down. I may also suffer damage to my clothing, camera equipment, or any other personal items I bring with me. Although many others have entered the compound without harm, it does not mean I may not be injured. I hold the Siberian Tiger Foundation and its agents blameless and I accept ALL responsibility for anything that may happen to me."

People either didn't read the warning or didn't care. They would get nipped, go to the ER, come right back for another close encounter. Worse, a kid would get knocked down and pinned or scratched by a cat, and his parents would just move him along to the next animal.

We trainees were supposed to prevent guests from getting hurt. One of us kept an eye on the cat, while the other stood on the chain until the customer could fuck with the animal and back away. I wondered how a 110-pound human – or even two humans – was supposed to stop a 600-pound tiger if he decided to tear someone up. Our "emergency gear" consisted of a few fire extinguishers and bottles of vinegar to spray in the cats' faces if they got feisty – that is, if smacking them on the nose and scolding them like naughty school children didn't work.

Diana claimed that the cats had been declawed and defanged, but some still had their equipment. She also said her cats were "trained, not tame." That claim was nonsense. They weren't trained, the chains were too long and there were no barriers between the cats and the customers. Since there were never enough volunteers or interns, the walk-up groups were much too big.

One day, Diana took a group in with Joseph, a squirrelly young lion who loved ice cream and scaring the hell out of people. He was hooked to the fence. To be safe, you had to stay outside the arc of his chain, but several customers came too close when no one was paying attention. Joseph grabbed a guy's shoe, and all hell broke loose.

Big cats are unbelievably quick and powerful, and they have the attention span of gnats. They're also possessive. Once they grab something, you can beat them senseless, and they will not let go. That's what Joseph did with the guy's foot. Only dumb luck saved it. The guy's ball cap fell off; Joseph released the shoe and went for the hat. Believe me, no one tried to take that hat from him.

Another time, Imara, my favorite tiger, put 50 stitches in the leg of a 10-year-old boy. A college student who saw the attack was so freaked out that she stumbled into Joseph, who knocked her down and bit her back. Volunteers sprayed him with vinegar to get him off her.

Joseph almost nailed me, as well. Diana and I were in his cage, when she suddenly said, "I'll be right back" and wandered away, leaving me alone – a position you should never be in with a big cat. I stepped back, too, and blundered into Joseph's range. I turned around; he was within a few inches of my foot, staring dead at me. Our eyes locked.

Joseph had the crossover look, just like Jewels did when she came after me. The crossover look comes the moment your couch snuggler turns into a killing machine, and someone is in a world of hurt. I've seen it in humans, too – the drunken slob at the bar who's been watching you dance finally slams down enough Jose Gold to convince his dick it's time to do business; the twerp who takes you shopping and out to dinner suddenly wants more than witty conversation and a dazzling smile, and you don't get a vote; the tweaker gangster who's been telling you he loves you and wants to marry you is about to beat holy piss out of you.

As we stared at each other, seconds became eternity. Joseph had me. He knew it; I knew it. I felt faint. I gasped and jumped back out of his reach. He went unhinged. His roar felt like someone was pounding on my chest with a sledgehammer. The concussion knocked the breath out of me, or, to be real, scared me shitless. I don't know why Joseph didn't kill me when he had the chance. I can only guess that the treacherous prick was savoring my fear before tearing me apart.

David and Ellen Martin Chester, the head trainer, had been teaching me Big Cat 101. They emphasized that I should never turn my back on a big cat, particularly an adult lion. My close encounter with Joseph certainly reinforced that lesson. After Joseph tried to jump me, I became deathly afraid of lions. Every time I got around one at the Siberian Tiger Foundation, terror instantly overcame me: shortness of breath, pulse pounding in ears, sweating, trembling, confusion. I tried to tell myself it was all in my imagination, that one lion wasn't reason to be frightened of every lion. I couldn't help myself, though; lions freaked me the fuck out.

CHAPTER THIRTY-SIX

This Might Be Kansas, But I'm Sure as Hell Not Dorothy

Dr. Burton told me that if I wanted to be legit in every way, I should register Jewels with USDA. I filed the paperwork and paid for Animal Welfare Act license 31-C-0135. Even though my new Class C Exhibitor's License allowed me to charge the public to look at Jewels, no one from USDA checked me out before I received it – not that I had any intention of letting civilians inside my gate, anyway, but I could've been nine different kinds of nutcase, for all USDA knew.

Once I registered, my information became public. I was immediately flooded with calls from police departments saying they'd confiscated big cats but had no idea what to do with them, private owners saying they were too sick or scared or old or broke to care for their animals, sanctuaries saying they were shutting down. I hated to do it, but I explained to the callers that I was in no position to adopt six or 10 or 16 dangerous wild animals.

When I told Dr. Burton about the calls, he said that there were probably thousands of exotic cats in the hands of private owners in Ohio alone, probably tens of thousands across the country. Since exotic owners are CIA secretive, no one knew exactly how many tigers and lions and cougars and leopards were being kept in backyards, barns, chicken coops, dog runs, basements and bedrooms. Hundreds of breeders sold them as pets to clueless people who bought adorable babies without ever thinking about how big and dangerous and destructive that animal would become in a year, as well as to cheapjack roadside zoos, walkup outfits like the Siberian Tiger Foundation, traveling "photo-baby" attractions and pseudo hunting ranches – "canned hunts" during which rich shitheads in safari outfits pay to shoot exotic cats. At least I had the excuse of being drunk and high when I accidentally bought Jewels.

Dr. Burton explained that the United States had no comprehensive regulations about owning exotics, just about importing and transporting endangered species and exhibiting dangerous animals to the public. In many states, like Ohio, only native species were regulated by a department of wildlife or natural resources. People were free to have as many "exotic pets" as they wanted and to treat them however they chose. Dr. Burton said USDA didn't have nearly enough field agents to supervise the scum who were abusing animals to make money. Many of them didn't bother to register, so they were never inspected, he said.

He blew me away. I'd been royally pissed at Mt. Hope but hadn't grasped the full implications of the auction. It was actually held three times a year and wasn't even the only one in Ohio. Animals were sold on consignment, and no one asked where they came from. As long as buyers had the cash, nobody cared who bought them. The scariest and saddest thing is that so many exotics ended up with people who shouldn't be allowed to own a guppy. Who dreamed that the eccentric hermit with all the property down the road could legally be keeping massive apex predators, or that the government cared a thousand times more about garter snakes and cottontail bunnies than it did about domestic-born mutt lions and tigers? This was *Through the Looking Glass* insanity – except with Cheshire cats that can turn a human being into a grease spot in minutes – and I'd landed right in the middle of it, just as Dr. Burton warned when I got Jewels.

A creep named Floyd Wells* called me from Kansas one day. He said he wanted rid of a young tiger. Wells didn't give me any options or ask for any advice. He simply said, "Come get this cat or I'm going to dispose of it."

Wells sounded serious, but I was just learning about cougars and getting my feet wet with other big cats. What would I do with a tiger that was going to end up four or five times bigger than Jewels? I made some calls. USDA essentially told me to get lost, Dr. Burton warned me not to swim any deeper into the exotic cesspool and I didn't want Diana chaining the cat to a fence for assholes to pester. PeTA and The Humane Society of the United States said they might look into the situation if they got a chance. There was no one else available. I told Wells several times I couldn't do it, but he kept calling and growing more threatening toward the little tiger.

Finally, he said, "If you don't come for him, I'll just drown this cat in a rain barrel."

He even set a deadline for killing the kid. Wells sounded so vicious that I knew he was going to murder that cat. It wasn't fair. 'The hell with it! I'm going to do this,' I thought.

I went to Walmart and bought the biggest wire kennel cage they sold. I removed the rear seats from the Land Cruiser, put the kennel in and called David to check on Jewels for a day or two. I had a cooler with some ground turkey in it, a few bottles of water, a bowl and a leash. At the last minute, Ellen, who was game for anything, offered to come along.

Ellen said that Wells likely wanted to dump the tiger because it was too old, too big and too dangerous to sell to the photo-baby operators who no doubt formed his customer base. He didn't want to be stuck with an adult cat that could cost 10,000 bucks a year in meat, specialized veterinary care and labor. If he couldn't get rid of it, he'd kill it, she said. That bastard was blackmailing me into covering his butt with the USDA, in case someone happened to come around asking questions about the cat.

Although the brakes on the Cruiser were already down to metal on metal, we rolled out for Kansas. I calculated the trip was 17 hours one way. Even if we went 90, we could miss Wells' deadline. There was no time for motels or drive-through meals or rest stop catnaps. We blasted out at 100 miles an hour and made it in the nick of time.

Wells was a tall cornshucker with a scraggly ZZ Top beard and long, tangled hair. When he shook my hand, he scowled and gripped it as hard has he could, trying to scare me. I almost laughed in his face. I'd seen a lot worse than that hick. His farm smelled like stale vinegar and rancid garbage. Thinking about it still makes my stomach churn. He must have had 25 leopard cubs in an area no bigger than a hallway. They were climbing all over each other, desperately trying to get our attention.

Even though he was still a juvenile, the tiger was a pretty big boy. He certainly didn't want anything to do with Wells. The cat met me and started chuffing like, 'Dude, let's get the hell out of here!'

I wasn't going to dart the tiger, so Wells hooked him up to a leash and tossed the other end at me. He snarled, "This is a man's cat," like I was going to piss my pants. I shook my head and led the cat to the Land Cruiser and got him into the kennel cage by offering him some turkey. We hauled ass out of that dump.

Now, I'd peeked behind the curtain and seen the real, ugly face of the exotic animal business. High on caffeine and exhaustion and anger and disgust, I was on a backwards *Wizard of Oz* trip, with an abused tiger, instead of a cowardly lion, as a travelling companion. If Dorothy kept clicking the heels of those gauche red shoes because she wanted to get back to a shithole farm in Kansas, she's the one who needed a brain.

Wells had barely fed the tiger, let alone named him. When I got pregnant that time, I was scared to death, but fear hadn't stopped lists of kids' names from running through my head. I thought if I had a son, I'd name him Gage, after the cute blond kid in *Pet Sematary*. Gage tiger became my first little boy.

Gagiepoo was a bouncing baby who had terrible diarrhea. Within an hour, the Cruiser smelled almost as bad as Wells' farm. Even with all the windows down, we couldn't outrun the funk. A highway patrol trooper stopped us right at the "Welcome to Ohio" sign. He walked up to my open window and got a whiff of the cargo bay. Then he saw Gage and asked what in the world was going on. I told him we were doing a rescue and showed him my USDA credentials. He checked things out and said that he stopped us because we were speeding and sparks were flying from the front wheels.

Leaning back from the window, his face pinched, he thrust my paperwork into my hand said, "God speed," and hurried away to his patrol car.

That trooper wasn't fooling me. Tiger piss and shit are their own kind of eye-burning, throat-clenching, gagging, acrid, ammonia stink. He wanted to get away from that window before he barfed his lunch all over his shoes.

I'd ducked the ticket but still had another serious problem: I was transporting a tiger that was in no condition to go home with me. I had to work up the nerve to call Dr. Burton. He'd done everything he could to talk me out of keeping Jewels, he was already irked at me for becoming involved with the Czirakys and he'd ordered me not to go to Kansas. Now, I'd driven halfway across the country with a sick baby tiger. I couldn't give him a chance to say no, so I went to the only location that made sense. I parked, rolled the windows down and dialed the clinic, thinking, 'Go ahead and chew my ass, man.

I'm too exhausted to care.'

I got him on the phone and said, "Hi, Dr. Burton. It's Ang. How're you? Holy heck! You'll never guess what just happened."

I ran the story down for him, and he flipped: "Angela! Angela!" He yelled at me for three or four minutes then said, "Okay, where are you now?"

"Uh, um, could you go to the, ahh, side door, please?" I said.

The door opened. Dr. Burton stopped it from closing with one hand and held his phone to his ear with the other, trying to process the scene in front of him. The Cruiser smelled like putrefied tiger butthole. My hair looked like I'd brushed it with an electric mixer. My mouth tasted like I'd been chewing scabby gauze bandages for two days. Ellen was slumped onto the floor, her head on the seat, passed out. Gage was jumping around in the back, like, 'Are we there? Are we there? Is this it?'

I'm pretty sure that was not how Dr. Burton expected his day to go; he looked like someone had just thrown a glass of ice water in his face. I felt like laughing, but I was too exhausted to even grin. He turned his head and said something over his shoulder. An army of staff surged out and took over. Gage became the clinic's top priority. He weighed about 50 pounds and had every problem imaginable: pneumonia, worms, pain in his right shoulder, an injured, seeping eye. That sick little kid cost me $891.30 that day, including x-rays, a half-page list of meds and a "tiger castration."

When I took the Cruiser into the shop, the mechanic looked at it and said, "Holy shit! What the hell did you do to this thing? That's the first time I've ever seen brakes welded together." His bill was just as steep as the one from the clinic.

At home, it was adjustment time again. Joshie checked the newcomer out, and they immediately became buddies. Trinity sulked and grumbled in the loft. I have a lot of pictures of Gage and Jewels getting acquainted. She doesn't have a happy face in any of them, but she never really despised Gage, or she wouldn't have gotten that close to him. She didn't understand what he was doing there. Shit, I didn't either.

Until I could get the contractor back out to the house, all I had for Gage was the big kennel cage. I walked him for hours just like I'd done with Jewels. I usually kept the lead on him, but I let him free once in a while, because he had pneumonia and I wanted his lungs to work. There was a stockade fence around the property, so he couldn't escape. When he started feeling better, Gage would bolt crazily back and forth through the yard. I bought a baby pool for him. He'd take off and tear around and come back and jump in and out of it. Once he got rolling, it was hard to put the lead back on him. I'd chase him, then I'd turn around, and he'd run after me, knock me down and jump on me. 'Are you still Gage?' I'd wonder. 'Are we still playing? Have I kicked something in and you want to hurt me, like Jewels?'

At night, I brought him inside, because I worried that he might develop pneumonia again. He slept in bed with me and didn't cause any problem, except when he had to go. When

Gage wanted out, he went to the back door and scratched like a dog. He didn't care what time it was; he wanted to go when he wanted to go.

Early one morning, he started fussing at the door. I dragged myself out of bed, more asleep than awake, and let him outside. It was just dawn, so misty that I could barely see. I followed in my pajamas and slippers as he bounded down a trail. A big black round mass rose up very slowly in the middle of the trail and made a God-awful screech. I stopped, thinking, 'Oh, oh! We're in deep shit now!' Then a bunch of little black roadrunners scampered from under a mother turkey who'd been sitting on her brood.

I looked around for Gage and couldn't find him. I heard him crashing along the path behind me, already halfway back to the house. When I got to him, my little boy was shaking on the porch – a tiger terrified by a turkey. I'd brought a cowardly feline back from Kansas, after all.

CHAPTER THIRTY-SEVEN

Flavor of The Month

Now that I had Gage, learning anything I could about big cats was doubly important, so I kept going to the Siberian Tiger Foundation, even though I thought that things were screwy there. I also didn't want to lose my relationships with the cats, particularly Imara.

I'm not sure why I loved Imara so much, but we definitely had an instant mutual attraction. She was all tiger baby – rough and beautiful and full of energy. Everyone else hated her, because she still had her fangs and claws and liked to nip and scratch. I'd pull on leather welder's gloves and tussle with her, which David didn't approve of at all. He said he didn't want me wrestling with her because she'd weigh 500 pounds someday and still want to roughhouse. I ignored him, of course, and Imara and I had a lot of fun play dates. Even though her nickname was "The Piranha," and she had several bad incidents with guests, she never tried to hurt me.

Although I still thought Diana was flaky, I became cozy with David and her. We went out to dinner, and I hung there after hours. As I became more involved in their operation, I started to see that even though David did almost all the work, he had no say in how the business functioned. Diana had zero interest in his opinion or anyone else's. She believed she was smartest person on the compound.

She certainly had every money angle covered. In addition to the one-time close encounter fee, she charged people who didn't want to do internship hours $2500 to be "preferred customers." Anyone who had limited time or a light bank account could fork over $200 to be a "day trainer." She supplemented that haul with donations by claiming to rescue abused exotics.

Diana didn't wait for customers to come to her. She exhibited cats in public places, which trusted her to keep everyone safe. I dressed in a ridiculous safari outfit and was part of the show. We'd be in an elementary school auditorium filled with excited kids and clip Joseph on a lead and walk him onto the stage. I was worried to death he'd get away and charge into a crowd of children; no one else, except Ellen, seemed bothered by that possibility.

Apparently, even that wasn't enough for Diana. One evening, she booked an entire dining room at Joe's Crab Shack for a team party. We took the place down, ordering massive everything, laughing and shouting. One of the last things I remember is Diana goading me into a shot war. I'm a terrible drinker, but she egged me on until I said, "Okay, babe, let's go." From then on, I come up with blurs: dancing on a table, a conga line, a lot of loud drunks singing in each other's faces. I woke up three days later, deathly sick, on the Czirakys' couch. David had been caring for Jewels and Gage.

When my American Express bill came, I saw a charge for hundreds of dollars at Joe's Crab Shack. Diana had dug in my purse and paid for everything with my credit card. When I asked her about it, she said, 'Oh, listen, funds fell through. We're expecting a lot of visitors. I'll get it to you soon.'

After I swallowed that explanation, Diana started confiding in me: 'My cats need food. I can't pay the utilities. The house is in foreclosure.'

I told her I could hook her up, no problem.

She borrowed more money, telling me she had $10,000 coming from here or $10,000 from there and would pay me back soon. I believed her every time.

Once again, I should've listened to Dr. Burton. The animals at the Siberian Tiger Foundation were healthy and well-fed and clean, but lot a of that was his doing. At a certain point, though, he refused to come back, because she wouldn't pay her bill. Diana owed him a bundle. Her fallback plan was to work that money out of me, which I was unwittingly allowing her to do.

Ellen finally wised me up. She told me that everyone at the Siberian Tiger Foundation called me "the flavor of the month," because I was the latest in a long line of suckers. Ellen said Diana would feel people out, seduce them with the cats, act like she was their BFF and then bleed them. I didn't want to believe Ellen. Like the paying customers, I was so high on intimate contact with dangerous predators that I would swallow just about any lie. One morning, I spotted Diana walking into a hair salon. I realized she wasn't using my money to feed the kids or improve the enclosures or pay on the mortgage. She was spending it however she pleased, with no intention of paying me back. She'd sniffed my weaknesses – out-of-control compassion and an inability to say "no" – and used them against me. I thought, 'All right, bitch, it's on.'

I also finally had to admit to myself that it wasn't all hunky dory for the animals there. After she attacked a little girl, one of the tigers was confiscated and beheaded to check for rabies. The cats weren't given breaks between close encounters. Some of them got so stressed that they would hide in their dens when they heard cars coming up the driveway.

I got intensely nervous when the biggest tiger, Nikita, wouldn't come out for Diana to chain him up. Nikita was huge. I have a picture of me wearing a Santa Claus hat, lying on his back. He makes me look an elf. At one time, she let Nikita roam around free. Now, he was older, cross-eyed, almost blind and had trouble breathing. He wanted nothing to do with strangers. When Nikita didn't want to come out of his den, she started taking people into that tight space to pet him and take pictures of him. I just knew he had chaos on his mind. Thank goodness, he didn't do anything naughty. We were all lucky something horrible didn't go down with Nikita.

Fed up, I left the Siberian Tiger Foundation for good and tried to figure a way to recover the $26,000 Diana ripped me for – or at least get some serious payback. I decided to go right for her jugular – I stole David, which wasn't hard to do to someone with a face like a praying mantis. It's a girl thing; she pushed first, and I straight-up did it to screw her over. I flirted and flounced and enticed and sealed the deal. David asked if he could move into the log house with me.

When I told Dr. Burton David was coming to live in Lancaster, he wasn't pleased. He didn't say anything specific against David, but he definitely discouraged me from having him around. However, David knew a lot about animals, and I could use help with Jewels and Gage. Not long afterward, his battered Chevy van creaked and smoked through the gate. He showed up with nothing but an extra pair of underwear. He left everything else in Gambier. He had the same bewildered and frightened look as every other rescue I took in.

At least I was honest with David. I told him, "I don't like humans, and I especially don't like dudes. I'm the thing your mom should've warned you about. I'm big trouble. You don't want to get serious with me."

He stayed anyway.

CHAPTER THIRTY-EIGHT

Rescue One

I was registered with USDA as the owner of one kitty named Jewels. After the Gage rescue, the Diana craziness and the phone calls that continued to pour in, I realized just how right Dr. Burton had been when he said there were thousands of unwanted cats trapped in the exotic animal netherworld. I knew I couldn't stand by and twiddle my thumbs while they suffered and died. I foresaw what my property would turn into and how expensive it was going to be.

"Oh, man, we'd better go non-profit to try to raise some money to take care of these kids," I told David.

To become a 501(c)(3) charitable organization and start taking in animals and accepting contributions, we needed volunteers and a steady meat supply and secure caging and extensive vet care, which Dr. Burton agreed to provide. We also needed a catchy name. I was driving in the Cruiser one day, playing with names for a rescue. I wanted to be the first one called when there was an emergency involving an exotic animal. I was thinking "Rescue" this, "Rescue" that, then the simple solution hit me: "Rescue One."

I took the name and wrote the mission statement: "Rescue One is dedicated to the preservation and conservation of exotic wild cats. We help by providing a refuge where unwanted and/or abused captive exotic cats can live out their lives in a safe, carefree environment."

Rescue One's goals were simple: to provide a lifetime home for rescued exotic cats; to never breed any animal; and to educate the public on the stupidity of owning dangerous wild animals. I'd barely finished the arrangements – except for the donors, of course – when an insane custody battle over a tiger began to play out on the nightly news. I saw the cat in question on television and thought, 'What the heck? I know that tiger. That's Sammy!'

I'd met Sampson because of the actress Jenna Elfman, of all people, at the very end of my time in Gambier. Elfman, David and Diana were Scientologists. Another Scientologist, who donated to the Siberian Tiger Foundation, had told Elfman about us. As a present to her husband, Bohdi, Elfman made arrangements with Diana to do a surprise close encounter for his birthday. David said Elfman paid $1500 for that one session.

Diana hired Dan Pablo's to cater the birthday party. We were told not to approach Elfman or even speak to her. The woman is an incredibly beautiful Nordic princess. Bodhi was like a Hobbit. In fact, he looked a lot like David. He was short and had a 5 o'clock shadow and was exotic, athletic and gorgeous. Bohdi was also cool. He sat on the couch with us and ate Mexican food, while Elfman walked around flipping her ponytail and talking on her phone to Hollywood.

The deal was that Bohdi would have a chance to play with Sampson, who was a great big Bengal/Siberian mix. Sammy was sweet, but also rambunctious. We all went outside to watch the encounter.

David took Bohdi into the enclosure. Sammy was chained to the fence, but he wanted to play, tiger-style. It took all David had to keep the tiger from getting to Bohdi and turning Diana's money grab/publicity stunt into an international incident. It only went on for about five minutes. David got the workout of his life. Bohdi never stopped smiling, but his smile wasn't quite as wide after he'd seen how much fun pet-and-play time really was with a full-grown cat.

Diana and I were barely speaking by then, so I didn't know much about Sampson's background. He just showed up one day. The nightly news filled me in on the crazy path Sammy had taken to Gambier.

A construction worker named Bob Sturm lived with his wife, Scarlett, and three young kids on a farm around Mantua. One of Bob's buddies bought two tiger cubs at Mt. Hope, and Bob paid him $1000 for one of them. Bob had volunteered with big cats, so he should've known better, but he said his family "humanized the heck" out of the tiger. Sampson bathed with the kids, watched his favorite TV shows and enjoyed belly-rubs.

The problems started when Bob told Scarlett he wanted a divorce. Scarlett threw him out and gave Sampson to a man named Josif Bean, who had Animal Haven HideAway, an exotic shelter in an industrial park across from Mentor Mall. Scarlett said she wasn't able to handle Sampson, she was afraid he might hurt one of the kids and the tiger was "common property" that she had a right to dispose of.

Bob went to Mentor and demanded his cat. Bean refused to give the tiger up. He accused the Sturms of not caring properly for Sampson. Mentor officials and the Cleveland Zoo made the same charge against Bean and said they wanted the "ticking time bomb" out of town.

A judge granted Bob custody, but when cops came to remove the cat, Bean handed them a press release that said, "Sampson was transported to an undisclosed big cat sanctuary to live out the rest of his life happily and peacefully." The truth is that Diana Cziraky had called him, and Bean sent Sampson to the Siberian Tiger Foundation on the downlow. Bean would not tell the judge where Sampson was, because, he said, Bob was unfit to own the cat since he owed back child support and had missed visitations with his kids. Bean said he'd rather kill Sampson than turn him over to Bob. Cops handcuffed Bean and took him to jail for contempt of court.

Bean kept complaining that he feared for an animal that had been turned into "a media spectacle." Diana said she was Sammy's legal owner and vowed to get permanent custody. Scarlett said that it was all a mistake and she wanted her property back. Bob said, "You hate to be without your kids and your tiger."

It got nuts. A guy showed up outside a court hearing, wearing a tiger suit and carrying a sign that said, "I WANT MY DADDY BACK!"

I watched the nightly freakshow, thinking, 'What the fuck?'

Diana wasn't about to surrender Sammy. She knew a good PR thing when she saw it. She figured taking in Sampson was a perfect chance to pose as the concerned owner of a legitimate rescue. Bob's lawyer got a writ ordering Diana to turn the tiger over. Bob, Scarlett and Bob's brother showed up, but Diana wouldn't obey the writ. The Sturms stayed there two days, claiming that Diana was trying to sneak Sammy off the compound.

Finally, David put Sampson in his van and pulled out of the Siberian Tiger Foundation. Bob and a caravan of cops and media followed. Things went very Secret Squirrel. At one point, Bob doubled back to Diana's place because he suspected David had a decoy tiger in the van. David took Sammy to the Knox County Courthouse. Diana made a last-ditch effort to keep the tiger, but a judge ordered Sampson turned over to the Sturms right there in the parking lot. As soon as Sampson saw him, he jumped up and slung his front paws over Bob's shoulders.

This was no happy reunion, in my eyes; it was a train wreck that would end with a dead tiger. I called Bob and tried to buy Sampson from him. He said he was determined to keep the cat. However, the strain of living away from the farm in an apartment and worrying that the tiger might hurt the kids finally got to him. Five months later, he turned Sampson over to me. Bob had learned something from the ordeal, because the agreement we signed sounds just like the one I had for Joshie and Trin when they were in foster care: "Bob Sturm has full visitation rights with courtesy advance notice."

Within weeks of taking in Sammy, I got a call about another cat who was in trouble because of a bad marriage. Sheba lion came from some bumblefuck place around Barnesville. The guy who owned her got into a big fight with his wife. He grabbed up a gun. The wife called the cops and took off with their kids. By the time the emergency response team got there, the husband had killed himself.

No one other than the wife and kids knew about the lioness, although a county detective, Bart Giesey, had heard rumors about her. Det. Giesey followed a path that led up into the woods behind the house and found Sheba in a tumbledown corncrib with some cyclone fence around it. The county sheriff wanted to shoot her. I couldn't really blame him. His officers had no training in dealing with dangerous exotics, no emergency protocol or equipment and no connection to the lioness.

For almost three weeks, Det. Giesey held off the sheriff, as he tried to find a home for Sheba. He called the Columbus Zoo, the Pittsburgh Zoo, The Wilds, The Good Zoo in Wheeling – everyplace he could think of – but municipal zoos will almost never accept animals from private owners. Most of those kids are bred by greedy idiots, so they aren't actually Bengals or Siberians or whatever. They're mongrels, and the zoos don't want wildcard blood lines introduced into their gene pools. Usually, privately-owned kids also come in with every kind of problem imaginable – diseases, parasites, genetic deficiencies, compatibility issues with other animals, aggression toward humans. Their care is incredibly costly. No one wanted Sheba.

The dead guy's wife told Det. Giesey Sheba ate chicken. He caught some live hens and threw them into the pen; when he went back, they were walking around pecking the ground. The wife said Sheba wouldn't kill chickens, so Det. Giesey found a chunk of venison in a freezer and gave it to her. At one point, the Gieseys were even considering adopting Sheba, but he'd been a canine officer, and his wife owned an exotic bird rescue. They knew enough to know they couldn't take care of a lion.

Without asking my permission, one of the zoos turned Det. Giesey on to Rescue One. When he called and asked if we'd take a lioness, I said, "Yes, yes, we're on our way," even though I had major misgivings.

There was a big drive-in theatre pretty close by to use as a marker, but the place was still hard to find. We pulled up into a crapscape of overgrown property and ramshackle buildings. Sheba's time was running out, so we tried to act like experienced professional animal rescuers. The sheriff was skeptical. He worried that we were a fly-by-night operation that would take the lioness and handle her improperly, and she would kill someone. He wasn't far from right. We'd made some conversions to turn David's van into a transfer vehicle, but it was still basically a hunk of junk with a shotgun clamped inside the back doors in case things went sideways. The sheriff had little faith in us; however, he also didn't want to kill the lioness in front of the media and the crowd of gawkers who'd shown up.

While we sized up the situation, Det. Giesey tried to control the chaos that was breaking loose. David and I walked up that narrow path to check things out and devise a game plan. As we climbed toward the lioness, the memory of Joseph tensing for the attack, his bottomless yellow eyes fixed on me, stuck in my head. We got to the top and checked the cat out. Sheba was a juvenile, about 18 months old, as best David could tell. She sure looked full-grown to me. She made my heart race. I was jealous of the hens calmly scratching around in the back of the enclosure. The lioness was a little starved out and crying and rubbing her face against the fence. She seemed calm enough. She was still a lion, though, and David had told me never to trust a lion. Even lions that are raised around humans are lethal. They're all instinct. They'll break your neck and then look for you at feeding time, he'd told me.

Things were not good. We didn't have a tranq gun and couldn't get a vehicle up that hill. We were going to have to go into the enclosure with Sheba, put a leash on her and walk her several hundred yards through cops and reporters and rubberneckers to the van.

We went back down and told everyone that we were going to walk Sheba out. The sheriff wasn't cool with it at all. He insisted that because of liability, some of his officers had to accompany Det. Giesey and us when we went back for the lion. If the situation got out of hand, they had orders to shoot the kid. We had to accept the sheriff's terms, so I gathered Ellen and several other volunteers who'd come with us.

"We don't want to scare this cat by sending a bunch of people in," I said. "David and I will go in with her. If she's happy to see us, she's going to jump up on us. These cops are going to misinterpret that, and she's going to be dead before we can do anything for her. Here's how we're going to handle this."

I laid out my plan: While David and I walked up, the volunteers would follow along to distract the cops.

"Accidentally, purposely stay in their line of fire as we're hooking her up and bringing her back," I said. "If they have to worry about hitting you guys, they can't take a shot at the kid."

While we climbed the path, cops sprinkled around us, nine millimeters drawn, automatic rifles ready. About halfway up, they started dropping off and holding their positions. My guys milled around, trying to seem preoccupied with their duties.

I had guns all around me and a lion waiting for me. Even though I was shivering like a cold breeze was blowing, I started sweating. I was afraid I'd hyperventilate if I even tried to talk, so I didn't open my mouth, which doesn't happen very often. As we entered the pen, we could tell that Sheba was weakened but still very dangerous. Even Det. Giesey drew his gun and kept it down by his side.

We tried to be quiet and gentle so she knew we weren't going to hurt her. David talked softly to her for several minutes, then slipped the thick leather leash on her. I forced myself to focus on what had to be done, not on Joseph's scary eyes burning in my memory. Shoulder-to-shoulder – David on one side and me on the other – we led Sheba down through the brush and rocks and trees. Cops maintained a moving semicircle around us, weapons raised. We were afraid Sheba was going to react to something and guns were going to start going off, so we tried to keep our bodies between her and the cops. Looking like they were going about their usual business, Ellen and the rest of the team played it perfectly. David and I walked Sheba to the van as fast as we dared.

She was happy to get out of there. We put her in a cage in the van. She lay down and drank some water. Dr. Burton was on stand-by, and I put the $2856.16 for her physical and shots on my platinum MasterCard.

Det. Giesey took home a sickly-looking silver fox from the farm that day. After he nursed her back to health, he brought Foxy to Rescue One and visited Sheba. The day he came, Shebee was playing with a Boomer ball, Gage was chilling in his pool, Sammie was napping and Jewels was hanging out in the office with me. Det. Giesey was amazed.

I still have his business card. It says "Pet Detective" in big red letters and identifies him as Bart "Ace Ventura" Giesey. That might seem a little presumptuous, but Det. Giesey turned out to be a sincere animal lover and a level-headed, kind, honest man. He was super-sweet, which is rare in law enforcement.

I never did know where all the media following David and Sampson and Bob around Knox County were from, and I'd been too busy and nervous to notice cameras filming us in Barnesville. Footage of both incidents ended up on an A&E program called *Investigative Reports*. "Pets or Predators?" aired on Christmas Day, 2004. A lot of it was about Sampson and Sheba and Rescue One. After the presents and turkey and trimmings and football, all of us were on television screens for the whole world to see – Sammy, Shebee, Bob Sturm, Det. Giesey, David and me, looking like I'm brain damaged.

A producer had borrowed some still photos from us to go with the video. All the Rescue One people are in the last picture in our segment. Everyone else is smiling nice. I'm right in the middle of the group, making an absolutely hideous, goofy face. My eyes are crossed, and my mouth is scrunched up. I look like a crazed doofus. I thought, 'Holy crap, I help save the lives of two beautiful exotic cats, and this is the geeky picture of me you show the world? I deserve this? Really?' Oh, well, didn't some famous dude say, "No good deed goes unpunished"? I think I remember that shit from college, but I might be making it up.

CHAPTER THIRTY-NINE

Snitch

Losing a tiger and a husband were the least of Diana Cziraky's problems. The Ohio Department of Agriculture and the state Department of Natural Resources, USDA and Knox County officials were sick of her and trying to dig up dirt. They wanted her for fraud, endangering the public, back taxes, you name it. She owed hundreds of thousands of dollars. Creditors wanted to kill her. However, no one could do anything about the animals because she was still USDA-licensed.

I called her one day and said, "Just give me Imara, and you won't owe me any money."

Diana couldn't handle that girl and couldn't sell her because of all the problems with USDA. She knew I loved that kid dearly, but because of the David thing, she wouldn't give Imara to me. Even though it was all crashing down around her, she was keeping the cat away from me out of spite.

That was the last straw. The USDA came to David and me about Diana. Like anyone else who grew up in the streets, I don't like to snitch. I made an exception in her case, ratting about everything I knew. The USDA, the Animal Protection Institute and *20/20* all did undercover investigations. David, Ellen and I coached them on how to play as if they were excited visitors looking for a close encounter. Diana and the Siberian Tiger

Foundation ended up on national television. It didn't help her that *20/20* showed a tiger attacking a guy during a close encounter.

The USDA charged in court that the cats had attacked 10 people in just 12 months. One of their investigators also testified that no actual "training" was ever done – with animals or humans – in Gambier. Our $2500 certificates were as worthless as used toilet paper. In addition to putting our lives on the line, all of us "trainees" had been paying Diana to milk free labor out of us.

I spent a lot of money at the Siberian Tiger Foundation to learn just some Big Cat 101 stuff: always keep your head higher than a cat's, never make sudden moves around a cat, don't turn your back on a cat, don't run from a cat, don't try to pull away if a cat mouths you – the simple shit they told every group before a close encounter. Talking to experienced keepers, like Ellen, helped, and the Czirakys did give me access beyond what most people got to their animals, but I certainly didn't learn anything substantial there.

Actually, though, Diana *had* been doing education at the Siberian Tiger Foundation. It wasn't about how dangerous or endangered big cats are or about how to care for them properly. It was about how stupid and gullible humans are. She was shrewd enough to know that if you act like you're legit, customers will happily pay any amount to walk into a cage with a huge animal that sees them as toys, prey or pains the ass. Diana, like so many other big cat owners, sold people their own illusions, creating a mass hallucination in which dangerous wild animals magically turn into Disney cartoons.

The USDA suspended her license to exhibit twice. She changed the name of the place to the Siberian Tiger Conservation Association and went right on having close encounters. Her license was permanently revoked, and she was fined $34,000. She was allowed to keep the cats, though, because what was the United States government going to do with them? She wasn't completely shut down until the landlords of the property evicted her. She had four tigers and two lions at that time. She fought to keep the cats for a little while, even tried to move her entire operation to Carole Baskin's Big Cat Rescue, in Florida. Baskin said she'd take the cats but not Diana. Eventually, she abandoned the cats and booked. County humane officers took control of the kids. She was never even arrested.

When we heard Diana had lammed, David and I prepared to take all the kids, even Joseph. I got very loud about it and paid my attorney to get involved. The government told him, "We'll get back to you." Because of how bad the situation had been and how much attention it had gotten, they went around us and shipped the kids out to other sanctuaries before anyone could do anything about it.

If it seems like I slapped Diana pretty good, she managed to hit me with one more painful shot. Imara was not among the rescued cats. I had no idea what had happened to her.

CHAPTER FORTY

Bart The Fart

A local cop asked me to take in a confiscated blue and gold macaw. I've dug exotic birds since my conversation with the scarlet macaw in Costa Rica, and the cops said this one's name was Bart, which reminded me of Det. Giesey. Everything seemed to be lining up, but I was still not quite sure, so I asked Dr. Burton what he thought. He was deep into birds, specializing in them at his practice, running a bird-watching club and taking trips to Costa Rica to check out the same exotic species I'd seen there.

"Oh, Ang, take him. They're exquisitely beautiful birds," he said. "They're very intelligent. They can learn hundreds of words. They're extremely rare. He must be worth at least $5,000."

The macaw's whole name turned out to be Bart the Fart, and Dr. Burton was right: Bart the Fart was gorgeous, with a lime headcap, fluorescent yellow tuxedo vest and cobalt cape. He was also much bigger than I thought. Even though I'd seen lots of macaws in Costa Rica, I had no real idea how big they actually are until I was face to face with Bart. I was afraid of him. His feet were bigger than my hands, he had talons like curved knives and, Dr. Burton told me after the fact, macaws' bills are so sharp and strong that they can easily nip off a finger.

He came with a perch that I put just off the kitchen. As soon as I set him up, Bart the Fart started spouting a bunch of gangsta crap. It was nonstop: "Fuck you, bitch"; "I'll kick yo ass, motherfucka"; "I'll gank you with a nine, punk."

They say birds who can talk just repeat whatever they hear and have no idea what they're saying. Bart the Fart knew exactly what every word meant. I'd taken in a little dog called "Ali," which was short for "Alibi." Once Bart the Fart heard the dog's name, he started bullying her: "You ain't shit, Ali;" "I'll slap the fuck out you, Ali, you bitch"; "I'm a buss a cap in yo ass, Ali."

The first couple times she heard him say her name, Ali barked and growled at Bart the Fart. His wings were clipped so he couldn't fly, but he climbed down off his perch and strutted across the floor like a midget gangbanger in a gaudy pimp outfit. He was surely going to kick Ali's ass. He was croaking, "Bring it, mothafucka" and a lot of other stuff I could barely understand, even though I'd spent so much time on the streets. Ali scurried out through the doggy door and sat on the porch shaking; I had to drag her back in by her collar.

I'd get frustrated and yell at Bart the Fart, "Shut the hell up!"

"Fuck off, bitch!" he'd say, cocking an eye as big as a quarter at me.

Bart the Fart would not shut up. He needed one of those Hannibal Lecter masks. After a couple weeks, I was willing to pay someone five grand to get that thugbird out of my house. I told Dr. Burton that he had to take Bart the Fart. When he didn't agree right off the rip, I did just what he'd done to me: "Oh, take him. He's an exquisitely beautiful bird. He's very intelligent. He knows hundreds of words. He's extremely rare. He must be worth at least $5,000."

Dr. Burton relented and installed Bart the Fart at his clinic. He immediately started cursing and threatening the clients and their pets. When I went up there, everyone blamed me for teaching him all that stuff. It was, "Hey, Ang, your bird told me to fuck off." My bird?

Dr. Burton was so offended by the vile language that he got mad at me, too. I thought he was going to gas that damn bird, and if a churchly person like Dr. Burton wants to gas your ass just for talking, you've got a really dirty mouth.

Dr. Burton had to get Bart the Fart away from his clients before his business crashed, so he took him home. He hosted Bible study meetings at his house every Thursday. Bart the Fart did the same thing to the church people and Susan and the girls. Susan wanted to wring my neck. They put him in a back room until Dr. Burton found him a home with someone who wasn't scared of him and wouldn't be upset when he told them to fuck off. Bart the Fart didn't ruin his love affair with birds, but Dr. Burton never mentioned that particular bird again. Neither did I.

After he was gone, I ran into the cop who asked me to take Bart the Fart in the first place. He told me that some drug dealers had trained Bart the Fart to protect their stash. Anyone sneaking around would hear him running his beak and think someone was home. They said he was more effective than any

Doberman.

Macaws can live to be a hundred, so I'm sure Bart the Fart is somewhere in the world right now, running smack on someone who wishes he would shut the hell up. That gang-bangin' bird had some serious street cred, man.

- Tiger Swim Time for Gage -

- Strolling with Sheba -

- Bachi, Charger, Tashara and Penny-

Cherry Angels and Earthly Predators 239

- Jewels – Angela's first love and first animal attacker -

- Nakobi -

- Exercising a sickly Gage -

- Wrestling with Imara at the Siberian Tiger Foundation -

- Tyson – who drew the wrath of the state down on Angela –

- Nyla – Defender of Special Needs Jabouhti -

– Nannok and Yukon – Wolves or Wolf Dogs? –

– Left-Right – Bachi, bartered out of a foul pet shop with Charger and Tashara, two of seven cats rescued from a madhouse in Georgia –

- Angela snuggling a rare and valuable white Tiger Cub –

- Mother's Milk – Angela bottle feeding young Gage -

- Zeus – One of the twins rescued from Georgia –

- China and Rosco-

– Apollo – chillaxing on his favorite log –

– Maximus – The rescue Lion who almost killed Angela –

– Cota – On her favorite log –

- Angela – All dressed up with a young tiger at Animal Care Unlimited -

– Montana – Saved from a corn crib and a pack of dogs –

– Jacob – Rescued during a blizzard –

- Nyla -

Angela – Radiantly happy with Ellen Martin Chester's dog

- China and Rosco just being happy –

CHAPTER FORTY-ONE

We Drove to Kokomo to Pick Up a Humongous Timber Wolf and Then Things Got Weird

I did my best to anticipate where the next problem would come from by spying on the dirtbags who were harming animals the most – breeders and dealers and roadside zoo and photo-baby swine. The only way to do that was to go underground where they dwell, and I couldn't go there as Rescue One. I combed through *Animal Finders Guide*, the magazine that advertises exotics for sale. I contacted people and talked to them for hours. I don't like to lie, so I didn't say anything about who I was. Somehow, John Brady* slipped under my radar. One of our donors had been to his dismal little zoo in Kokomo, Indiana, and spotted Nakomas wolf there. Ellen, who was now volunteering with us fulltime, was an artist into painting wolves. The woman brought Nakomas to Ellen's attention; she got in my face about him. I didn't know shit about wolves but told Ellen we would go get him.

I called around and learned that Brady was ready to dump the wolf because the animal was in bad shape, and he didn't want a dead kid on his hands. We already knew USDA was a no-go, so Ellen and I drove five hours to Kokomo to see if we could rescue the wolf.

He was a humongous, scary creature, like something out of a fairy tale. On all fours, that kid looked me right in the eye. He was also a mess: ears bloody to the scalp, emaciated, living in a tiny cage, fleas swarming all over him.

I thought I'd finally become noseblind to big-cat stink, but Brady's place dropped it to a whole new depth. That dump was so rank that I told myself I should make gasmasks standard issue for rescues. Looking at those 2000 square feet of foul cages stuck together in a makeshift roundabout, I thought, 'Why don't kids ever get to pick their own Hell?'

Brady was a slippery, kinky shyster who blatantly said, "Oh, yeah, I breed."

Like Ohio, Indiana didn't regulate exotics, so no one was preventing him from breeding and selling, and Brady was absolutely not worried about us. He ordered us to take the wolf and go.

While we were figuring the best way to get Nakomas out of there, I saw a tiger as big as Sammy across the roundabout. Sybre was a mutt-mix of some kind, too, with short bowed legs and a gigantic head. Although Brady said he was eight months old, the cat looked like a mature adult.

We didn't know if Brady would give Sybre up, but we took Nakomas home, and while David settled him in, Ellen and I turned right around and went back for the tiger. Sybre was in a middle cage, pacing and grumbling. There was a black leopard in a cage right behind him. Her name was Dakota. I could see in her eyes that she was a very sick kid. That jerkoff wanted money, though.

He said, "Why should I give them to you? I'm USDA. Nobody's going to touch me."

"Well, what're you feeding them?" I asked him.

He wouldn't tell us what his meat supply was – always a red flag for an exotic owner.

I kept badgering Brady about Sybre. He wouldn't relent; neither would I. Brady didn't want to give the tiger up; at the same time, he was griping about the cat. I guess he finally had enough of us pestering him, because he abruptly said we could have him.

I wouldn't quit about Cota, either. Brady got frustrated and said, "The hell with it. You want her, take her. She's a man-eater, anyway."

Honestly, I was intimidated. I'm only as good as the kids are kind, and those two cats didn't seem very friendly. Sybre was a lively, fabulous kid, but he was very big. I looked at him and thought, 'Whoa, I don't want you manhandling me. If I can just get you in the Cruiser and get you to Rescue One, you can manhandle David.'

Cota hissed and spat and clawed the air when Brady went near her cage. I had no experience at all with leopards, either, so I assumed that she was wicked and showing us how badass she was. 'Fuck, how're we going to do this?' I thought.

I ran into Kokomo, located a PetSmart, paid retail for the

biggest carrier cage they had and hurried back to load Sybre and Cota. By the time I returned with the cage, that numbskull had knocked Cota down with tranqs. We didn't even have a chance to bait her into the carrier. I didn't like how she was breathing, and I didn't like Brady. I just wanted to get the hell out of Kokomo.

When Brady jumped into the cage with Sybre, he looked like a circus midget next to the tiger. He managed to put a leash on the cat, but Sybre kicked his butt the whole time. Ellen backed the Cruiser up, and we opened the bay and put down a few pieces of chicken, and Sybre jumped in for a snack. He was so big that the Cruiser sagged on its suspension.

We put Cota into the carrier and laid her on the backseat. Ellen and I crammed into the rest of the space. We took off on pins and needles, running 90 miles an hour down the interstate again. On the way back, I became concerned about Cota's breathing. I called Dr. Burton. He figured that Brady had overdosed her, and we should be prepared for her to die before we got her back. I took a deep breath and punched the gas.

Cota threw up in the cage. It smelled foul, but I finally saw the meat supply Brady fed his animals. He was going to places that process poultry for human consumption and boxing up the scrap that falls on the floor, because it's free. Thank goodness Cota puked; she threw up just enough of those meds to skate the OD.

Even after all that, I wasn't done collecting animals on that trip. As I was dropping Ellen off, she told me about a stray cat that dogs were chasing around her neighborhood. When I pulled up in front of her house, guess who was cruising down the street with a pack of dogs on her tail. I opened the door and said, "You want a ride?" She jumped in. I'd gone to Kokomo for a timber wolf and ended up with the huge wolf, a sick leopard, a massive mutt tiger and Abby the alley cat. Rescue One was becoming an animal orphanage.

David had moved Sybee into an enclosure. He was a good boy, but he'd given David a run for his money. Dr. Burton said he didn't want Cota to travel again, so we ran bags of meds on her all night. The next morning, we carried her in the kennel cage onto the back porch. Cota was trapped there when she woke up.

We were very leery about going out there with her. I'd always heard that leopards will eat you alive, without exception, and this one probably had a nasty tranq stoneover. We had to move her into a clean cage, though. We used fence panels as shields, like gladiators, opened the carrier and backed up. That's the only way you can protect yourself and still make a big cat go where you want her to. Cota was nothing but an angel. She came out and walked up to David and let him pet her. They were pals immediately. She ambled into the big cage, jumped up on the ledge and lay there. We watered and fed her. She never made a move on us.

I offered Cota to the Columbus Zoo, but because she was sick, older and her tail was broken, they didn't want her. Within six months, I turned that kid into gorgeousness. Word got back to the zoo that I had a healthy black leopard. They didn't have one, so they called to talk about Cota. They'd already shown me how much they didn't care, so I told them to kiss my ass and hung up.

CHAPTER FORTY-TWO

The Short, Happy Life of AJ The Dumpster Baby

When we first brought Sheba, the lion whose owner shot himself, to Rescue One, we could hook her on a leash and take her for long walks around the property, like I'd done with every new kid. As time went on, though, she got rougher and wilder. We had to cut out the walks and lock her down in an enclosure just to the right of the back porch.

One day, some cops called and said they'd found a tiger cub in a dumpster in Tiffin. That's how much respect some people have for life, even the life of such a beautiful, helpless creature. By then, Dr. Markin had become our USDA rep. She was a veterinarian who inspected facilities for over 30 years. When she first came to Rescue One, she and I hated each other. We walked my property for hours, screaming. She'd order me to fix this and change that or she'd write me up, which could lead to fines. I wanted to jump on her. Over time, though, we called a truce, became friendly and cooperated for the good of the animals.

She kept telling me, "Ang, Ang, you're getting heavy on kids. Ang, Ang, details. Ang, Ang, you're getting too big."

I nodded every time, even though I had no intention of heeding her advice. Dr. Burton had been singing the same song.

I heard through the exotic tap system that a circus elephant somewhere in northwestern Ohio wanted to get out of show biz. That interested me, but Dr. Burton was plugged into the same grapevine. He beat me to the punch.

"No elephants, Angela," he said. "I can't reach that high, and I don't want to get stomped to death."

Then he ran down the species that were banned from Rescue One, because they were too dangerous, difficult to care for or expensive: hippos, rhinos, polar bears, grizzlies, hyenas, jackals, zebras, kangaroos – the list went on and on. In fact, he didn't want me to take any more animals at all. I just couldn't say no to the little dumpster tiger in Tiffin and risk his death, however, so when the cops called, we bounced right up to get him. He was barely four months and cute as heck. I named him AJ, but I called him my "Dumpster Baby."

I took AJ to Dr. Burton, endured the lecture, spent the money and got him into place. He slept in the house at night and went outside during the day to hang out in a paddock directly off the back porch that we kept free as a baby playpen. AJ still had a cone on his head from being neutered, but the kid was a tiny, happy, playful guy.

There was a fence between the playpen and the big-boy enclosure where we had Sheba. Dr. Markin had already warned me that Sheba could get a paw under the gate between her enclosure and the paddock. She wanted us to pour a cement slab under the gate, because Sheba was digging a rut and might be able to grab something and pull it into her enclosure. When AJ came in, things were hectic, as always, so much so that I put off having David install the dig barrier between AJ and Sheba.

I came in the front door of the log house after a supply run one morning, loaded with bags. I heard Ellen's piercing scream. I dropped everything and ran to the back porch. Whoever came in early that day had let AJ out to get some sun. Just as Dr. Markin feared, Sheba had reached under the gate and pulled AJ into her enclosure. We couldn't tell if he was alive or dead. No matter, we had to take him away from Sheba, and we didn't have any time to think things through.

"Screw it! We're going in!" I said.

I yelled for David, and he came running. We all knew that entering an enclosed space with a loose, Level-Five, Code-Red cat is jumping into the fight from hell. We threw the door open and went in to face Sheba. She had the crossover look; she'd turned into a lioness who'd tasted blood and was going crazy. Now, she *had* to kill. It could easily be one of us.

We each took a corner of the enclosure. I smacked Sheba's rump and faced the brunt of her charge, while David and Ellen attempted to grab AJ. She snarled and spun and roared. Over and over, we hit her and ducked and tried to scoop the cub. It was a split-second dance with death, and we still couldn't tell if AJ was alive. When Sheba finally got winded, we snatched the little tiger and ran him out of there. Unfortunately, it didn't turn out to be a recovery/rescue. AJ was dead.

It wasn't Sheba's fault. She was only doing what lions do. It was my fault. Dr. Markin said it, and I ignored her like I do anyone who gives me advice. A hot second later, it happened. Fuck. We had to bury that poor kid.

We never let a gate go without a dig barrier again. That mistake was easy to fix, but I'll never forgive myself for being stupid and irresponsible and costing my gorgeous little Dumpster Baby his life.

CHAPTER FORTY-THREE

Asthma, Ass and Ankle

Rescue One was never easy or as much as we tried, completely safe. We had daily cleaning, watering, feeding, fence repairs, sight checks, grass cutting, weed whacking, basic veterinary care, schmoozing potential donors, intakes and calls to place rescued animals. It was upgrade, fix, we need to move this kid, we need to expand, this isn't going to work, we're short on staff, we've got to get this cat to Dr. Burton.

We were so busy it became hard for me to see Granny. I felt bad that she was alone, so any time I happened to be near her neighborhood, I dropped by. She was a trip. She never just sat on the couch and watched TV with me and talked. As soon as I came through the door, she jumped into the kitchen. She hovered over the stove and the oven, cooking and baking and chitchatting. Even though I ate almost nothing, she always packed up the leftovers for me to take home. David and our volunteers loved them.

I couldn't see her as much as I wanted, but I phoned Granny so often that the number of her old landline – 6142763855 – is stamped into my brain. I'd wake up in the middle of the night, hear her calling "Ang! Ang! Come down and eat!" and catch myself answering her from my bed. Usually, I just rolled out and start the day's chores. There was no time to waste on sleeping.

To make things harder, I'm very allergic to cats. The bigger the cat, the worse my reaction. My skin catches fire. My eyes swell. I wheeze like I have pneumonia. After I was around any of the tigers at Rescue One, I had to hurry into the kitchen, fill the sink and wash with Dawn dish detergent. I never went to an allergist, because if you take anything that makes you drowsy around big cats, you could end up as steak *tartare*.

One mistake – one momentary loss of concentration – could literally cost you your ass. I woke up one night and felt something pressing down on my head. I turned on a lamp and opened my good eye. When it focused, I saw David holding his pants around his knees. His bare butt was hanging a few inches above my face.

"Dude, what are you doing?" I said. "It's the middle of the night. Get your ass out of my face!"

"Is this all right?" he said, pointing at his rear end. "I just wanted you to check if it's all right."

I finally saw what he meant – a line of perfect stitches running across his butt cheek.

"What the fuck happened to you?" I said.

He told me that he fell behind on his butchering and feeding that day and didn't get to some of the cats until after dark. Rushing, he set food down for one of the tigers and turned his back. She bit him. He propped a mirror on a kitchen chair and sewed himself up with a stitch kit an EMT friend had given me.

I said, nonchalantly, "You're good to go, buddy. Nice job," but it really was impressive.

The Gage kid in *Pet Sematary* dies and is reincarnated as a killer, but my Gage tiger never became vicious. That doesn't mean he wasn't dangerous. I worked so hard to save and care for them that I savored any chance to just enjoy the cats for a few minutes. I was in the enclosure with Gage one day, petting him, and, as usual, he was all chuffy, chuffy. Trying to be cute, he leaned against my leg and fell on his side so I'd rub his belly. Unfortunately, he was too close and too heavy. He landed on my ankle.

My foot got very hot, like I'd stepped on glowing coals. Pain knifed up my leg. Gage was still lying there, looking up at me, waiting for his belly-rub. I'm not sure if he caught my vibe or what, but I could tell by his face that he knew he'd hurt me. I was afraid the pain might trigger some lethal instinct in him, so I choked down a scream and held onto the fence, gritting my teeth. Gage sat beside me with his belly down, chuffing, as if saying, 'Oh, Mommy, I'm so sorry.' As I limped away, he paced the fence, whining.

I went to the ER and made up some cock-and-bull nonsense about stumbling on the steps. Luckily, it was a clean fracture right above the ball joint, so they believed me. They wrapped my ankle and put a blow-up cast on it. When I came back, I wanted to lie down, because walking was agonizing, but I wobbled over on one crutch and sat beside Gage's enclosure. I put my cast against the chain link. He went right to it and started sniffing.

"It's okay, Gage," I said. "Look at it. It's cool."

I let him check out my leg and feel my vibes until he calmed down.

CHAPTER FORTY-FOUR

In Which Gomez and Morticia Get Hitched by an Elvis Impersonator – No, Really!

I've often thought that if I'd married one of my wealthy Beach Babes clients, I'd be a rich bitch lounging on a beach in the Caribbean right now, checking the Dow Jones and wondering where that damned cabana boy is with my margarita. With the exception of Fred, I never regretted not marrying any of those jerkoffs, though. Hell, all I had to do was stay with Grant, and I'd be a princess living in Europe. I heard through the grapevine that after I left, he got married, bought a real *chateau* and fathered the heir he'd nagged me about for so long.

What happened with Sammy and Shebee confirmed how I felt about marriage. If being married meant giving my tiger away to live in someone else's backyard or shooting myself, I didn't want any part of it. Then I did it, anyway.

Even though David had been staying at Rescue One, I told him I'd never get married and live the Sheep Life; he insisted that it wasn't fair for him to do so much work yet have no official standing. I finally had to admit that he was right. He knew a lot about animals, worked very hard and was a skilled handyman. David also had a subtle sense of humor and was very compassionate. He was dedicated to the kids, and they loved him. Besides, I needed a legal way to hold and protect my animals. If something bad happened to me, I didn't want local authorities or the state or the USDA to waltz in and seize my kids and ship them wherever they wanted or put them down. Marrying David would protect the cats and shut him up. He would be an instant security blanket.

"I get it," I eventually told David. "I see why it's important to you, and I understand how it could be important to the kids. It takes a big worry off of me. Okay, dude. Let's do it. Let's get married."

We were married a week later, on Halloween eve. Every year, Reeni and Steve, lovely salt-of-the-earth volunteers from Delaware, Ohio, threw a big costume party. They rented a hall and had the bash catered. Reeni said it would be fun to integrate our wedding into the party. David and I filed the paperwork, and Gomez and Morticia Adams got hitched during a rowdy Halloween shindig. I was smashed. I love Elvis impersonators, so they found one to perform the ceremony.

David always knew it was about taking care of the kids and nothing more, just business. I even continued using my own last name. I told him, "I'll always do exactly what I want, and if you get in my way, I'll slap you into your next life."

That had always been the deal with me, and I wasn't about to change.

CHAPTER FORTY-FIVE

A Cosmic Wake-Up Call

Sybre, the mutt tiger from Kokomo, had adapted perfectly to his new home. He shared an enclosure with Gage. They wrestled and played with their Boomer Balls and slept side by side. However, one midsummer day, Sybre suddenly flopped down like he had bubonic plague and didn't move. Mystified and alarmed, I called Dr. Burton. He sent Andrew, a very good young vet and very cool guy, who rushed to Rescue One. We put Gage in the lockout, and Andrew took Sybre's temperature. The dude was running a brain-cooking, 107-degee fever. Andrew drew blood, gave Sybre injections to try to pull his temperature down and hurried back to Animal Care Unlimited with the samples.

David and I waited for the blood work to come back, speculating about what could've hit the tiger that hard and fast. We were baffled, and an animal can't tell you what's wrong with him. It took almost a whole day to get the results.

Dr. Burton called and said, "Ang, go to the store and buy every bag of ice you can find and a lot of rubbing alcohol and put it on his paws. We have to lower that temperature."

I spent almost a hundred bucks on a case of rubbing alcohol and a backseat full of bags of ice. We poured alcohol on his pads and packed ice around him. He was limp and barely conscious.

'Damnit! We're losing my big boy!' I thought.

Dr. Burton called again and said the bloodwork looked normal. Andrew returned and gave Sybre another injection. We stuck medication up his rectum to get it into his bloodstream quickly. Even after all the tests and ice and meds, the fever barely changed. None of us had any idea what was going on. Sybre was a sack of meat. He looked like he would die at any second. I was petrified.

That night, I went out into the enclosure and sat down beside him and stroked his fur. I was exhausted and resigned to the terrible fact that Sybee would die any second. At around five in the morning, I woke up to Sybre's fuzzy, fangy, tonguey, beach ball-sized head in my face. He was looking down at me, nuzzling me and chuffing. I thought, 'Whoa! Whoa! What? What happened?' I was so scared that my stomach did a bump and grind. He stood over me, as if he was saying, 'Hey, hey, I'm hungry. Hey, hey, hey, I want to eat now.' I could see 'Hi, Mom' in his face, like Jewels after the episode in her enclosure. I was so happy I started crying.

I spotted David and called, "Get some food in this kid! He's hungry! Get him some water!"

I kissed Sybre and hugged him and checked his temperature. His fever was down. His eyes were clear. We gave the boy something to eat and drink, then let Gage out with him. They sniffed and nuzzled each other. Sybee was fine.

While I was gathering up the rubbing alcohol bottles and

empty ice bags, I called Dr. Burton and said, "You won't believe this!" He was incredulous. Something mysterious had reached out and touched Sybre and me. I didn't understand it, and not even Dr. Burton couldn't explain it. It was a cosmic wake-up call. 'No matter how huge and powerful you are, life is fragile,' I thought. 'Never forget that every second is precious.'

CHAPTER FORTY-SIX

Dressage Boots and Taxidermy

I knew Dr. Burton and Dr. Markin were right when they insisted Rescue One was growing too fast. I wanted to say "No," but when trouble came knocking, I thought, 'I can work it out. I'll move them around and make space for another one.'

The money it took to just to keep the cats alive every day was becoming astronomical. We were spending tens of thousands every year just on food. We bought beef from packing houses in Pittsburgh and Toledo and as a side dish, frozen chicken quarters at cost – 30 cents a pound – from Vitale Poultry in Columbus. For dessert, we served "bloodsickles" – cubes of blood and bits of meat that we made in a chest freezer. Farmers started calling us when one of their animals died; state and local cops turned us on to road-killed deer. David picked up the carcasses and butchered them in one of the garages.

I hate to say it, but the cats' favorite food was horsemeat. Every Friday, David took a big trailer to an auction in Sugarcreek, where they shot horses that were unwanted or too badly injured to sell. David hauled them back whole and spent all night processing them. It was a lot of grisly and disturbing work with machetes and mallets and power saws, but we needed the meat.

In addition to the muscle meat, Dr. Burton said, the cats

needed vitamins and calcium. We went through two or three $500 tubs of powdered supplements a month. We needed money for utilities, cleaning supplies, equipment and fencing repairs, gas, new enclosures, insurance, our own household stuff. Every time a new cat came in, it had to be quarantined and undergo a thorough examination, including bloodwork and inoculations so that it didn't infect the other animals with a killer disease. My vet bills began to look like invoices for human cancer treatments or heart transplant surgeries.

Even the domestic animals could be incredibly expensive. Joshua became very sick. One minute, he'd be fine and then his eyes would turn ice-white and he couldn't move. Dr. Burton said it was kidney failure.

"Ang, come on," he said. "You've got to let him go."

But I was a stupid young mommy fooling herself: "No, no. Look at him. He's better today."

I spent $6777.89 on Joshua before Dr. Burton finally convinced me to put him down, for the sake of the cat.

It wasn't as if we were swamped with donors, either. It's all talky-talky when people are in the limelight pretending to give half a shit, but once the 6 o'clock news is over, they go away. Unless you hit the lotto with some super-rich animal lover, donations are minimal. Most exotic owners are broke, so no one wrote us a hefty check out of gratitude for taking in a big cat.

There was still enough left from my Hidden Lake days and in my trust fund to last a little while, I was selling off jewelry and a few donations were trickling in; however, what we earned wasn't nearly enough to create any margin of safety. We couldn't raise money like the big animal rights organizations. Those phonies slap some heartbreaking pictures on TV accompanied by sad soundtracks, wait for the donations to roll in and then spend almost none of the money helping animals. We were making do as best we could, but I knew that when my nest egg emptied, every creature at Rescue One would be in deep shit.

Eventually, my credit was trashed and the property was in jeopardy. Reeni and Steve were generous enough to charge two or three of our mortgage payments on their credit cards when we got behind; even so, Rescue One slid into foreclosure.

Everyone was waiting for me to come up with an answer, but I didn't have one. I had to get the property out of foreclosure, so I refinanced with a shady company under horrible terms that were like a noose around my neck. I knew that wasn't a good idea, but at least I'd saved the compound and the kids for the time being.

One year, I got involved in a huge charity event called the New Albany Classic Invitational Grand Prix and Family Day. It was an equestrian show-jumping competition combined with music, carnival rides, food trucks, a classic luxury car show and lots of activities for kids. It was put on by billionaires Les and Abigail Wexner. She's a high-powered attorney. He founded the Limited clothing chain and bought Victoria's Secret and Bath and Body Works. They own an estate in Franklin County, a

$100,000,000 superyacht in Florida, a private jet and a mansion in England. They are also philanthropists, supporting Ohio State, Jewish causes worldwide, animals and, particularly, The Center for Family Safety and Healing, which helps victims of domestic violence – something I know more than a little about. The match seemed perfect.

Along with many other charitable organizations seeking help, we applied to have a booth in the Wexners' 300-acre backyard. Thousands of people, including many of the Wexners' wealthy chums, attended the event every year. I fervently hoped that we could cozy up to some big-time donors. Applying involved a rigid, confidential and official process. After we submitted the application, we took follow-up phone calls and fielded questions. We were accepted and had t-shirts and brochures printed.

For this once-in-a-blue moon opportunity, I violated my most sacred rule – absolutely no public contact with the cats. At the time, we had a pair of little lions and two tigers who were young enough to be frisky and cute without being dangerous. We hooked them up and took them to the gig with us.

They were a smash hit. People flocked around them, petting them and asking questions and taking pictures with them. They caused such a commotion that Abigail Wexner descended from her private perch. She wore tan riding breeches, tall, shiny black dressage boots and a white shirt with a flared collar. If he ever got so close to a woman that rich, Grant would have a premature ejaculation.

Surrounded by her security team and a gaggle of girlfriends, Abigail told me how beautiful the cats were and how wonderful it was that we were saving them. She said she was sure that people would rally to our cause. She gave me a card and told me to call the number on it so we could "start the paperwork."

'Finally,' I thought, 'we'll be able to put our heads above water and breathe.'

I called that number . . . and called it. When someone finally answered, he informed me that not only would we receive no donations, but we were not welcome at future events. Soon, an official get-lost letter arrived. It said the liability presented by the kids was "unacceptable." I was bewildered. It's not like we'd been walking rabid wolverines and Nile crocodiles around. They were playful kittens who might grab your shoelaces or hiss at your Yorkie. It had been a one-off, anyway. My cats were neutered, and I certainly wasn't going to run out and grab more cubs for the next year, not that anyone bothered to ask.

I'd spent enough time around rich people that I should've recognized the 48-carat brushoff when I saw it – the vague language accompanied by the batted lashes and the horsey smile and the eyes that look everywhere except directly at me. After Abigail had left, security stayed close to us for the rest of the day, whispering into their walkie-talkies. My desperation blinded me to reality.

For a while, I thought Abigail Wexner might've been jealous over the amount of attention we attracted. I told them beforehand that we were bringing the cats, but maybe their actual presence kicked her lawyerly training in. The more I pondered it, however, the more I smelled the Columbus Zoo in that freeze-out. They had a petting zoo there, and they had been very aware of Rescue One and our kids. They would be pissy about anyone cutting into their donations, and Jack Hanna ran in the same circles as the Wexners. Given the chance, the zoo would've eagerly submarined any exotic owner, no matter how small the operation or how unselfish its motivations.

Ironically, public zoos were part of the reason Rescue One had to exist at all. Jack Hanna was almost a regular on *The David Letterman Show*, which had a huge audience then. God only knows how many dimbulbs saw darling Jungle Jack cuddling a cub in the chair next to Dave and rushed out to buy one – or three – for themselves. Believe me, we're not talking about the AKC Pomeranian and Pekinese crowd here. Record-keeping is so shoddy – or nonexistent – that it's impossible to trace the *provenance* of most exotics. I wouldn't be surprised to learn that I'd been killing myself to care for animals that had once been owned by Jack's dumbass acolytes.

A car came up the driveway one afternoon, carrying the opportunity to solve some of my financial problems. A smiling yokel got out and introduced himself. He had a hedge-clipper haircut and wore a wrinkled Sears suit and a too-short polyester tie. Flecks of brown snuff peppered his lips and teeth.

Thinking he was a door-to-door salesman, I started to run him off, but he said, "I'll give you $10,000 cash money for any lion or tiger on the property, living or dead, sick or healthy."

I chewed on that for a few seconds, then asked him what the hell he was talking about. He repeated the offer and took a wad of bills out of his pocket. He fanned them in my face. I still didn't get it.

"You want the animal for what?" I asked.

"I'm a taxidermist," he said. "I'll mount it and display it in my front window as advertising."

It took me several more seconds to comprehend what the guy had said. When I finally had it straight, I punched him right in his moronic grin. Bills and snuff spit flew. He ran back to his car, a hand plastered over his mouth. I chased him down the driveway, throwing rocks and calling him every name I could think of. I didn't even pick up that cockroach's money, just let it blow away. From that day on, when an animal died, we spray-painted its coat bright orange and buried it deep with a front loader, in case someone tried to sneak onto the compound and dig up the body.

CHAPTER FORTY-SEVEN

Games People Play

At last, I came up with a fund-raising idea.

"Hey, why not have a bingo game?" I asked David and Ellen. "We're nonprofit, so we can do that."

I'm not sure what led me to an old lady's pastime, but I couldn't believe the money it attracted. We took out a state license and rented a hall. Just like rescuing animals or escorting, our bingo game took on a life of its own. You either go all in or don't go, and our game turned into the biggest and best around. Three hundred players showed up two nights a week.

I needed staff to set things up, run tickets on the floor, cook. I needed ball callers and accountants to tally the money, keep track of the tickets and disperse cash to the winners. We hired parking people and a cop to direct traffic. I needed door prizes, food, kitchen stuff. I bought very expensive electronic boards that flashed every time a number was called. We hung TVs all over the place.

We were underfunded, undermanned and overwhelmed, but the condition of the license was that the government could step in and take a bite out of what we were making. They knew nothing, did nothing, contributed nothing, but the state had a legal right to bleed money from my kids. I had no choice but to eat their shit.

To make matters even more complicated, since I'd copped to "menacing" after the dustup with Phil, my name couldn't be on the license, and I wasn't allowed anywhere near the game. I slunk in and out, doing what I could. A lecherous old drunk who managed the hall came on to me. When I shut him down, he squealed to the state. An investigator busted me carrying food into the kitchen and fined me 10 grand.

A ton of money went through that place, but because of the cost of running the games and the bureaucrat extortionists, hardly any of it was making it to the kids. In fact, the kids were being neglected because we were all exhausted from bingo. I needed help, but everyone was already pitching in. I didn't know where to turn, except to my family, messed up as they are. I called Mom and asked if she and John could help. They surprised me by showing up for every game. Mom worked the door, and John cooked.

I was astonished and overjoyed when Arletta walked through the door one night. Luke was still close to Johnny, and she'd heard about the bingo game through him. Arletta turned out to be a fanatical player. She jumped right in, helping me with all kinds of things. She never mentioned my taking off with Grant without telling her.

Of course, when that kind of cash is involved, there's scads of competition. Other bingo halls were putting out rumors that we were cheating, that we didn't pay our winners. The lies compounded the stress. Even with the new help, we couldn't make bingo pay like it should've. After three years, I had to shut down the vicious circle of crap. The money got very tight then, but, of course, the phone didn't stop ringing. I was flipping.

CHAPTER FORTY-EIGHT

Cherry Angels

We needed money – a lot of money – and we needed it in a quick minute. David kept saying, "We're in trouble here. Work your magic, Angie. Get us out of this mess."

Nothing seemed viable. The stress was unbearable. I'd been fighting to contain it, but my bulimia was raging, sapping my energy and concentration just when I needed them most. I was walking down the hallway from my bathroom one morning, wiping my mouth on a hand towel and wondering what I could do to avoid the tidal wave that was about to crash over us. Suddenly, it came to me: 'Wait a second, I know how to make $1000 tonight. I've made way more than that before. Ang, you've been using your body to make money since you were a kid. The hell with it, you have to go back into the nightlife. Just go to work and do your thing.'

I never explained what I was up to, just told David and Ellen, "Don't worry about it. I'll handle it. I'll be bouncing in and out and dropping off money."

They returned to their schedules, and I went to my fallback options – dancing and prostitution. I'm not being completely accurate when I say that 'I' started hooking again. I actually put out my own call for help. I didn't need someone with compassion or morals or scruples. I needed someone who knew that in a world that rewards ruthlessness, kindness is worth jacknothing. I needed Heather. Running in that world is just as dangerous as walking into a tiger cage, and that's why Heather resurfaced, strong and fast. She wasn't afraid of anything and didn't give a damn what anyone thought about her. Heather wasn't going to waste time fretting about animals; her only priority was getting paid.

At first, I worked only on weekends. I stayed in motels in Columbus and danced with a bunch of mutant crackheads at a trashy joint called Fantasy Island, which was essentially a big storage unit in an industrial park. I spent so much time playing mommy to the young, burned-out chicks there that I couldn't make the money I needed, so I quit to go freelance.

There are different ways to announce that you're in the business: newspapers, specialty publications, the phonebook and, eventually, online. I didn't need to hustle party money from horny substitute schoolteachers and assistant hardware store managers like Arletta and I used to. Now, it wasn't about getting high and having fun; it was about my kids' lives. I needed to make bank in a major way.

Before print died, the real pros were in the Yellow Pages. That's how you attracted the heavy hitters. The phonebook ads meant executives with big money, travel, fancy evenings out, expensive gifts, huge tips. However, the big ads started at $10,000 a year. I couldn't afford that, so I looked to see which escort service placed the biggest ad in the phone book. The agency was called Doll Set. A woman named Becky ran it. She'd been in escorting for a long time, then had a kid with a guy who placed a big ad every year, so she retired from the day-to-day business. This dude rented a house and ran a bunch of girls. I talked to Doll Set on the phone, and Heather went to work for them.

As always, Heather came with her own habits and needs. She stayed in her own place. She associated with her own friends. She wore her own clothes. She immediately had to have another Mitsubishi 3000 GT VR-4, this one blood red instead of the more sedate burgundy model. Now, we had to pay for Heather's gas, her car, her rent in Columbus and the Nextel phone that was my lifeline to Cherry Angels and Rescue One.

Heather worked at Doll Set for about a year. Becky and I were both alphas, though, and that never works out. We both knew we couldn't coexist. Phonebooks come out once a year. If you miss that print date, you're out of luck. I took her crap for a year, stashed as much money as I could and then told her to stick it.

I took out an ad for my new escort service, Cherry Angels. There was a lot of competition around, and I wanted to be the first escort service dudes called, just like I wanted Rescue One to be the first exotic sanctuary anyone contacted. That ad ended up costing close to $25000.

Doll Set operated with a house full of assets: an office where two chicks answered phones and booked appointments; a waiting room filled with girls; drivers who made certain the girls collected the money and came back safe. I wanted to involve as few people as possible, because if what I was doing ever got out, it could ruin Rescue One. When I had Beach Babes, I didn't bother with drivers or bodyguards. I walked blindly, night after night, into I didn't know what. I was naïve then. Now, I was experienced enough to know that going it alone was stupid and perilous. I tried to hire drivers – 50 bucks to deliver me to the location, walk me up to the door, look tough, wait outside for an hour and bring me back, a bonus if you get me out of trouble. Because I worked so much, though, no one could hang with me.

I certainly wasn't going to pay any pimp to steal food from the mouths of my kids; they needed too much of it – like 10 pounds of raw meat per cat, per day, no exceptions. It wasn't New York strip, but it wasn't slaughterhouse floor trash, either. Although our suppliers were all nice people, they did business strictly cash-and-carry. We had to have the money up front, so I flew solo, took the risks and kept everything I earned. I heard Heather say it a thousand times: "If you weren't there helping me suck that cock, you're not entitled to any of the proceeds."

For obvious reasons, I couldn't do in-calls, which made things far more dangerous. No one knew where I was going or who I was meeting, yet I needed to stay safe and get paid at the same time. I had to create the illusion that Cherry Angels was a major operation. Ang was never in the nightlife, and Heather couldn't answer the phone and go on the calls, too. I invented an office manager named Lisa, who didn't sound anything like Heather or Angela. I made Lisa up from scraps of raw material and some imagination, just like I had with Heather. Lisa was never as strong a character as the others, but since the production opened with her, she was crucial.

Lisa kept 3x5 file cards in the Mitsubishi's glove box and booked Heather's gigs on the fly. Her job was to sort the freaks and jokers and setups from the real money. She had to be able to tell quickly if a caller was worth fishing for an appointment. She listened carefully to how he greeted her and spoke, what he talked about and where he was located, exactly what he wanted and what he was willing to pay. Then she quickly calculated if he was legit cash and, more important, sane.

I love live theater, so I wrote an opening speech for Lisa to deliver to potential clients: "Good evening, Cherry Angels; this is Lisa speaking. How may I help you? Certainly, sir, there are numerous gorgeous girls available tonight. Please hold while I see who's in right now."

Lisa took her time, as if checking a roster; of course, she steered every client to Heather. Things became very fast and very full, with a lot of moving parts. Ang was responsible for Rescue One; Heather was working the money; Lisa was doing the administrative duties. All three women had to concentrate every second on who was doing the talking, scheduling, feeding or screwing. If any of them made a mistake, a deranged client might rape and kill Heather or a 600-pound tiger might tear Angela to pieces.

The Cherry Angels clientele was a mixed bag: married locals bored with old habits, freaks hiding all sorts of perversions, businessmen traveling for work, lonely older men looking for company. The ultimate goal for any call girl is to rack up the frequent flyers – the return customers who are less risky and more dependable than first timers.

Some of my clients were amusing. I saw a prominent Japanese industrialist about a half-dozen times. Mr. Himura* was a handsome, cultured, pleasant millionaire who happened to have a weird fetish. Heather would get dolled up – always including her most provocative and expensive fuckme heels – go to an upscale hotel, knock on the door, strip down to just the footwear, kick him throwing-up hard in the balls, dress and leave him curled on the bed, gripping his crotch and moaning. The appointment took a few minutes and paid a grand, sometimes more. I had to resist the temptation to ask Mr. Himura if it was as good for him as it was for me.

Mr. Himura wasn't even close to my wackiest client. I had a cute little guy who must've been 80. He lived in a house out in the country. His wife had died, and he was starving for affection. He was also a masochist who wanted Heather to beat him with a wire coat hanger until his back bled. He became obsessed, calling her endlessly just to check on her. She finally cut him off. Those freaky sessions weren't worth the money.

I had a Russian crossdresser. In the daytime, he was a respected professor, but on some nights, he became Jennifer. He wore spike heels that he had made to fit his gigantic feet. When Heather arrived, he was always dragged out, looking at himself in the mirror and smearing on makeup. He wore a wig and the spike heels and a very short jean skirt.

He'd say, in his Russian accent, "Heather, do I *luke* like I will get date tonight? I am going to be reel *sloot*."

He'd pose, trying to see in the mirror if his hairy ass was hanging out of that jean skirt. Although he could barely get in it, he always worried that the skirt wasn't tight and short enough. He reminded me of Buffalo Bill in *The Silence of the Lambs*. Maybe that's where he found Jennifer, or maybe she was always inside him somewhere, like the wild cougar was always in Jewels and Heather was always in Angela.

"Jennifer, did you do your make-up in the dark?" I'd ask him. "I hate that green eye shadow, babe. We have to do something with that mess."

I'd go in my purse for some decent makeup, redo Jennifer's face, adjust her wig, fix her outfit, give her a pep talk and some pointers on seduction, collect my money and turn her loose to hunt for her date. The Russian was a screwball, but he cracked me up.

The Rice Krispy Guy, on the other hand, was a sick, sick man. He was a stubby, pear-shaped, middle-aged dude with a pencil-thin black mustache, black Vitalised hair and black horn-rimmed glasses. Something had happened in his childhood that wasn't right. I think he's dead now, but for the longest time he rented a room and called Heather.

When she showed up, he'd say, "How many do you think I can do tonight?"

As he concentrated on shoving tampons up his ass, Heather

sat on the bed, counted them and told him how amazing he was. His personal best was five big ones. It gets even weirder. He always had a bunch of junk in the room: a five-gallon bucket, family-sized boxes of Rice Krispies, a wooden spoon and packs of new pantyhose. He poured the cereal in the bucket and added water until it turned into goo. Then he brought out five or six pairs of pantyhose. Every time he put a pair on, he stuffed them with saturated Rice Krispies. When he was done, he looked like a bloated Elephant Man. Then Heather filled the bathtub with scalding water and put him in it. He sat in the tub, while she told him what a loser he was, how worthless he was, how he'd wasted his life, how sorry his little dick was.

I suppose he was punishing himself for something, but I'm actually not sure what the thrill was in all that. I have no clue what happened after the hot baths, because, by then, the hour was up. Heather grabbed the money and boogied. After my first session with the Rice Krispies Guy, I could never look at cereal again.

Except for the assholes who tried to hurt me or cheat me, the johns I hated worst were the ones who wanted me to tell them dirty stories. Their own sessions weren't enough for them. They wanted to know who I fucked, when I fucked them, where I fucked them – with a full XXX description of every intimate detail. The problem was there was nothing "intimate" about what I did. Most of it was the farthest thing from erotic or sexy, whatever those words mean. It was boring, sickening and, a lot of times, pathetic. But they wanted to hear it all; well, that's not right – what they really wanted was for me to confirm their own vile fantasies. At least as long I was talking, they weren't touching, so I made up a lot of *Penthouse* Forum whoppers, while they jabbered at me: "Oh, my cock is bigger than that, right? I fucked you harder than that, right?"

I'd say, "Yeah, oh yeah, baby. You're the best I ever had," the whole time thinking, 'Where'd you say left that money, dimwit? Oh, did I mention the 20% upcharge for the fractured fairy tale?'

Even if my childhood hadn't been so fucked up, those perverts would've made the thought of sex gag me. The way I saw it, I never let any of them fuck Angela, anyway. They never touched her; they never even met her. They were all humping Heather and the spankbank between their own ears and their own palms. No wonder Silky called men "mushrooms."

I was too cynical to believe anymore in magic gardens and enchanted castles. I convinced myself that every blowjob was another trailer-load of meat; every hour Heather spent on her back with her legs spread, pretending, while a sweaty fool humped away at her was another emergency visit – or two – from Dr. Burton; every night wasted listening to some gasbag ramble on about his booming business or his frigid wife was another payment on the predatory mortgage that was strangling me; every act of perversion was a chance to rescue another abused cat from a hellhole.

I was not worshipping Mammon; I was protecting my kids. Heather's flesh was willing, and Angela's spirit didn't give a fuck about anything but saving animals.

CHAPTER FORTY-NINE

That's Just the Way It Is, Bitches

If I don't refer to my whoring notebooks, I can recall only my kindest, strangest and most vicious clients. The rest are as nameless and faceless as listings in an out-of-town phone book. I found one of those notebooks the other day and opened it to an entry for the Drury Inn on Stringtown Road in Grove City. That's one geek I'll never forget.

Lisa took a call at almost 3:30 in the morning. Heather had already done several appointments that night and made about $1500. She was in her pajamas, bone tired, but the caller said he was CEO of a construction company that did major jobs in big cities all over the eastern United States. The Drury Inn was also a nice location. Lisa told Heather to get her butt out on the call.

The client was around 45, with a shaved head and sleeve tats on his arms. He was friendly, but he was tweaking. His face was twitchy, his movements jittery, his eyes unfocused. He'd pulled a drawer out of a desk and turned it upside down so that he could snort this big pile of yellow coke off it. I started wondering if he was money or just a zero hallucinating in mid-jag.

I did the usual spiel about my rates, then told him I had to see a bank statement or a credit card. He showed me his corporate checkbook and plastic. Like all cokeheads, he had word-vomit.

His thoughts were bouncing all over the room. He told me his real name, where he lived, all about the buildings his company was working on. He invited me to hit the pile, but the last thing I needed in that sketchy situation was a headful of questionable blow.

I took a second to size him up again. He looked like Gollum from *The Lord of the Rings*, except bigger, and was so high that I thought he was going to start climbing the walls and crawling across the ceiling. The money seemed legit, though.

Heather finally figured out what he wanted and stripped. Luckily, he was too ripped to get an erection. He just wallowed and slobbered on her and felt her up for about 45 minutes. She worked him for $700, which included tip. He said that was all the cash he had. I was headed out of there, but he begged me to stay. The bars were closed, and he was fighting the crash, frightened of being cooped up in that little room alone. 'Man, I am wiped out, and this goofball is driving me completely out of my mind,' I thought. 'I know he's going to be pissed, but I have to get out of here.'

"My driver's on his way. I have to go," I told him. "The agency gets mad if I spend too much time with one client."

"Oh, Heather, I talked to Lisa," he said. "She likes me. I'll give her another call. I know I can convince her to let you stay longer. I'll go to the bank in the morning and withdraw the rest of the money."

He reached for his phone to call Cherry Angels. My Nextel

was in my purse on an end table right beside him. If it rang, even that wasteoid would've figured out that I didn't have any backup. I couldn't gamble on what might happen next.

"I have to use the bathroom, dude," I said. "You go out and get us some ice and sodas, and I'll call Lisa. I'm her best friend. We'll work something out."

After he pulled on his trousers and left, I had a minute or two to figure out whether I should bolt. I opened a drawer and peeked in his wallet: no cash. I almost grabbed my stuff and ran, but I thought, 'If he burns me, the hell with it. It's a risk, but I'm here, and we need the money.'

He came back with a bucket of ice and two cans of soda.

"I talked to Lisa," I said, "and it's okay for you to write a check, but I have another important thing I'm supposed to do. I'd probably make a couple thousand. I can't stay for anything less than $2500."

He sat on the bed and wrote a company check for that amount to "Cash." He even gave me his driver's license and car keys as collateral. Heather pretended to call her driver to cancel pickup. She stayed while he laughed and babbled and stuck his face in that pile of coke and fondled her store-bought tits.

His bank branch was on Stringtown Road, too. When it opened at nine, I had my hand on the door. He said he'd go in. I hesitated, but I had his license and keys, so I let him go. He grabbed the check, went inside and came back out with a pretty decent payday. The four grand Heather made that night held

Rescue One together for one more week.

Heather told Lisa she was never going on another call that late, when the client was almost sure to be loaded. However, the truth was she had to do the work. Hooking is like carpentry or driving a truck – if you're not on the job, you don't get paid. There are no vacations, no paid holidays, no personal days, no sick time.

Once I got things up and running, there weren't enough nighttime hours to make the money that Rescue One demanded. The Cherry Angels number never stopped ringing. David, who knew nothing except that we needed money, wanted me to open Rescue One to the public and charge people to take pictures with the animals. I told him I'd jump off the highest cliff in the world before I let a bunch of pussnut Sheep Worlders treat my kids like circus freaks. Every night, Lisa had to work the phones to score at least one call that would pull in 250 to 500 bucks; on better nights, she would schedule three or four calls, and I came home with $1500 or more; on the best nights, Heather fulfilled some rich guy's wildest fantasies and made more in a few hours than she normally did in a month.

After work, I went back to the office, showered Heather away, fell on the couch for an hour or two, woke up, called Rescue One to see what they needed, bought supplies on the way in, put out fires, did a sight check on the kids, gave everyone their marching orders and emptied my pockets for David to bank. Then the cycle started over.

I had to be careful about reaching out to my old clients,

because the last thing I needed was someone in the wrong position connecting me with the sanctuary. Besides, Rescue One had become so expensive that I couldn't cherry-pick reliable and well-to-do men like I used to. At the very time Heather should've been growing more cautious, the need for money was forcing her to become more reckless. Ang couldn't take a break, because animals needed her. Heather couldn't take a break, because the money had to keep coming in. Lisa couldn't take a break, because she had to book gigs. It's like Angela and Heather looked at each other one day, shook hands and said, 'Okay, it's on. Let's go.' We agreed to do anything to protect the kids.

I was always sleep-deprived and exhausted, running on coffee, Marlboro Lights, Diet Mountain Dew and catnaps. Eventually, I started sampling the Tramadol that Dr. Burton frequently prescribed for my animals. He said that Tramadol, which is basically synthetic codeine, was good for pain and to quiet the cats when they were agitated. These were huge animals that required massive doses of whatever drug they needed to take. Trammies were not a controlled substance at the time, so a lot of doctors prescribed them like aspirin. We had big bottles of them all over the house. They helped when I was hurting, killed my appetite, kept me awake and sharpened my focus. At first, I took only half a pill daily, but that quickly accelerated until I was eating four or five of them four or five times a day. I needed them just to get by.

My resistance was always low, so I frequently had colds or flus. I'd be on my period, doubled over with cramps, but I couldn't curl up in a ball in my bedroom and eat ice cream for a week. I chose my gigs carefully, used extra tampons, avoided wearing light colors, squeezed my bloated body into spandex and gobbled even more Trammies.

If Heather or Angela ever faltered or complained, Lisa was there to say, 'Hey, get your ass out there. I don't care how you feel, I don't care how deep the snow is, I don't care that it's Christmas time and everybody else is singing carols and drinking eggnog. Guess what: You're on the clock 24-7. Get used to it. That's just the way it is, bitches.'

CHAPTER FIFTY

Duane in The Lion's Den

Heather messed up one day and took a Rescue One call in front of a client named Duane*. Duane was a shy, highly-paid diesel mechanic who was completely infatuated with Heather. He was extremely generous and worked on my vehicles for nothing, so Heather had granted him a peek into her life. Duane wasn't aware of the whole Angela Harter thing, but he knew that Heather Smith was somehow involved with an animal rescue. The caller said that some people who were doing a photo-baby gig at a mall about three hours from Columbus wanted to dump young twin lions. It was urgent, the caller said, because the traveling shit-show was moving on that night.

There was no time to transform Heather into Angela. At least I wasn't dressed in full-on Heather-leather; Duane preferred tight jeans, tube tops and high-heeled pumps. I told him I had to get moving to take care of an animal emergency.

I hesitated, though. The photo-baby business is like the drug trade: To photo baby operators and drug dealers, product – whether it's China White or a white tiger cub – is just product. Their involvement is financial, not emotional. Operators buy cubs from dirty breeders and haul them around to county fairs or pet expos or mall parking lots. The cubs are in the sun for 10 or 12 hours a day, being pawed over and sitting for pictures.

When kids get too big, operators dispose of them, one way or the other. If no one will buy the cubs or take them for free, the photo-baby freaks drown them, break their necks, shoot them, feed them poisoned meat. They either buy more or grab them out of their own fresh litters. It's a sickening but common practice. What makes it so sinister is that the photo-baby operators hide the true evil of what they're doing behind cute little babies.

I was wondering out loud about what kind of dirtbags might be waiting for me at that mall. Duane overheard me muttering and volunteered to go along, even though he'd never owned so much as a guinea pig. I thought, 'Ang, just this one time, you might need some backup.' I called David and told him to expedite the paperwork, ran to Rescue One to grab it, and Duane and I headed for the Ohio/Indiana border in Mitzi.

As soon as we got to the mall and found the photo-baby operation, I saw that I'd been fretting for no reason. Pat and Robert Engesser, the older couple who ran it, were perfectly lovely to me. They said they had a walkup compound in Florida called, simply, "The Zoo." To pay for all the animals there, they traveled constantly in a big RV. As they went along, they ditched the older cats with whatever USDA-approved sanctuary or private owner was available and willing. Runners brought them supplies from Florida, including new kids. The Engessers did have their problems with USDA, including a leopard that jumped on a young girl about 25 years earlier, but from what I saw, they fed primo food, had primo caging and paid plenty of staff to kiss the animals' butts. They also knew the lingo and handled things properly: "Are you non-profit? Are you USDA-licensed? We need your completed paperwork before you take possession of the cats and transport them."

Still, the Engessers and I had reservations about each other. They weren't eager to turn their cats over to someone who looked like Heather, and I'd totally screwed up by not finding out exactly how old the lions were. The "cubs" were much bigger than I expected. Maximus and Gemini were at least 25 or 30 pounds. They had claws and teeth and lots of muscle and energy. Meanwhile, I'd brought only a few bottles of water and an ice chest. I had no carry cage, not even a doggie gate to put between the front and back seats. I was stuck, however, and so were the Engessers.

"Oh, this is no problem," I lied to them. "I got this."

We loaded the twins into Mitzi and headed for Rescue One. The interior was tight quarters, and Max and Gem were not happy. They squirmed, fought and squealed. They dove from the front into the back, came flying up at us again. They beat the crap out of poor Duane, who was in the passenger seat. They knocked his glasses off and tried to chew them. His arms and hands were decorated with bleeding pinpricks and raw welts that looked like jailhouse tats. We tried to stop the lions from ripping up the interior, but they fought back. I pulled over to let Duane drive, while I managed the cubs; it didn't do any good. Those kids were impossible to control. Duane had to dodge tractor trailers for three hours on I-70 while two lions kicked his ass.

When Duane got out of that car, I thought, 'I don't care how much he digs Heather, you better find a new frequent flyer and another mechanic.' He didn't even ask for a discount on future sessions, though. In fact, he chuckled about his ordeal in the mobile lions' den and eventually started volunteering at Rescue One so he could hang with the cubs. Of course, he was a mechanic, not an upholsterer, so Mitzi's interior is still scratched all to hell.

I set Max and Gem up in the living room of the log house. They had scabs and fresh rubs all over their cheeks and noses from the stress of travelling in small cages, but they soon calmed down. They were cute little butterballs who smelled exactly like chocolate-chip cookies. All they wanted to do was play with each other and their toys and sit on my lap and gaze up into my eyes.

CHAPTER FIFTY-ONE

Heather Unleashed

Along the way Heather started running with Linda Friday and Dani Sexton, porn stars who were about her age and moved in the same circles. Friday and Dani introduced her to Lisa Lipps, whose boyfriend was a wealthy oral surgeon named Peter*. He owned a four-story house in an exclusive part of Long Island, where they hosted upper-level, orchestrated, underground *soirees* for rich clients and porn stars. Lisa invited Heather to join the party.

As long as Heather limited her hunting ground to Columbus, if David or Ellen called and said, "Someone wants us to take in a juvenile tiger"; or "Gem isn't eating right"; or "Dr. Burton wants to see you at the clinic immediately," I could shed one skin, put on another and be there in minutes. I hated to be so far from the kids, but Friday and Dani said the payout for Lisa's trips was huge, and Rescue One was a bottomless money pit. While Heather took care of business, David and Ellen would have to get along without Angela.

Lisa and Peter flew us first-class into JFK. We were assigned bodyguards who drove luxury SUVs and were armed with credit cards. They were under orders to keep their entertainers happy. On my first trip, my bodyguard was waiting at baggage claim. He was a little hottie – an 18-year-old Italian kid wearing a wife-beater and a bunch of gold and calling me "Baby." He carried my bags to a white Escalade that was parked illegally at the curb. Dani Sexton was in the backseat waiting for me. We screeched and hugged. I hadn't seen her in a while, so we were excited about having a great weekend together.

Dani immediately offered me a "bullet" – a little cylinder, obviously shaped like a bullet, used to snort cocaine. Lisa put the bullets in a party bag, like stars receive at the Emmy's. The bags were filled with a lot of cute little things: an eight ball of coke to get you started, a couple bullets in different colors, because once you got rolling, you always lost them, a cell phone, different varieties of condoms, a huge bottle of Gucci #3, my favorite.

I took the bullet from Dani, knowing I had to be cautious with it. Those girls lived in a blizzard, and they didn't mess around with mediocre coke. Their stuff was brutal. It wasn't powder. It was one solid crystal chunk that flaked off like fish scales. It was milky, but if you moved it around, a funny rainbow of color flashed through it. It was called Rocket Fuel, and it probably ran her $600 an eight ball, six or seven times more than street-issue street blow. A fat rail of the generic stuff wouldn't even get me close to a tiny bump of Rocket Fuel. I had to be extra-careful with Rocket Fuel, because Heather had a nose for blow just like she did for cash; she'd go full Hoover in a heartbeat.

Other than the necessary Trammies, I never touched drugs around the animals – it would be suicide – but I figured a little Rocket Fuel would help put my head in the right place to handle the craziness Dani and Friday described. I took the bullet from

Dani, did a hit the size of two pencil leads and waited for my head to freeze and my heart to race.

The bodyguard cranked the stereo up, and as we were pulling out of JFK, he said, "Anything you need? Any stores you want to hit on the way?"

Naturally, we wanted to shop on someone else's credit card. Dani bought a bunch of stuff – lingerie, licorice whips, red thigh-high slipper boots to go with one of her outfits. We were nicely buzzed and enjoying a sunny afternoon.

Dani said Friday, who was a real maniac, was waiting back at the house. Some other girls I knew were going to be there, too: Plenty Up Topp, Suzette, who has tits like watermelons, and Lala, the badass from Boston. She said Lisa Lipps's mentor, Jenna Jameson, was there, too.

Those chickees are all third-generation porn stars. In that industry, you have the end of the '60s and the '70s, when it first kicked off big, then every few years, it turned over a new generation. The first generation was John Holmes and Linda Lovelace and all that freaky '70s shit. You can clock the generations in the industry by the names of the biggest stars and the highlights of the movies – swinging became okay, then bondage was cool, then anal. We're in the seventh generation now; you can figure out what's okay in those movies, because I don't ever watch them.

We made it to the house about four hours later and looked around for Lisa. She and Peter had decorated the house to look like a swanky *boîte de nuit* from times-gone-by Paris. There were round, two-seater pub tables with cute, single-candle arrangements on each one. Down a few stairs, in a lower pit area, there were waitresses and bartenders and entertainment. They had custom-made, tufted-leather couches shaped like crescent moons, low lighting and big TVs. There was a stage with dance poles on it.

As we checked the place out, Dani and I laughed and carried on – until we saw Lisa descending a big white staircase in a long, see-through negligee and a robe that flowed behind her, like Mae West. She had long brown hair and exaggerated Jessica Rabbit features. She spent over $100000 on her face, butt and boobs. She was also a vamp who partied all night and slept all day. She had her own suite in the house; manservants who followed her around like guard wolves prepped it by blacking out the windows. Afraid we'd awakened her, Dani and I immediately shut up. Lisa was smiling, but we never knew if she was going to kiss us or eat us.

She spread her arms and said, in her sweet, absurd, over-the-top, Maria Carey way, "Oh, I'm so glad you guys are here! We're going to have so much fun!"

She sent Dani and me upstairs to our rooms. We stayed on the second floor, two girls to every gorgeous suite. The top two floors were all custom-made rooms – for S&M, for hot-tubbing, for *ménage a trois*, for voyeurism, for all kinds of sicko fun and games.

By then it was past 7:30, and the party was supposed to crank up in a couple hours. We had to decide what to wear and do our makeup. Dani and I put on our finishing touches and went downstairs together in our best gear.

The high-powered clients were coming in and being greeted and shown to one of those little tables or down into the pit. Waitresses served them cocktails as they studied laminated menu cards that Lisa had printed specifically for those parties. Everything was on the bill of fare – literally. It was like ordering an appetizer or a bottle of wine, but on those cards were items like "Ménage a Trois, Starting Bid $1200" or "Single 45-Minute Session $700."

Everyone eventually congregated in the pit, where we mingled, introducing ourselves. That was the time to make deals. Heather migrated around, located a client, found out what he wanted, negotiated the price as high as she could and walked past a bodyguard, up the stairs to whatever room we needed. The bodyguard held the money, checked what the client was paying for and kept track of what went on. Heather worked the gig, then came back down to the pit to start another negotiation. If she needed to generate business, she jumped on stage, hit the pole and did a little naughty advertising. That went on all weekend.

Even though they were wealthy and operating under a cloak of secrecy, the men were pretty typical. Some of them were kindly and generous and said they wanted to help me get out of the life or marry me; some were horny, arrogant shitheads; some of them were spineless whiners who turned my stomach; almost all of them were drunk and ripped on flake that was way out of their league. Once in a while, one wanted to play rough; Heather knew exactly how to handle that.

I always got in trouble when I was with Dani. At the end of that first night, we were so cranked up we couldn't sleep. It was four in the morning. There was no Diet Mountain Dew in the house, and I was addicted to it. I threw a fit. We went out to the Escalade. My stupid bodyguard gave me the keys. I was flying on Rocket Fuel, and this was a very expensive car. Windows down, stereo obnoxiously loud, we barreled through Long Island. We were barely dressed, drinking champagne from the bottle and totally coking out. I don't know how the cops didn't stop us.

I pulled up to a Taco Bell drive-through window and said into the speaker thingy, "Yeah, I want a big Diet Mountain Dew."

My bodyguard paid for it, and I pulled up to the next window to get it. What the girl handed me wasn't Diet Mountain Dew. She insisted it was. We got into a tiff, and I threw the full cup into her face. Everyone leaned out and started yelling at the poor girl. She was petrified.

I hit the gas and ran up over the cement berms that led away from the window. The driveway took a sharp right, but I jumped the Escalade straight over the curb, plowed through the grass and steered back across the sidewalk onto the street. We tore out of there. Everybody was laughing about doing a *Dukes of Hazard*, but by the time we got back to the house, it was clear that the Escalade's custom rims were seriously fucked up. The bodyguard was flipping because he was in serious trouble; buzzed up as I was, I didn't see that as my problem. Dani and I walked upstairs and fell asleep.

After the second night of madness, we were drugged out and exhausted. I took Dani to our suite and put her to bed. The bodyguard followed us. Suzette, who is a freak, was with him. We weren't ready to go to sleep, so we wandered up to the third-floor theme rooms. We were drinking champagne and talking about getting in the hot tub. Out of nowhere, those jerks got pushy. They threw me on the bed, held me down and ripped off my boots. Suzette's way bigger than I am, and the bodyguard was being an asshole. I kicked and cursed and yelled but couldn't get them off me. Friday must've heard me screaming, because she came in and pulled me out of there.

On Sunday, after the clients were all gone, Lisa threw a party to thank us and see us off and tell us about upcoming events. Suzette stayed on her side of the house that whole day. The bodyguard had been fired. I thought, 'You gave me the keys, you moron. You deserve to be fired.'

Okay, I confess to willingly participating in a meat market that demeaned women. If the pun wasn't so bad, I'd say the work sucked. However, I could make 10-grand for just hanging around with some rich jackasses for a weekend. If I wanted to hustle my butt off, I could clear four times that much. Occasionally, I'd run into a client who wanted something particularly exotic, and I could buy myself a new vehicle. Angela just checked out, let Heather take the wheel and calculated how much horsemeat and cyclone fencing and vet care the cash would buy.

CHAPTER FIFTY-TWO

Sin City

Lisa Lipps was a Vegas baby, a big deal there. She had a grand scheme for us to headline a big porn convention in the city and basically do a western version of her Long Island bullshit: initiate, negotiate, fornicate, repeat. She arranged suites at the Bellagio, airplane tickets, Rocket Fuel.

I'd heard enough from my girlfriends to know that by going to Vegas, I was taking a step up – or down, again depending on how you look at it. Heather's usual clients had no chance against her, but when you're swimming with all sharks, the moves that work on minnows are no good. Everybody in Vegas is shuffling the same deck of cards, and they're all Magicians of Immorality. Friday morning, on the flight out, I consciously summoned Heather the Witch Whore from Hell into existence and for the first time ever, gave her total control. That turned out not to be a great idea.

I hated Vegas. It was too noisy and too bright and jammed with stoned-out porn actors flashing their tits, shaking their asses and hiking their supertight trousers up around their big cocks to freak out the Bermuda short crowd – tiresome PG-17 hijinks. I couldn't step on a casino floor without some idiot from Paducah or Peoria grabbing me and dragging me to his table to play Lady Luck and blow on his dice before he threw them or rub his head before his cards were dealt.

Vegas is another Temple of Mammon and another place where I felt that malevolent entity that had frightened me so much in Roma. Grant should've been declared Caesar of the fucking place. Just like the Vatican, Vegas pretends to be one thing but is actually another. Sin City has tried to rebrand itself as Fun City for the Whole Family, but if you're unfortunate enough to walk through the wrong door, you'll find the unbridled, hardcore carnage of real Vegasland, in the flesh – the beautiful evil you don't want to buy or even see. I didn't notice a foggy miasma in Vegas, but the city is one big miasma wrapped in a bigger mirage. Call me a hypocrite, I just wanted to make as much money as I could and haul ass back to Rescue One.

On Saturday night, we were in costume and going to private parties. By that time, we were all drunk, wiped out and aggravated with each other. Everybody was rolling on Rocket Fuel and locked down in a cage that someone else was paying for. In return for the parties and the business opportunities, we had to commit to do certain special things that Lisa and Peter had cooked up. No one could just get pissy and storm off. Now, we're talking about a bunch of "me, me, me" girls, and when a bunch of "me, me, me" chicks get stuck together, something's bound to erupt.

Peter was strutting around looking like Burt Reynolds – bald on top, big fur coat, shiny cowboy boots with pointy toes and a lot of fancy stitching. He was playing Sultan Shithead, barking orders at us like we were his personal harem. Heather had been amped up on champagne and blow for two days. She flipped and shouted in his face, "Fuck you, cocksucker! I'm not doing this shit! I'm out of here! Take this and shove it up your ass!"

He started on some kind of 'you owe me, bitch' tirade, but a couple girls jumped in quick, explaining that she was just cranky and would be okay after a nap. I let them walk me to my room and put me in bed. I pretended to pass out, and they left. I was so cranked up I couldn't lie there. That asshole Peter was not going to make me do a damn thing. I was leaving, whether he liked it or not.

Once again, we all had bodyguards. These dudes were nothing like that punk on Long Island or Melvin's iceheads. These were scowling professional badasses, simian brutes with thick steroid muscles and surly dispositions who weren't about to take Heather's shit or anyone else's. Two of them were holding me captive on a floor with just one elevator. The only other way out was the stairs, which were at the far end of the hallway.

Of course, what happens in Vegas stays in Vegas, but there's another popular saying in Vegas – a scary one: "Two and six." That's not gambling advice, like stay on 17, hit on 16. It's a how you dump a body: Two miles out in the desert and six feet under the sand. I didn't want to end up there. I turned out all the lights and stalked the Ape Twins by listening against the door and looking through the peephole as they came and went. For an hour or so, I timed their routine. Clutching my purse, I watched their shadows pass the bottom of the door and took off, leaving everything else behind, including a $500, handsewn white bikini that went perfectly with my thigh-high, black-leather boots.

I ran down the stairs and burst through a security exit. The door slammed shut behind me and locked. I was in a dark, vacant alley behind the hotel, trapped, the Ape Twins sure to follow. I thought I was screwed, but a taxi came down the alley and almost ran me over.

I waved it down and said, "Oh, my God, take me to the airport!"

The driver didn't want me in the cab, because I'm sure I looked like trouble on the hoof. I had to get out of there fast, though. I ripped the cab door open and dove in. Sure enough, the Ape Twins slammed through the exit.

I yelled at the driver, "Go! Go! Go!"

He put it in reverse and barreled down the alley the wrong way. He drove me to the airport in North Vegas, and I leaped out of the taxi. He took off before I could even pay for the ride. Thank God, I had my plane ticket in my purse. I ran into the airport, and as soon as I got inside, I heard those goons behind me. I ducked into a ladies' room directly across from a departure gate and peeked out. The Ape Twins blew past.

A ticket agent was standing at a little desk beside the gate, watching. He was very gay, so cute I couldn't believe it. As the Ape Twins walked down toward the concession area, checking every shop and waiting area, the ticket agent waved to me and hissed, "Come here, come here!"

I scurried over and told him, "I've got to get on a plane and get out of here, and those guys are trying to stop me."

"Get on! Get on!" he whispered, gesturing at the boarding gate.

I handed him my ticket, even though it wasn't for that date, time or destination. He didn't even look at it.

"I don't care. Go. Get on," he said.

A flight attendant showed me to a seat. I was totally wired, but I somehow fell asleep. I don't remember doing it, but, evidently, when we landed, I got off the plane, walked straight to a chair in a waiting area and passed out. When I woke up, I thought, 'Where the hell am I?' I stumbled around muddle-headed, reading flight information and advertising posters, until I figured out I was in Nashville. I booked a flight back to Columbus and called David to pick me up.

Lisa never spoke to me again. Since the other girls all followed her lead, they shunned me, too. Thanks to Heather, that lucrative revenue stream had dried up for good. Except for my white bikini, I didn't really care. I was tired of being led around by Lisa Lipps. However, I did have one serious concern about our falling out. She'd arranged to have head shots and group photos taken of us in Vegas. I ended up in the middle of some of them. I'd always refused to do porn because, once again, I hated to think what would happen to Rescue One if somebody ever matched Heather with Angela. Now, certain pictures of Heather were circulating. I worried that they would end up going public, and someone would put our two faces together.

CHAPTER FIFTY-THREE

Identity Crisis

Coming clean about the hooking stuff hurts. I worry that a charged-up mob of hypocrites will surround the log house, chanting "Whore! Whore!" and stone me to death like a witch back in Salem times. Maybe that's what I deserve. I did awful things, disgraceful things, things I'll wear like a tiara of thorns until I the day die. I'll tell you this, though: I'm no poor soiled fucking dove; I knew exactly what I was doing. To care for beautiful, defenseless kids, I preyed on people who didn't do anything to me. Even though they might be kind enough to forgive me, I'll never forgive myself. No judge could ever hand me a sentence worse than life behind my own eyes.

I got myself into legal problems that will never go away. I'm barred from even talking about some things. Other stuff is so painful that if I go back to those places and those faces, I'll drive myself crazy. Being normal, finishing my bachelor's degree and working at a desk would've been much easier. I just couldn't go that way. At least when I was whoring, I controlled when I worked and how much I got paid. This much is certain: If Heather would've done anything other than get down on her knees, a lot of kids would have died.

I tried to keep my two lives in sealed compartments behind locked doors; over time, though, I became obsessed with the fear that Heather, Full-On Vamp of the Night, would spill over into a rescue, or that Angela, Docile, Frumpy Zookeeper, would show up at a gig with sweat stains on her t-shirt and lion shit on her chukka boots. The Duane thing had been a necessary calculated risk, but another slipup could expose my most dangerous secret, so I was vigilant about who was doing what. I didn't always have time to think clearly, however.

Heather had just finished an all-nighter, when Ellen called Angela and said that an ongoing problem with an adult tiger named Jacob had boiled over. An old woman had the cat at a farmhouse up north, almost in Indiana. Her son had bought two tigers – a brother and a sister – at an auction. He got in some kind of legal problem – drugs, or the cops were after him or something – and split and left the cats with his elderly mother.

The woman called the cops and said, "My son is gone. I need these tigers out of here. They're starving. I can't take care of them."

At the time, I had an arrangement with a woman who owned a sanctuary down South to do a tit-for-tat on rescues. When one of us took a call, we would confer; depending on where the animal was and who had the time and means, one of us would save it.

She called one day and said, "There's a cougar over in Indiana. I can't get to it. Take him, and if anything else comes across, I'll take the next one."

She said and an informant told her the mountain lion didn't

have his claws or fangs; some hicks were going to tie a bag over his head, throw him in with a pack of dogs and bet on which one would kill him. Ellen and I drove all night to grab the cat. Those jerkoffs had him in a rusty corn silo. They called him "Buttwheat," of all damned names. The boy was in pretty bad shape. I took him home and changed his name to Montana. He turned out to be a darling, beautiful cat.

When the cops first called about the tigers and the old lady, I was getting full-up on kids and struggling to manage both sides of my life. Some unholy peckerwood breeder from Indiana showed up and took the girl tiger. I shoved the boy on the Southern lady's plate, and she agreed to take him. I considered the matter closed; now, 30 days later, the cops were calling Rescue One, asking, "What the hell's happening with this tiger?"

They were annoyed; the old lady was frantic. When Ellen called, she said the cops demanded that we come and pick up the tiger immediately, or they were going destroy him. 'That flake didn't even bother to call me and tell me she wasn't going,' I thought. 'Now these people are jumping in my face.' I was so furious that I didn't realize until I was bouncing up the driveway to Rescue One that I was in Heather's Mitsubishi, not Angela's Land Rover.

When I got out, I heard someone shouting in a harsh, scary voice at Ellen and David, who still had no clue about my night work, "Goddamnit! This dumbass is making us all look bad! Piss on her! Let's get the fuck going!"

I saw the surprise on their faces, then realized it was Heather yelling, not Angela. Instead of Angela's work clothes, I was wearing a black leather motorcycle jacket, black bustier and skintight black leather pants, and my hair was sprayed and spiked like Don King's. As I went inside to change, I didn't mention the voice or the vehicle or the outfit, just ordered everybody to get moving 10 minutes ago.

This was in the middle of winter and frigid. It was supposed to snow, and we had a long drive, but I called the cops and told them to give me directions.

"We're coming," I said. "That cat will be out of there tonight."

The tiger was full grown. We were going to need a big cage, so the Cruiser wouldn't work, and David's van wasn't running. We were forced to take Ellen's beat-up Voyager. David pieced together a cage, but the door on it was shaky.

The snow was coming down harder, so I said, "We have to leave now. Finish it, and let's get going."

Ellen I and had no sooner left the driveway than the full-on storm hit, forcing us to crawl along treacherous roads. When we finally made it there, the old woman said the cat was out back. The enclosure had been built into a dilapidated garage. There wasn't even electricity. It was just me and Ellen and an unfamiliar full-grown tiger in the snow, daylight draining away. I didn't know if we could even get the van through the gate to where the kid was trapped. Two curious hilljacks who worked the farms around there walked up and leaned on the fence to watch, too scared of the tiger to come closer.

We opened the gate and managed to back the van up to the garage, but we had to take the makeshift cage out and carry it into where the tiger was. We lured Jake into cage, but he was so heavy we couldn't lift it high enough to load it in the van. We were using cheap flashlights, shivering and dragging our feet through muck and snow so deep and heavy that if the tiger got loose, we wouldn't be able to run. Grinning like they were watching reality TV, the worthless hilljacks leaned on the fence.

The roads were becoming worse by the second. We had to load the kid into the Voyager and get him out of there. Finally, I talked one of the hilljacks into helping. He started this fork-lift thingy in the garage and moved it under the cage. When he lifted it, the cage teetered back and forth. Jake was tense. The yahoo raised the cage higher than the van's roof and got it stuck.

Finally, the other hilljack kicked in. They bumped the cage down just enough that Ellen and I could push it forward. We shoved until the bottom dropped out. Jake went backwards off the forklift and into the Voyager. We pushed him all the way in and shut the rear gate. He was super-pissed, growling and spitting and banging on the cage.

"Okay, how're we going to get out of here with all this extra weight?" Ellen asked.

We begged the hilljacks to push us, until we could finally escape that dump. Problem was we'd slammed the cage down off of the forklift so hard that its door was partly sprung. Even though the cage was wedged against the back of the Voyager, Jake could get his face and half of one shoulder out. He kept clawing at the window and snarling. 'If he gets all the way out, there's going to be a fucking bloodbath in this van,' I thought, swallowing hard.

My heart was in my throat as we crept along at 20 miles an hour for the whole bobsled run home, Jake scratching at the window and snarling the entire time. By the time we made it to Lancaster, it was almost morning, and Jake was a very perturbed boy.

Dr. Burton was supposed to neuter him, but the guy who owned her told us he was carrying the white tiger gene. Dr. Burton couldn't bring himself to do it.

"Ang, he's in his own cage," he said. "We're not going to allow him to breed. This is so rare; please don't make me neuter him."

We never did.

That peckerwood from Indiana had wanted Jake's sister so he could breed her for white cubs, which are extremely valuable. Even though I tried like hell to get her back, he wouldn't let her go. When I offered to buy her, he tried to switch out a couple other cats for her. I insisted that I wanted Jake's sister.

He said, "Oh, she's gone."

Heather was ready to drive straight to Indiana, kick that lying bastard's ass and take the cat. Angela talked her down.

"Sometimes, fucked is fucked," she said, "and there's nothing you can do about it."

For once, Heather listened to reason.

CHAPTER FIFTY-FOUR

Dr. Burton Battles Satan for Heather's Immortal Soul

The last two people on earth I wanted to know about Heather and Cherry Angels were Granny and Dr. Burton. I tried to keep Heather hidden from them; neither was stupid, though. Despite having no visible means of support, Ang was taking care of scores of exotic animals, and Heather, who loved extravagance, was driving expensive automobiles and wearing Zsa Zsa bling and throwing around platinum credit cards. Granny and Dr. Burton both knew the math was wrong.

Granny really liked The Florentine, a mom-and-pop Italian place on West Broad; every time I visited, I dragged her out of the kitchen and took her and anyone else who was around the house there and told them to order anything they wanted and tipped big. She was careful not to directly ask me what was going on; however, no matter how I dressed or talked or acted, I knew Granny could see right through me. I didn't want Heather to come between us a second time, yet the more money Rescue One needed, the more often she showed up, threatening to seep into Angela's life. I refused to put Granny through that hell again. I hate to admit it, but I started to avoid her.

Because of Rescue One, I couldn't duck Dr. Burton. At the clinic, I'd whip out a diamond necklace or ring to pay my bill and scram before he could interrogate me. He never made money on that jewelry. He sold it at the annual auction he held to support the Ohio Wildlife Center, his rehabilitation center for native species.

Dr. Burton was also an extremely devout Christian, an elder or lay minister or something at a big church right off 270 near Westerville. He quoted scripture all the time and worried about my relationship with God. He bought me the first Bible I ever touched. He paid hundreds of dollars for me to go to Bible-study classes, made me attend them during the summers and asked questions about them. It was like being back in college – textbooks and homework and sitting in class listening to lectures and answering questions and taking quizzes. Meanwhile, I was losing money by not working. I never wanted to disappoint Dr. Burton, though, so I did everything he asked.

For a long time, he handled me just like Granny did – he wouldn't straight-out ask what I was doing for money. Eventually, he caught me when I was tired and preoccupied. He ended up talking to Heather, who was listening to Lisa, who was running cover for Ang. He pinned me down; I told him the truth. After that, Dr. Burton bumped into Heather quite a bit. He despised her and what she did. She thought he should mind his own damn business.

Now, in addition to saving animals, Dr. Burton was out to save my immortal soul – or Heather's soul; like I said, it got confusing. The problem was he was preaching to Heather most of the time, and she didn't want to hear his Holy Ghost bullshit.

Dr. Burton began to wage war against Heather by fighting with Angela. He became intensely clingy, righteous and preachy. He never said it, but I knew he was worried to death anytime I was out of his sight. Just like Granny, Dr. Burton had a heartbreaking, impossible mission, and he was just as relentless as she'd been with me when I was young.

He'd call me while I was in mid-flight and say, "Angela, come up here to the house right now."

I'd immediately reschedule some gigs, scrub off my makeup, dress down and go, even though I knew "Come over to the house" actually meant, 'We're going to have food, and you better bring your Bible that I paid for, so we can discuss it.'

He summoned me to Animal Care Unlimited so often that the staff got used to seeing me come in through the side door, just like they did.

"Angela," he'd say. "Let's go into my office."

When Dr. Burton ordered you to go into his office and shut the door, you were in deep do-do. It was bad enough that he pulled me away from everything else I had going on, but everyone in the clinic knew what was going down. He'd lock the door, open his Bible and start yelling. People knocked on the door during surgeries, and he'd say, "Give me a minute!" and go back to scolding me.

I had too much respect for him to argue. Anyway, I had no defense for what Heather was doing, at least none that would satisfy him. I came out of those sessions, thinking, 'Oh, my God,

I'm going to hell for taking my clothes off in front of men for money because I don't have any other way to protect my kids. This is another layer of shit I don't need.'

Dr. Burton nagged me about attending a church service, which he was certain would remake my life and cleanse my soul. The thing is that despite a life overflowing with what Sheep People call "sin," I've always considered myself a child of God. I'm spiritual, though, not religious; I don't trust manmade institutions. In fact, except for my Bible classes and a bunch of old cathedrals in Europe, I'd never been inside a church. Sunday morning was also one of my peak business times. Clients dropped the wife and kids at church, saying they had to go to the office and finish some paperwork or meet an old friend for breakfast or get in a quick round of golf with a client. Then they hurried to a motel to worship at The Mortal Sin Hour – Rev. H. Smith Presiding. I couldn't tell Dr. Burton that, so I figured, 'What the heck? I can kiss his butt and get all dressed up in regular clothes and spend some time around normal people.'

I bought a conservative go-to-meeting outfit, right down to a stupid, church-lady, Easter-parade hat, called Ellen to go with me and drove up to Dublin. We walked in, found a seat and tried to be inconspicuous, which wasn't hard because the place was pretty crowded. Sunlight radiated through the tall, spotless windows and washed over my shoulders. I folded my hands in my lap, trying to mimic the pious faces I'd seen in paintings of saints in European museums. 'This is fabulous,' I thought. 'I'm going to get away with this, and I'll be turning a buck by three o'clock.'

I forgot about the phone sitting under my steepled fingers. It was a Nextel with the walkie-talkie feature, my only direct connection to Rescue One and Cherry Angels. It was never turned off. During a lull in the service, one of my nightlife girlfriends said, loud enough for the whole congregation to hear, "Hey, Heather, you fuckin' or suckin'?"

Her voice echoed four or five times in that quiet church, like a tolling bell. Everyone turned around and stink-eyed me. Ellen slid away from me as fast as she could. Up on the stage, Dr. Burton went from saintly to fuming. He turned purple and glared at me. They had a halftime at that church, when everyone drank cappuccinos and talked about their favorite Bible verses. As soon as it started, I bolted.

Okay, not turning my phone off might've been dumb, but the bigger question is, 'What the hell was that vampire skank doing calling me so early on a Sunday morning?'

The maddest Dr. Burton ever got at me was when I showed up late for my own baptism. It was a scheduled thing, but I was running behind because I was on probation and not supposed to be travelling that far from Lancaster, an excuse I didn't dare use to him. I tried to Ninja my way in and act like I'd been there all along. He spotted me immediately, but he couldn't start yelling in front of the whole congregation. I watched several people go under the baptism pool. Dr. Burton barely dunked them. They hardly even got their hair wet.

When my turn came, he jerked me into in the water and held

me under until my lungs were exploding. He dunked me three times. It was like an exorcism. I thought, 'Oh, man, after all I've been through, he's drowning me just like that cornshucker threatened to do to Gage!'

He finally pulled me out. My hair was sopping. I was sputtering and choking, sucking air, barely conscious. He looked at me like, 'This is for your own good. Do you get it now?'

Dr. Burton never stopped fighting the devil to redeem Heather. He swore up and down that Satan was always chasing me. The pitchfork, the scaly red skin, the *eau de sulphur*, the pointy tail, the brimstone eyes, the horns, the bat wings – when I say all that out loud, it sounds absurd, but the image haunts my nightmares to this day. I loved Dr. Burton, but that man could be a pain in my butt. I can only imagine how much aggravation I was for him, because he never once complained.

CHAPTER FIFTY-FIVE

A Little TLC

The exotic animal world is like a combination of junior high school and the Underground Railroad: part of it is ridiculously petty – rumors and jealousy and backstabbing over nothing important; the other part is deadly serious – animals suffering in hellholes, only the most fortunate ones bought or stolen or seized or traded and moved into safe homes.

The comparison with slavery isn't as crazy as it sounds. Tiny cubs, like Jewels, are ripped away from their mothers and siblings and turned into sources of income for heartless shitheads, some of whom are the last people you'd expect to be so cruel. I once got a tip that a zoo in South Carolina was about to sell an older, unwanted tiger to a canned hunt. I drove down there, snatched the cat up just before the owners of the hunting ranch arrived and brought it north.

We were forever taking calls from spies, informants, anonymous USDA or state employees, angry former volunteers, owners looking to settle old scores, neighbors who wanted the big cats next door gone. The day after Thanksgiving one year, a man left us a message about TLC, a pet shop in Cambridge that was trying to sell a tiger for $900. The Concerned Citizen, as he identified himself, said the same store had sold dangerous wild animals in the past. He wondered if they were doing it legally.

Of course, I knew there were no laws in Ohio about private ownership of exotics; however, I wasn't sure if a business could legally sell them.

I did my best to contact someone who had the answer. Since it was a holiday, I couldn't reach anyone at USDA. An investigator returned my call on Monday morning. He said that if the business didn't have the proper licenses, selling exotics was indeed against the law. He said they'd heard about TLC but were so understaffed they hadn't had a chance to visit the place.

Once something like that catches in my craw, it won't stop bothering me. The next morning, I lined up everybody for the day and said, "You know what, guys? I'm going to go over to Cambridge and see what's going on."

TLC turned out to be a dreary dump near a fast-food joint and a heating and air conditioning shop. I posed as a Sheep World customer who'd wandered in to browse. Sure enough, a little male tiger bounded down an aisle. He was about eight weeks old, not much bigger than Trinity. Maybe the man and woman behind the counter thought it was good PR to let him roam the store. I didn't see a cage anywhere, but the cat's appearance and behavior told me exactly what was up.

'You're a mess,' I thought. 'You're sickly, and your face is ripped up. I know they throw you in a cage in the back when they leave, and you spend all night rubbing your face against the bars, because you're lonely and afraid. The shit packed between your toes tells me they never clean your cage. You're covered with fleas and fly-strike bites.'

I wrote the man's name – Steve – in my incident notes; I never heard the woman's name. Even though they didn't have any sort of license, they'd bought "Tigger" at Mt. Hope to sell at a profit. They also said they bred bobcats, bears and cougars at their home. Steve said they took the cub from his mama and put him directly on raw meat. He thought it was funny to tease Tigger with food. It wasn't one damned bit amusing. The kid was so hungry he'd take off one of your fingers if you moved the wrong way while you were tormenting him.

I didn't tell them who I was and said nothing about exotic animal laws. I just flew home and came right back. I brought some of the junk left over from my life with Grant: a full-length black mink and an expensive gold watch. The coat was worth about $6000. The watch was broken. I had no use for either of them.

I walked back into TLC and said to Steve, "Listen, I don't have the cash you want for this animal, but I do have this, and I have the papers to prove it's real."

I handed him the fur. Watching from behind the desk, the woman, who was about my size, perked up. She knew what it was and that it was worth a lot of money. She snagged it and stroked it.

"All right, is it a deal?" I asked.

Just like I figured he would, Steve looked at my wrist and said, "What about the watch?"

"Yeah, it's gold," I said.

"Give me the watch, and we have a deal," he said.

I gave the useless watch to him without telling him it didn't work. As he fussed with the watch and she drooled over the coat, the cat ran up to the counter. I picked his little butt up and slung him over my shoulder. They didn't know who I was. They didn't know where the kid was going. They didn't ask me to sign any papers to transfer ownership.

"Oh, just give him some raw chicken wings," Steve said.

'At that age? Are you nuts?' I thought.

I changed Tigger's name to Bachi, if only to take the stink of TLC off him. The dried poop under his toes was so bad that fungus was growing on all four paws. Dr. Burton had to cut it out.

It turned out that those people weren't even the registered owners of the store, so the whole deal was shady. I called USDA again to inform them what had gone down in Cambridge. They said they would investigate the situation. That pet store is not there anymore. I'm pretty sure USDA didn't shut it down. They're forever dealing with messes they aren't equipped to clean up. They let suckers like me do their dirty work.

CHAPTER FIFTY-SIX

A Couple Cubs

Just a few days after I rescued Bachi, a guy named Speedy Mathis called and said he had very young tiger cubs that needed to be placed. Speedy and Rhonda Marx owned Big Cat Haven in Dawsonville, Georgia. We'd taken in one of their full-grown cougars. They seemed cool, like nice people who cared about animals. Speedy explained that he'd made a deal for the cubs with another owner in Georgia. He hadn't taken possession of them yet because he was concerned about their health and worried that they might contaminate his other cats. He said the cubs needed help right away and asked us to meet him at Big Cat Haven.

I called a number Speedy gave me and talked to someone who mentioned "a couple cubs." The person didn't give me an exact number and was evasive about everything else. Nonetheless, I put three transport cages for small dogs in the back of the Land Cruiser, and Ellen, Reeni and I headed south. We drove all night to Dawsonville.

Speedy asked us to follow him to where the little tigers were. We drove deep into the land of three-fingered snake-handlers, itinerant faith healers and unemployed shade tree mechanics who speak in tongues on Sunday mornings. The weathered billboards and staticky AM radio stations were all for guns and the Second Coming and against abortion and liberals. By the time we made it to the second location, it was getting dark. We'd been on the road for felt like 18 hours. My butt was hurting, my one good eye was blurry and if someone had told me we'd driven all the way to Costo*fucking*Rico, I would've believed it.

What Speedy didn't know – or didn't tell us – was that the place was being raided. Armed officers stopped us outside the gates.

"We're with Rescue One," I said.

"Okay, yeah, we know. Go ahead," a cop said, waving us in.

Spotlights had been set up on the grounds. To this day, I don't know the name of the place, but it was a freakshow compound with a lot of shelters and foot bridges – a little theme park, one step up from a roadside zoo. The property seemed to lack everything – secure fencing, food and water containers, covered enclosures. Speedy told us the animals were being bred. The ones we passed looked sickly and scared in the light from portable towers that had been set up all over the place.

The cops weren't just local sheriff's deputies. Armed officers in black tac gear were flowing all over the place. I'm not sure if USDA was there, but there were a lot of people in uniforms and a lot of guns. We reached a house at the center of the compound and got out. An older man was on the porch, mad as hell. He had blow-dried, snow-white hair and wore a gold necklace and rings and a thick gold chain on his wrist, like those Mafia dudes all had. Everything was so chaotic that I could only pick up on snippets of information and try to put them together: The guy was a fun-park, drive-through, buy-a-tiger-for-500-bucks, canned-hunt scumbag who'd been a thorn in everyone's side down there for years. Apparently, he finally screwed up enough to let the authorities come onto his property.

He was screaming, "You have no authority! Get out of here! I have rights!"

'You have rights, asshole?' I thought. 'What about the rights of all these poor kids?'

As if he'd heard my thoughts, he pointed right at me and yelled, "Who's she? What is she doing here? She has no authority here. I'll sue you!"

The whole time he raved, a white tiger with a broken front leg limped back and forth in a cage on the porch beside him.

A lady who was obviously in command rushed toward me and said, "We need you over here right now!"

She led me around the house, toward the back of the compound. I asked her about the white tiger with the broken leg.

"Oh, that's one of the reasons we're here," she said. "He refused to get veterinary care for that tiger, and someone reported him."

She said he kept the tiger there for months with a broken leg so people would feel sorry for it and donate. I wanted to go back and kick his sorry ass. The lady asked me what I thought they should do about the cat. The leg was broken right above the ankle, but he'd learned to walk on three legs.

"Baby, you cannot fix a broken leg on a tiger," I told the woman, hating my own words. "You cannot cast a big cat. You have to amputate or put him down."

I already had Dr. Burton on the phone. I let her talk to him, and he confirmed what I said.

When she got off, I said, "Please, don't shoot him full of bullets. Can't you just dart him and then euthanize him?"

She was noncommittal. I was upset, but I kept my mouth shut, and when the lady started walking again, I followed her toward a big metal building. By then, it was full night. I was worrying about how sick these cubs might be. A couple hundred feet away, there was a line of bushes on the property's border. Eight or nine guys dressed in black and carrying machineguns and shotguns ran up and shined flashlights over the bushes.

A radio squawked. The lady shouted, "Get down!"

We ducked between two nearby sheds. Someone yelled an order. I heard gunfire – a lot of gunfire. A full-grown African lion had somehow gotten out of its enclosure. The cops had the lion cornered in the bushes. They were trying to contain him. When he barreled out, they opened up.

Oh, God, I was close enough to smell the smoke and hear the lion's snarls and screams. There was nothing I could do to stop the white lights flashing in the darkness and the explosions going off like clusters of little bombs. The lion went down; they still held the flashlight beams on him. He crawled 20 or 30 feet while cops blew chunks off of his head and body. It seemed to take forever to kill that lion.

When the shooting finally stopped, I started to walk over to the lion. Cops tried to lift the dead cat, but he fell into pieces. They had to pick up the bloody parts. It was a scene straight from Hell. I wish I could burn that memory out of my head. I don't know what I thought I was going to do about the cat, but the lady stopped me from approaching it. I also don't know if they went there to shoot that lion or if the guy let it out after they came on the property or what. The lady told me only what I needed to know; obviously, she wanted me to take the cubs and get out.

The guy had a nursery in that big building. The "couple" cubs were three babies about eight weeks old. They were so sick I was afraid they would die before we got them back to Rescue One. I was already losing it, when the woman said, "Listen, we've got these two that are just a couple days old. We don't know what to do with them."

I thought, 'Damn it!'; but I said, "Okay."

Then she said, "Hey, you've got to come over here and see this."

I walked over to her. Twin tigers four or five months old, about as big as medium-sized dogs, were quaking in a corner.

Listen, we need them out of here, too," the woman said. "We have no way of taking care of them."

'Oh, my God!' I thought, 'I only brought one car!'

A "couple" cats had magically turned into seven. I was flabbergasted. The woman was hoping that I was the real deal I was pretending to be. I didn't want to admit we weren't prepared to transport so many animals or care for them once we got them home, and I sure didn't want to leave those little guys there to die.

'Damn it! Here we go!' I thought.

We put a dog gate behind the front seat, threw all the carriers out and removed the rear seats from the Land Cruiser and ditched them right there. We loaded the tigers, the woman signed my USDA documents and we were out of there. We had the two tiny babies up front. We cleared a spot right behind the driver's seat for the three eight-week olds. The twins, whom we immediately named Zeus and Apollo, were in the back. During the whole long trip back to Ohio, Ellen and Reeni and I were going to have to switch off, two of us sitting in the front and one lying in the cargo bay with the twins.

We'd brought a plug-in warmer and some bottles of formula, so we could feed the smaller cubs. We stopped and bought more KMR and some baby blankets. We fed the five babies as we drove, and they went right to sleep. The twins, on the other hand, were excited – all bouncy, bouncy, because they were going on a field trip. I hoped they were good boys, because they were going to be confined for a long time with three strange humans and five other cats.

CHAPTER FIFTY-SEVEN

Georgia On My Mind

After a few hours on the road, the twins needed a snack, so we pulled into a Wendy's. It was late, I was exhausted, and we were in a hurry. When we got to the drive-through, I rolled my window all the way down without thinking. The cubs would likely throw up cooked meat, so I told the high school chick who waited on us, "I need about 10 pounds of raw hamburger."

I'd intentionally bought the Cruiser with the darkest tinted windows Toyota made so no one could see Jewels riding shotgun in town. I never considered that the girl would be able to see directly down into the car, where the twins were freaking out. She took one look and ran. Seconds later, the manager came to drive-through window, a perplexed expression on his face.

"I know this looks strange, but we're a rescue facility," I said. "I need some raw meat for the two older tigers, and we're a little hungry, too."

I watched his face and waited, envisioning state cop cars flying down the off-ramps at us, sirens wailing.

"No problem" he said and hurried away.

Several kids who worked there came out and stuck their heads in the windows, thrilled to see all the baby tigers. They kept petting the little ones and handing me stuff and saying, "Here, do you need this? Do you need this?"

The manager hustled back with the raw meat, sacks of burgers and fries and a big white foam container filled with ice. It was way more than I'd asked for. He insisted we take it all and wouldn't let me pay for any of it. That man truly was *gallant*, and the kids were darlings. I wonder how many times they've told that story over the years.

We gave the twins their snack and some water and kept putting ice in Styrofoam bowls for them to play with. We only stopped once, for gas and to potty. When they got bored with the ice, the twins wrestled, ripped the headliners, chewed the moldings, clawed the sides of the bay and pulled hair of whichever one of us was riding with them.

Just at daylight, we were coming around a mountain in the rain, and I almost hit a little dog. She was a quirky, mixy something that someone must've dumped, standing in the middle of the road like she was directing traffic. I had to slam on the brakes to avoid killing her.

"Reen, go get her," I said.

Reeni jumped out, and that skinny dog ran straight to her. Reeni carried her to the car and got in.

"What do you guys want to do?" I said. "If we leave her here, she's going to get hit. We don't have time to deal with this."

"This is my new dog," Reeni said. "I'm going to call her Georgia."

Georgia rode on Reeni's lap, her paws on the dash, watching the road, happy as heck, all the way home.

I arranged transport to another facility for the two youngest babies. After we got Zeus and Apollo and the three eight-week olds settled in, I called Dr. Burton. He went through the mandatory, three-minute bitch-out session and then said, "Okay, get those kids in here."

Rescue One was already full of needy animals. We had Cota, the black leopard, Nikomas wolf, the cougars – Jewels, Sapphire, Neko, Nakia, Nakobi and Montana. We had Gage, Sybre, Jake, Bachi and Sammy, the big tiger. We had Maximus and Gemini, the twin lions, and the lionesses Sheba, Nyla and Serena. Now, we had the twins, Zeus and Apollo, and what we came to call the North Tigers, because that's the side of the compound we put them on – Penelope, Charger and Tashara. I'm sure I'm forgetting someone; we rescued so many animals over the years, it can be hard to keep them all straight.

Bachi had only been there for a few days, but Dr. Burton had cured his parasites, treated his other issues and cleared him. He was happy, clean, eating the right diet and getting healthy. That kid and his new siblings had a blast.

On the other hand, I was dead tired and facing even bigger bills. Helping made me feel good, but the more I helped, the more I struggled, the more I worked, the more I amped up. Keeping my bulimia at bay was becoming almost impossible; I was pigging out on junk food and Trammies with a vengeance. Every time I jumped without thinking it through, I was hurting myself, everyone around me and, worst, the very animals I was trying desperately to protect. I was drowning, but instead of turning around or calling for help, I kept swimming away from shore, and the water kept getting deeper.

CHAPTER FIFTY-EIGHT

Super 8

On the positive side, I was still alive and in one piece, so my method acting for Cherry Angels was effective. The show didn't always go smoothly, though. One evening, Lisa sent Heather to a Super 8 in north Columbus. Heather wore her slutty professional outfit – a black pantsuit that I bought for 25 bucks at a consignment store. It was easy to take off and put on, as were the zippered boots that matched it. The long-sleeved, double-breasted jacket hid the lingerie show underneath. I'd also picked up a black, soft-brimmed hat that I could pull down over my eyes so no one who passed me in a lobby would recognize me.

I didn't dig the location, but when the client talked to Lisa, he sounded to be around 30, mannerly and educated, and Rescue One needed every dime Heather could turn. His room was on the second or third floor. I knocked. He stayed hidden behind the door when he opened it, which immediately put me on edge. As soon he closed the door, I saw by his expression that I wasn't what he was expecting. He thought he'd opened up for a 19-year-old rockhead hoping to make 40 bucks to score another piece of crack, not a woman in her mid-30s, alert and dressed for business.

There were two double beds in the room. I put my back

against the wall next to the door, while he slunk around the bed near the air-conditioning unit and stood there. I checked him out. He was at least six feet tall, broad-shouldered and had on a tan, lined windbreaker, jeans and white running shoes. His hair was blond and fell in bangs over his forehead and almost crewcut-short on the sides. He was pale, his cheeks flushed. He looked like the klutzy graduate students I'd seen around campus during college. He was extremely jumpy. As I recited my rates, he didn't say anything and didn't seem to listen. He kept glancing at the floor under the bed on his side of the room. From where I was standing, I couldn't see what he was looking at. The vibe was all sour; the hair on my nape rose. Heather immediately became loud and assertive.

"Obviously," she said, "this isn't going to work out. My driver's in the parking lot waiting for me. If I don't give him the okay in five minutes, he's coming up. I'm going to need my agency show-up fee, and I'm leaving. Forget the tip."

He didn't wait for me to tell him how much the imaginary show-up was. He crouched and starting rummaging under that bed. I knew he wasn't going through a wallet or a briefcase, because I could hear keys and what sounded like makeup containers, lipstick tubes and loose change clinking. He took a long time. I got the distinct impression that he didn't know exactly what was in the backpack or tote or purse he was searching. Holding the doorknob behind my back, I held my breath, waiting to see what he'd have in his hand when he straightened up.

He stood, tossed a folded wad of cash onto the bed in front of me and said, "For your trouble."

Without taking her eyes off him, Heather growled, "Stay on that side of the room, motherfucker! I am *not* fucking around!"

She snatched the money and hauled ass, slamming the door behind her. I didn't run, but I hurried down the hall and used the stairs, not the elevator, so I didn't end up trapped in another confined space with that hinky asshole.

When I got back to my house in Canal Winchester, I counted the money. He'd thrown me $600, when 150 was the show-up I'd quoted him. For some reason, he wanted me out of that room very badly. I chalked it up to a goofball getting cold feet. Several months later, I saw that same guy's face on the news; I recognized him immediately. The reporter said his name was Phillip Markoff, a medical student who'd robbed and murdered some prostitutes around Boston. They were calling him "The Craig's List Killer."

Dumbfounded, I wondered again why he'd been so nervous about that bed. 'Did that son of a bitch already kill some girl and take her purse?' I thought. 'Did he have a body under there? Was he trying to double his fun?'

For the next few weeks, I paid close attention to the street chatter and talked to my nightlife girlfriends to see if anyone else had run into that creep. A few girls thought they might've recognized him, but I heard about so many dead, missing or brutalized single, young women – overdoses, suicides, strangulations, stabbings, sexual assaults, fatal beatings, unexplained disappearances – that it was impossible to tell if Markoff ever operated around Columbus. Of course, if you work in the sex industry, you're literally a thousand times more likely to end up murdered than any woman from Sheep World. Cops don't spend a lot of time on hooker murders, either. They do the basics, file it under NHI – "No Humans Involved" – and move on to people who actually matter. After too many hours of listening to too many horror stories, I gave up, sickened.

Markoff committed suicide in jail, so I'll never know for sure if the guy in the Super 8 was the Craig's List Killer. I'm certain, however, that if Markoff and that dodgy asshole were in the same room, you couldn't tell them apart. Thank goodness for Heather.

CHAPTER FIFTY-NINE

The First Resurrection of Gemini

Until they hit puberty, Maximus and Gemini, the twin lions we took from the Engessers, were very content in the enclosure David built for them. Even afterward, Gem was mellow, but Max became a clever, naughty boy. Anything could trigger him into holy crap. Like Joseph, terrifying people entertained him. If you were walking past his cage, he'd sneak up and startle the hell out of you with a big lunge and an ear-busting roar. Someone reacting to his silliness overjoyed Max.

The only problem we had with Gemini was that he ate odd things. He'd eat his toys and any other plastic or rubber he could get. We kept that stuff out of his enclosure, but he managed to grab a water hose someone left hanging over his fence, pull it into his enclosure and eat some of it. After that, he was lethargic and sick all the time. Dr. Burton examined him and said Gem needed immediate surgery.

I was outside the operating room, pacing and watching through the window. Dr. Burton split Gem from his ribcage to his groin. I could see every organ. I knew by the frantic look on Dr. Burton's face that he couldn't figure out what was going on.

'Fuck! They're losing my Gem!' I thought.

About three hours into it, Dr. Burton came out and said, "I don't know how it's going to go, Angie. He has an intestinal blockage. We're trying to track it down."

Two hours later, Gemini died on the table. When he told me Gem was gone, Dr. Burton was apologetic.

I slammed my fists down on my thighs, jumped up and screamed, "You get your ass back in there! My kid is not dead! Bring him back!"

Dr. Burton told me later that he didn't have any idea what he was going to try next; he just thought, 'I'd rather face whatever is on that table than Angela.'

Still wearing their masks, his little penguins followed him back into the operating room. I stood there and glared at them through the glass, like, 'Do it, damn you!'

After a few minutes, someone shouted, "Paddles! Clear! We got him!"

I calmed down, but after the surgery, Dr. Burton was more like Dr. Frankenstein. He came out with a bewildered look on his face and said, "Oh, God, I've never done this before. Ang, I don't even know what we did here. He's back, but what did we bring back?"

Dr. Burton explained that a piece of hose had torn Gem's intestine. It was like letting the fluid out of a car's brake line, except this fluid was toxic to the cat, he said.

"I had to remove almost seven feet of his intestine," Dr. Burton said. "I don't know how his digestive track is going to function. I don't know how he's going to process food. I don't know how this animal is going to live. He's going to be a lot of work. He has a snowball's chance of surviving."

"That kid is here, and we have to deal with it," I said. "I'm good with whatever, as long as my kid's back. I'm going to keep the cat. Stitch him up."

CHAPTER SIXTY

The Second Resurrection of Gemini

Gem spent two weeks at the clinic and then came back to Rescue One. He'd been in intensive care, so we had to recreate that sterile environment. Dr. Burton sent the drugs we needed, with instructions on how to administer them.

Gem was home and up, but he was unhappy and so was his twin. Max smelled the incision. He knew what critical condition his brother was in. He wanted Gem, but his instincts were kicking: 'I smell blood. He's weak. I want to kill him.' Max became 450 pounds of pure nasty. To keep him away from his brother, we duplicated their den in another enclosure and moved Gem into it.

We still had our every day – and night – work; now, we were also running a medical center around the clock. Of course, none of us had formal veterinary training, so Dr. Burton had to download his education on us. We struggled to learn as we went along, and Gem gradually improved.

It's not like Max and Gem were our only problems. I had a thin crew; we were heavy on kids. The questions were maddening: 'Who's turn is it to watch over Gem? Where's the next rescue? Which animal is arriving? Did that sanctuary in Florida call back? When's David making the Sugarcreek run? Where's Heather supposed to be?'

And then Gemini went down again.

Dr. Burton said Gem almost certainly had another blockage. He needed a second surgery immediately. If we waited for someone to arrive or tried to rush him to the clinic, he'd be dead. We had to do it ourselves, even though we were completely unqualified to perform such a delicate procedure.

We turned the den into a MASH ER, hanging IV bags and restricting entry to David, Ellen and me. We scrubbed in, and I prayed as I gave Gem the anesthetic. Too much, he'd die; too little, he'd wake up in the middle of the procedure and kill one – or all – of us. We were on the phone with Dr. Burton, inserting, cleaning, navigating, as if we had veterinary degrees. It was dead-on serious. I had no choice but to control my nerves and force myself to think clearly. Working by flashlight and listening to Dr. Burton over speaker phone, I found the new blockage, scalped it, removed it and then stitched Gem's intestines back together. When it was finally over, I almost passed out from exhaustion and relief.

After the surgery, we took turns watching over the den, around the clock, all summer. We had to administer injections to the minute, on the hour. Gem ate a special diet that we ground very fine in a blender. We slept in the den, marked our charts, kept our radios on.

Somehow, Gemini pulled through again. Dr. Burton was amazed. To this day, I don't know how we managed to resurrect that lion twice.

CHAPTER SIXTY-ONE

Going After Imara

Dr. Markin was finally able to help me locate Imara at Tiger Ridge Exotics, a USDA-licensed place near Toledo. She knew how important that cat was to me. Rescue One was already popping at the seams, but I had to have my tiger-girl.

A guy named Kenny Hetrick owned Tiger Ridge. I didn't know Hetrick at all, and you run into all kinds of kooks in the exotic world. Even so, Ellen and I drove up to his property unannounced. Tiger Ridge was a tiny zoo right up against Route 20. Hetrick had a bunch of lions and tigers and cougars and leopards and wolves and a huge liger and two massive Kodiak bears, all in cramped cages. There was just a low perimeter fence around the enclosures and a couple donation boxes nailed to posts. Anyone could stop in and wander around unaccompanied without paying anything. David, who knew him a little bit, told me that Hetrick bred and sold exotics. I wasn't dealing with that issue, however; I just wanted Imara.

When we pulled up, Hetrick's wife, Roberta, greeted us. Hetrick was talking to a good ole boy with a mustache so wide it looked like the horns of a Texas steer. A sign beside the driveway said something about guns being bought and sold. The guy had a wad of cash in his hand, so I supposed that's what was going on. The moment we stepped out of the Land Cruiser, he put the money in his pocket and walked away.

Hetrick turned around and growled, "Who the hell are you and what the fuck do you want?"

Hetrick was an Incredible Hulk, weightlifter/boxer/cop with red hair and a red face. He outweighed me by 150 pounds, but I hadn't driven all that way and gotten so close to Imara just to tuck tail and leave. I resorted to mental judo.

I introduced myself and said, "Clara Markin notified me that you have a tiger named Imara here. David Cziraky lives with me, and we want that cat."

I knew Hetrick had been having problems with USDA. I ran the whole thing down for him: "Your compound has 16 USDA violations, and Dr. Markin says you have no business taking any more animals."

He dug his heels in. I got pushy: "Hey, man, I know exactly what's going on. You don't like Clara, and she doesn't like you, and I know where you stand with everything. You don't need that cat. That cat is important to me. I want her now, or you're going to get some heat. Don't piss around with me."

He knew that if he didn't give Imara to me, I'd be on the phone to USDA. I had him, legally, so we got down to brass tacks.

"Yeah, we're looking for a walk-in freezer," he said. "I have the walls, but I need the cooler part."

"Dude, I can hook you up," I said.

I think I threw some fencing into the deal, as well.

Just like Floyd Wells, Hetrick must've thought I was afraid of the tiger, because he said, huffily, "She's in the barn. You go get her."

Imara was a very cheeky, rip-you-a-new-ass kind of girl, a mean, mean cat. I'd raised that kid, so I knew her tricks. Hetrick had her stuck in a little cage inside a dark barn. When Ellen and I went in, Imara looked up, instantly recognized us and came running.

"Ellen, back the Cruiser up, dude," I said.

I went into the cage. It was just me and Imara. She was very excited. As Ellen pulled the Crusier up to the barn, I put a leash on Imara. She was a good girl and jumped right up into the cargo bay. Later on, I heard Diana was raving mad when she found out I had Imara. That news made me even happier.

CHAPTER SIXTY-TWO

Buddy

My stepbrother Johnny called me out of the clear blue one day and asked if I could help rescue his dog. Over the years, I'd lost track of him. Johnny said he'd been living in a trailer park in Florida with some people who'd moved there from Lockbourne. He was trying to become a professional bass fisherman, of all things.

He got into a hassle with the Lockbourne people, and they threw him out; then he got into trouble with the law. He said his little Jack Russell mix, Buddy, had been seized and dumped into a pound. They were going to gas him if Johnny didn't come up with $94 in the next 48 hours. He didn't have the cash.

I told Johnny I'd try to figure things out. I called the pound. Something very bad must've gone down, because they wanted nothing to do with Johnny and were determined to gas Buddy. The person abruptly hung up, leaving me to wonder how I was supposed to save a dog I didn't know who was on death row 1500 miles away. I'd spent most of my life in Ohio. Who the heck did I know in Florida who would be willing to run out and save a mutt they'd never even seen?

The Engessers, of course. I didn't know where their zoo was located or if they were out on the road in the RV, but I dialed their number.

Pat picked up immediately and said, "Oh, hi, Ang, honey.

How're you?"

I explained my predicament, and she said, "You're in luck, girl. We're just getting ready to leave for my sister's house in Georgia. We go right by that pound. We'll stop and pick him up."

When I promised to reimburse them for Buddy's bond, she said, "Don't worry about it. Consider it done."

Johnny was supposed to call me back, but I didn't hear from him for a few days. Before I did, Pat called and said, "Angie, listen: my sister's family all love Buddy. They have a big fenced-in yard and a lot of dogs. He's having a blast here. Please let him stay."

I had no idea what was going on with Johnny, so I thanked Pat and gave her my blessing.

When Johnny eventually called, I told him what had happened. I expected him to be grateful to me for finding a perfect new home for Buddy. Instead, he cursed me for giving his dog away. He demanded to know where Buddy was.

"No way, man," I said. "He got taken away from you once, and he'll get taken again. He's where he needs to be for the rest of his life."

Johnny yelled until I hung up on him. He kept calling. I wouldn't answer.

CHAPTER SIXTY-THREE

Throughout This Land, A Plague Upon Your Lions

After his second new lease on life, Gemini was doing fine. He was up and moving and even eating a little bit of meat that we ground in the blender. One day, though, he threw up and collapsed again. He was running a high fever. Dr. Burton rushed to Lancaster, but he couldn't find out what was causing it. Within 48 hours, Gem faded. There was no bringing him back a third time.

Gem's death didn't sit right with us. That cat had health problems, but he'd been improving all the time. Then he shut down like someone had unplugged him. Things became more mystifying and frightening when some of our other lions started dying young. The cats were waking up one morning with something that played havoc with their systems. It came out of nowhere and was completely debilitating and shocking. We were in a state of utter fuck.

Nairobi made it to eight months – about when our lions hit the wall. He became disoriented, started having seizures, quit eating. Dr. Burton hit Nairobi with a load of heavy steroids, a harsh intervention that can make cats doubly mean. Nairobi was up and aggravated. We tried to work with him, but he died.

Kenya was six months old when it hit. I was tearing up Rt. 33

with her in the van, headed for the clinic, talking to Dr. Burton on the phone.

"Ang, prepare yourself," he said. "You could lose her on route."

"No, I'm hurrying," I said. "We're going to save her."

"Everything's ready for you here, but, please, prepare yourself for what might happen," he said.

Kenya was fading fast. I stopped along the busy expressway and did CPR as traffic blew past, but she died.

We thought it might be some contaminant in the food, the water or the soil, but only young lions were dying. The tigers and cougars weren't affected. We couldn't figure it out. Then we started hearing reports about the same thing happening in Texas, Florida, California, North Carolina.

Dr. Burton was brilliant and had connections with top-dog vets and scientists all over the country. He went to every one of them. They were working overtime to solve the mystery, but the cause eluded them. They looked for diseases, poisons in supplements or medicines, toxins in the environment. We were all searching desperately for a hard cause.

This was freaky Old Testament stuff – 'Throughout this land, a plague upon your lions.' I started to blame myself for what was happening. Maybe Dr. Burton had been right all along, and God had pronounced a curse on Angela and Heather to punish us for our sins.

Working with researchers in California, Dr. Burton finally

figured it out. The one constant in the cases turned out to be the Engessers. We'd gotten all our lions except Sheba from them. They were handing lions over to other sanctuaries as they did their photo-baby gypsy trip. The never-ending exotic swap meet dispersed the lions around the country.

An essential building block was missing in those cats. The Engessers had probably been breeding an old lion with his own children and grandchildren. As the inbreeding progressed, the original DNA mutated until the cubs became copies of copies. Entire sentences and paragraphs of the strain were missing. The Engesser lions had a major vitamin B deficiency, which compromised their immune systems. The plague came from that simple cause. We had all overlooked it because it was so obvious. The lions just needed an additional vitamin supplement.

David insisted that the Engessers had figured out the perfect way to keep breeding without having to take care of cats once they became too big and dangerous for public contact. He said they intentionally bred the lions to die young, then signed off on them and let someone else deal with the fallout.

I don't know if the Engessers even suspected that anything was wrong. They never offered any clues; that's what finally ticked me off. I didn't jump in their faces, but they were aware they'd crossed a line with me. I've spoken with them since, and I could tell they felt bad. They've invited me to come to Florida, but I think I'll pass, even though I still consider them friends.

CHAPTER SIXTY-FOUR

Who Are You to Play God?

Jabouhti lion came from the Engessers, too, but he was messed up from jump. When they're cubs, all lions are clumsy and flop around, but Jabouhti never grew out of that stage. He didn't put on weight, develop and get his act together the way he should've.

When Jabouhti was about five months, Dr. Burton did an MRI on him. He called me to the clinic to show me the pictures. His spinal cord should've curved down, with all the connections coming off of it – the muscles, the ribs and other bones, the nerves – in an orderly pattern. Jabouhti's looked like a steering wheel ripped out of a car; his wiring sprayed all over the screen.

"Ang, I can't fix this, honey," Dr. Burton said, tapping the MRI. "See all those nerves going everywhere? Something went very wrong when this kid was born. There's no technology, no procedure, nothing. It's over."

We stood there fixated on that image, sick.

"He's got no weight now," Dr. Burton finally said. "Let the kid enjoy the summer, Ang. Let him smell the flowers and play with the other kids."

Dr. Burton said Jabouhti was probably not suffering, so we didn't have to jack him up on painkillers. We decided to give him as much time as possible by shooting him with cortisone, like a human with a bad knee. Dr. Burton gave us the vials, and we kept them in the fridge. He taught me exactly how to inject Jabouhti, even marking the needles so I didn't go too deep. I'd pinch his skin three or four inches on either side of the spine, stick the needle in, hit the plunger and count like Dr. Burton taught me.

Jabouhti wasn't thrilled with the shots, but there was no choice. At first, he just dragged himself around on his front legs; however, he learned to walk in his own funny, corkscrewing way. He could get to his food, pooh pooh and play around with the other lions in the common enclosure outside their dens on the southeast side of the compound.

Everybody doted on the special-needs kid so much that he became an entitled little brat. Nyla mothered him. Anytime a scavenging bird swooped down on the food bins, he hollered, and you'd better not be anywhere near him, because if Ny-Ny came out of that den, you were in a world of trouble. Jabouhti ran that game on Serena all the time. When she wanted to play rough with him, he knew all he had to do was scream. Ny-Ny would fly out and knock the crap out of Serena. I watched him do it time and again; he knew exactly what he was up to.

Despite the cortisone, he eventually got very bad. Some days, he couldn't stand. I'd think it was over, then he'd get up and weave over to the water bowl or the feeding bin. Everyone said I should put Jabouhti down, like I had Joshua. I refused. 'Who are you to play God?' I asked myself. But I really wasn't playing God. I knew better. God paints glorious sunsets forever. I was just trying to extend the liferoad of one doomed kid for as long as I could.

CHAPTER SIXTY-FIVE

Dr. Burton Battles Maximus for Angela's Mortal Ass

I'll find out soon enough if Dr. Burton saved my immortal soul from hellfire and damnation, but I can tell you for sure that he saved my mortal ass in more ways than one.

We were chatting over breakfast at Bob Evans one day, and he asked, "Hey, Ang, do you have any idea what we've done here, kidwise, moneywise, effortwise? Do you have a number?"

I'd been sipping black coffee and watching him eat and daydreaming; things suddenly turned serious.

"Are you kidding me? Do you?" I asked.

"No," he said, "and I don't want to know."

I said, "Me neither, man."

Neither of us ever asked that question again.

We both knew I could never pay the whole freight at the clinic, no matter how hard Heather worked or how much jewelry Angela dropped off. After that morning, he began sending me a flat bill for $500 every few months. He stopped billing me altogether for a lot of stuff, or he would charge a nominal fee, like $1 for "cougar castration" or "nursing care." Eventually, the invoices were marked "Professional Courtesy." I'm pretty sure that he was trying to get rid of Heather by making her unnecessary. Even so, I spent at least in the high hundreds of thousands, maybe as much a million and a half, on Rescue One. Dr. Burton matched my money, if not more. That man never failed me; in fact, I wouldn't be telling this story if it weren't for him.

When Gem died, I tried to hide it from Maximus, but Max knew. He saw me hanging out in the den while Gem was sick. He saw me carrying Gem's body away. That quick, Max hated me. There was no way back for the two of us. Even though the twins were big guys, I'd always walked right into the enclosure with both of them. After Gemini died, Maximus charged me once, so I stopped going in with him altogether. If I even walked by his enclosure, he roared and rushed the fence. Even when he just stood there and watched me, his eyes were chilling: narrowed, fixed, murderous. Except for that miasma in the Vatican, I was never more afraid of anything than I was of Max. I still loved him, and he was still gorgeous, but that boy straight-up wanted me dead.

We were updating all the cats' shots one morning, which was a pain-in-the-ass production. Dr. Burton would pull in at daybreak, and we were lucky to finish by dark. We went cage by cage. We knocked the kid down, moved all the equipment in, stabilized the animal, drew blood, inspected feces and examined the kid from nose to tail. Then we reversed the drugs to get the cat back up, because if you let a lion or tiger stay down for too long, it will stop breathing, suffocated by its own weight. We had to do that for every animal on the compound. It was a series of lengthy appointments. It was not fun.

Sleepy as hell from working all night, I zoned and drifted a little too close to Max's enclosure. Like I said, he was a clever boy. He turned his paw vertical and stuck it through a gap between the fence and a post and stabbed a claw behind my right ear. Max was hooked into my skull. We were connected; a lion prowled my thoughts; I could feel what he was feeling. I'd felt lust – even predatory lust, like the night that psycho Melvin beat the fuck out of me in that motel room. That was human lust, though, the kind we all understand. What I felt from Max that day had nothing to do with anything human. It was bloodlust – wild and primal and completely terrifying.

My first instinct was to jerk my head back, but I knew if I did, his claw would sever my carotid artery; I'd be dead in minutes. Instead, I did a little crow-hop to my left. The claw popped loose. I gasped and slapped my hand over the spurting blood.

Dr. Burton was about 15 feet away with an OSU intern, prepping to move into another cage. He heard me, realized something was wrong and came running. He lowered me to the ground and swabbed blood from the wound.

"Ang, stay with me. Ang, stay with me," he kept repeating.

I felt my blood pumping. His voice sounded like it was echoing in a cave. He looked scared, like the nurses in the emergency room after the dog attacked me. 'Hmm, this is it. I'm going to die now!' I thought, dreamily. 'Okay.'

For some reason, I wasn't afraid at all, just sleepy.

Dr. Burton jumped in his medical bag and stitched me up right there in the field. That poor intern was at Rescue One for the first time; she was a trouper, though. She handed Dr. Burton his instruments and assisted him throughout the procedure.

I was lucky. Max had only grazed the artery. Another millimeter, and he would've ripped it. Nothing could've saved me from bleeding out then.

We had another problem, though. We couldn't have the intern telling anybody what happened. I was trying to act cool, but there was so much blood on my clothes I looked like I'd stepped out of a slasher flick, and I was so light-headed I was faint. Dr. Burton and I went into *Mission Impossible* mode. We had to browbeat the intern into silence. I wanted to tell her, 'Listen, this never happened. You didn't see that lion do anything. If that cat gets hurt, we'll ruin your career, bitch.'

Dr. Burton was much too dignified to even think something like that, let alone say it. He calmly explained to the intern that talking would only hurt everyone involved, especially the animals. She said, "Gotcha," and that was that.

I still carry that scar, in more ways than one. I'd sit on the porch, watching Max rub along the fence while David petted him. The minute he sensed me, however, it was on. He got all liony. His ears cocked; he stood up and glared at me, his chest rumbling. It was painful, because this was the same munchkin I'd held on my lap. I played with his feet until he fell asleep. If I tried to move him, he woke up and followed me around the house. He was the little guy who thought I was better than Santa

Claus. Then he wanted to kill me. I loved him all the same, though. Maximus was an incredible guy.

CHAPTER SIXTY-SIX

Sampson's Hygroma

I'll say this for Bob Sturm: He didn't just dump Sammy with us and run off, like every other owner did. For years, he was around Rescue One all the time, helping care for that tiger.

During one of our annual checkups, Dr. Burton used a tranq gun to knock Sammy down so we could do his physical. That little needle prick became infected. It started out as a kind of half-golf ball tumor. We tried to drain it by lancing it. Sammy started licking it. I kept detailed, daily notes on his condition, starting on the 10th of March that year with, "Sammy licked hygroma on back left leg raw – opened it up." Before we knew it, there was no stopping him. He wouldn't leave it alone. He was lying on his side all the time, licking, licking, licking.

We rinsed the wound and gave him drugs, trying to make him stop licking himself so we could heal it and get him up. Nothing we did helped. He opened that thing up so much it looked like a shrapnel wound.

Nothing else could be done. Like I said, there was no handbook. We couldn't keep him on the drugs anymore, couldn't keep him down any longer. Dr. Burton had to euthanize him.

I just reread my note for the 21st of April. It says, "Sam died today."

Talk about understatement.

CHAPTER SIXTY-SEVEN

The Great Sugar Bear Raid

A month or so before Dr. Markin sent me to do recon on the Thompson farm, a woman tipped me about some ignorant hillbilly jackasses who were keeping a young bear in horrid conditions somewhere out in the sticks. The snitch had a falling out with one of them. It had something to do with the woman being pissed at a girlfriend of somebody in the house or something equally silly. Even though she was around those imbeciles all the time, they didn't realize she was mad at them, and she seemed to know the inner workings of what was going on down there. She brought it to my attention; I brought it to USDA's. It was the same old crap: 'Whatever happens happens. Maybe somebody should do something about it.'

"All right, fine," I said. "I'm going down there."

They said, "Uh, okay."

The snitch lady called again and said, "Hey, they're having trouble feeding the bear. They have it in a nasty cage. The guy's running ads in *Animal Finders* and talking to his stinky hunting buddies about selling the bear for a canned hunt."

I didn't know that bear at all, but the thought of some yokel shooting him while he was tied to a tree or locked in a pen fried my terminals. We were full-up with cats, though, and I didn't know shit about bears – still don't, as a matter of fact.

The snitch lady kept badgering me. A week or so after she first contacted us, she called and said, "Listen, I think they found a buyer for the canned hunt. It's all going to go down here in a couple days."

'Oh, my God,' I thought, 'here we go again.'

The snitch lady had finally touched my last nerve; I had to make a split-second decision. The Land Cruiser was in the shop, so I walked across the road to ask my neighbor Lee Tipple if I could borrow his van. Lee's a super-sweet country boy with a wonderful, winning smile. He was in the Army reserves, but when he was home, he delivered mail out of a little beat-up thing that didn't have a prayer of running much longer.

I knocked on his door. When he opened it, I said, "Dude, can I borrow your van?"

"What're you going to do with it?" Lee asked.

"I'm going to go pick up a bear," I said.

"All right, Ang, fine," he said, like I'd said I had to do a grocery run. "I've got the early route tomorrow. Have it home by dawn and put some gas in it."

It was already late afternoon. David had taken three calls from cops for road kills that day. He had to pick up the deer carcasses and butcher them. We needed the meat. No one else was around. If I went, it would be me alone with the bear and the hillbillies.

I said, "Give me the keys, Lee," and took off.

The snitch told me the bear place was down near Marietta, on the southeast corner of Ohio. I found the trailer way out in Yahooville, in a maze of gravel roads and dark forest. It was so remote that I started to get hinky about this bear raid, but I thought, 'It'll be all right. These stumpjumpers won't be home, anyway. They're probably all hiding from Dog the Bounty Hunter. They're not going to do anything.'

As usual, I was wrong. There were lights on in the trailer; it sounded like some kind of roaring, kickass moonshine hoedown was going on. I got out and snuck around, looking for the bear. I found him in a crappy cage on the back of the property. The snitch lady told me that he sat on her lap and cuddled with her, so I was expecting a little guy. When I saw the kid, I realized I'd been conned again. He was a fat yearling, at least as big as a St. Bernard, his matted fur crusted with dried mud and accessorized with leaves and twigs. They must've been feeding him table scraps and stale donuts because that bear was seriously filled out and had very long claws. The kid didn't know me, and he was obviously hungry.

'Oh, man, I am in deep shit!' I thought.

Since I didn't have time to put together a Yogi Bear, pic-a-nic basket, I'd stopped and bought three little plastic bear bottles of honey, because I remembered Winnie the Pooh liked the stuff. I stood there in the gathering dark, looking at three or four times the kid I'd been expecting to find and wondering what the fuck to do with him.

'There's no time to come back here with reinforcements,' I

thought. 'By Monday, this kid'll be sold and shot. You have to do it now, Ang.'

I took a deep breath and whispered, "It's okay, you got this."

I scurried up the hill to the van, pulled it down the dirt road and backed it up as close to the cage as I could. I took out a squirt bottle of honey and started talking to him. I didn't know what to say to a bear, so I just chatted him up like he was a client.

"Hey, what's up, guy?" I said in my huskiest hooker half-whisper. "Oh, what a handsome stud you are. You are one hot dude. You want to party? Come with Angie, and we'll have a real fun time tonight."

There was no lock on the cage. I pulled the pin, opened the gate, eased in cautiously. He sat up on his fat rump, mummering, sticking out his unbelievably long tongue, watching me with the sad eyes of a dense, chubby adolescent.

"Okay, handsome, here we go," I said, slipping a dog leash around his neck.

Walking backward, I squeezed the bear bottle and talked him toward the van. The honey hypnotized him. He waddled along, licking and humming and snorting. I tried to hurry him up, but he was enjoying the stroll and the treat. As the bear waddled toward the van, I thought, 'Damnit, if they see us from that trailer and we're in rifle range, this's going to go all the way bad.'

He followed me right into the back of the van. Just as I thought we were out of there, we got stuck. On the way down, I didn't notice that the road was muddy in spots. The bear's weight, uphill, bald tires, rear-wheel drive, mud – I couldn't move.

I pounded steering wheel, yelling, "Damnit! Damnit! Damnit!"

I looked in the mirror. The bear was peering over the seat at me with his dull, close-set black eyes, licking his rubbery lips, like he was wondering how anyone could be so upset during such a fun outing. I left him in the van, climbed out and found a bunch of lumber scraps around his pen. I stuck the wood up under the wheels like I'd seen on TV. Meanwhile, I was waiting to hear the first rifle shot from the trailer and worrying what this big guy was thinking, because if we managed to escape, we had a long ride jammed together in Lee's little van.

This time, the wheels caught. I tore out of there and got back on the road. I thought I was going out the same way I came in. Oh, no, no, no. I hadn't planned anything through. I got lost in a jumble of dark backroads. I didn't know what else to do, so I held a bottle of honey behind my head and squeezed it. The kid sat on his butt, licking and grunting, while I tried to figure out which way home was.

To make things even more pleasant, I'd been in such a hurry that I hadn't put gas in the van, like Lee told me to; besides, I'd left my purse at home and spent my only cash on the honey. When I looked down at the gauge, I felt like someone kicked me in the stomach. By 10 o'clock, it was pitch black, and I was tripping on pure panic: no cell phone reception, tree branches hanging over winding roads that all looked exactly alike, afraid to stop at any of the rundown houses I passed because someone might shove a double-barrel shotgun up my nose. I drove around in circles; honey dripped in my hair; the bear licked it with his huge gross tongue.

Thank God, he didn't decide to chomp on me. The bugger got curious, though, and jammed his head and shoulders into the front seat. He turned on the radio and started switching the stations. I had to shut it off and push him into the back. He drooled all over my arm and shoulder and neck. My hair was matted up with honey and bear spit. He smelled like assfunk and severe halitosis. It was disgusting.

I finally blundered into the freeway and ran for Lancaster. The van didn't have tinted windows, so there was no way to hide that big kid from the traffic. I thought, 'If a cop sees you, this explanation is going to be very interesting,'

I can't believe the bear tolerated that nonsense, but he was totally chill. When I pulled up the driveway to Rescue One, I was down to my last few licks of honey and drops of gas. The tank was empty, there was honey all over the place, the bear had trashed the van's interior. Lee never said a word about it. If he hadn't flipped me the keys that afternoon, Sugar Bear would be dead. I talked to Lee just the other day. He's still as handsome as a country music star, and he never lost that old-school belief that his word is his bond.

David had set up a corn crib we'd bought from a farmer for 500 bucks. He was putting the roof on even as Sugar Bear was going in. A couple of weeks later, we moved him to a shift cage and laid a cement floor.

Dr. Burton wrote "a big ball of fat" under the Comments section of his initial evaluation. He prescribed worm medicine and some antibiotics for Sugar Bear's runny nose. Sugar Bear was too young to neuter, so we didn't touch that. Dr. Burton was concerned about the bear's weight; we searched the internet for a South Beach Bear Diet.

I kept thinking, 'We have to find somewhere for this bear to go.' I figured I'd rescue him and send him out to a place that knew how to take care of him and had some bear buddies for him to play with, but I wasn't plugged into the bear world. Dr. Markin tried to put him in a national park in West Virginia, where there were other bears. When the move fell through, we gave up, listed him under "Misc" on our roster and kept him.

I'd set out to help somebody who was going to be shot for money and ended up with another foster kid. I don't mean to gripe about Sugar Bear, though, because he came with a funny fringe benefit. Every time I think about The Great Sugar Bear Raid, I imagine those rubes coming out the next morning and standing in front of that empty pen, scratching their empty heads and wondering where the *hayall* that *bayuh* – and that wad of cash they were going to make for selling him off to be murdered – went, and I crack up.

CHAPTER SIXTY-EIGHT

Diana's Last Laugh

When we brought Imara to Rescue One, I came up with a plan to save time, space and money. We had Zeus and Apollo, the twin tigers from that madhouse in Georgia. They were only about seven or eight months, their enclosure was big and Imara was used to being social. 'We'll put her with the twins,' I figured. 'She'll slap them into line right quick, and they'll all live happily ever after. It'll be an awesome match.'

Everything worked out for a while, then a volunteer got sloppy. We had ponds in the enclosures that we filled by putting hoses, like the one Gem had grabbed, over the fences. It took all day to drain the ponds and refill them with fresh water. Somebody turned off the water and walked away and left the hose hanging down into the enclosure where we kept Imara and the twins.

One of the tigers grabbed it, and that ferocious possessiveness kicked in. Imara and the twins started fighting over the hose. It turned ugly. Just as we were coming through the gate, the twins took her down and killed her. There was nothing we could do. The tiger I loved the most and had worked so long to save had been killed by two of my other kids. I was crushed.

It wasn't the twins' fault; they were only following the law of the jungle. Imara was dead because of a human mistake. I imagined Diana Cziraky somewhere hearing about her death and having one last laugh at my expense.

CHAPTER SIXTY-NINE

The Solid Gold Volunteer

I never asked who left the hose in Imara's cage; I couldn't afford to alienate anyone over a mistake that was so easy to make. I just reminded all the volunteers that someone had made the same screwup with Sybre and issued them a blanket reminder: "Pay attention. I don't care if you're hungover or have a cold or are worrying about Mom's chemo treatments. Never take your eyes off the cats. Never take anything for granted. One little mistake can be deadly, to an animal or to you."

Like every exotic sanctuary, we lived off volunteers, and we never had enough of them. Volunteers could be more trouble than they were worth, though. Dangerous exotic animals attract the weirdest people, for all the wrong reasons. I never got over how willing otherwise intelligent adults were to take someone else's word for it and enter an enclosure with an extremely dangerous animal. Then again, a lot of Sheep People's lives are so shitty and boring that they'll do almost anything to feel the excitement of hanging out with 500-pound predators. That's the point – they'll do *almost* anything, anything except learn the safety protocols and follow them all the time.

One of our long-time Solid Gold Volunteers was a woman we called "Denny." Denny adored the cats. She also lived with a sugar daddy who didn't mind helping us out financially.

Although Denny had to drive over a half hour just to get to Rescue One, she was on the schedule almost every day. She brought presents for the cats and sat and talked to them and cooed over them. They loved her as much as she loved them.

Denny was also kooky-funny. She claimed to have multiple personalities, one of whom was a 7-foot black dude named Nonnie. Nonnie and David despised each other. Nonnie would intentionally bump David with a shoulder, then throw gang signs, square up, lean back, fold his arms over his chest and accuse David of "disrespectin" him. Even though Denny was almost as short as I am, Nonnie could somehow look up and down at David at the same time, while running vulgar smack like Bart the Fart. David is normally pretty meek, but he'd jump in Nonnie's face and yell back. Before someone started throwing punches, I had to separate them, while trying to keep a straight face.

Despite Nonnie and the other characters running around inside her, Denny was an extremely hard and dependable worker. One night, though, she violated one of my prime directives: she made rounds of the cages alone. I insisted that everyone work in pairs, double-check each other and carry walkie-talkies. For whatever reason, Denny went out by herself, and Serena, our feistiest lioness, attacked her.

When Denny limped into the log house, all I could say was, "Oh, shit!"

Her calf was ripped in a 'V' that went from just below her knee to just above her ankle. She looked like a Great White had grabbed her. The wound was so deep I could see everything inside her leg, like a drawing in an anatomy textbook.

We wrapped her leg in towels, but the blood soaked right through them. Even though I knew I would be summoning my own doom, I grabbed the phone to dial 911. Denny stopped me; she also refused to let me drive her to the emergency room, because, she said, the law would inevitably come out to investigate. I was in the same position when Jewels attacked me, but Denny's wound was much worse than my scratches and nips and bruises. I told her she had to go to the hospital.

"Hell no!" Denny said. "I'm not going anywhere! I will not hurt those kids!"

I finally convinced her that she needed professional medical attention before she bled to death. I said we'd work out the details of our bogus story on the way to the hospital. In truth, there was nothing to work out. No doctor would believe that a dog bit her or she fell trying to climb over a rusty fence.

As soon as we hit the ER, they grabbed Denny and rushed her into the back. I paced the waiting room, thinking, 'It's all over now, man. These people will know this is a wild animal bite, they'll know who I am and they'll know where Rescue One is. I'm screwed and so are the kids.'

A nurse came out and said Denny wanted to talk to me. I followed her to the major trauma suite, trying to devise a last-second lie, but it was futile. When I got there, Denny – or one of her alter-egos – was screaming in an Indian doctor's face, "Fuck you! I'm not telling you shit!"

"Ma'am," he said, patiently. "You will lose your leg."

"Look, fucker, I have Quadruple A insurance," she said, "and you're only here for the money. I need your services right now. This is an accidental dog bite, got it? Fix my damn leg, and that's that!"

The doctor squinted and scrunched his brows like he was trying to figure out what the heck "Quadruple A insurance" was. He nodded, turned to a nurse, said, "Okay, prep her for surgery," and walked out.

I don't know what went down between Denny and Serena that night. Denny said it happened so fast that even she wasn't sure how she got hit. She put in a lot of hours; maybe she was tired. Maybe her sugar daddy wanted her home, and she got in a hurry. I'm pretty sure Denny was covering for Serena, however. Serena was filled with manic energy; her crazy eyes watched every move anyone made. She brought back my fear of lions, and she knew it, which made her very aggressive toward me. Because of Serena and Maximus, I avoided the lion dens as much as possible. I believe Serena had been stalking Denny for some time. She waited until Denny left a gate unlocked for a quick minute, then took her shot. The mysteries are how Denny got away from Serena alive and why the cat didn't escape and raise a hundred different kinds of unthinkable hell.

Denny's loyalty saved me and my kids, but not her own leg. She had to undergo years of surgeries and therapy. Her leg was never right again. She became a visitor instead of a volunteer. I felt awful that she was hurt so bad, but the saddest part was that

Denny had to stop caring for her beloved cats. I know it broke her heart.

CHAPTER SEVENTY

Bratty Primates, Alleged Artic Wolves, Baby Gators and Giant Serpents – Oh, Shit!

A little while ago, I tried to do a mental headcount of animals who were already at Rescue One when we came back from Georgia with the carload of baby tigers. I knew I was leaving somebody out, but I couldn't come up with the name. Like they say, the memory is selective. I forgot about Coco, the holy terror Java macaque.

Heather was out working, when Ellen, whom I'd named director of Rescue One by then, called and said a Java macaque whose owner had surrendered was coming in. I called Dr. Burton and told him what was happening.

He went off on me like I said I was adopting a velociraptor: "Angela! A Java macaque? Do you even know what that is? You don't have the facilities or experience for him. They're deadly. He'll rip your fingers and your face off! They're also known to carry Herpes B."

As usual, he didn't stop me from doing what I wanted, no matter how loud he yelled.

Coco was about 30 years old when we got him. He was an elderly, smarty-pants, starved-out, parasite-ridden, hairy ET who was mad at the world. He showed up with a chain collar around his neck and a broken jaw. Dr. Burton had to cut the collar off and then wire his jaw.

Coco was terribly smart, and he never forgot anything. We put a little TV on the wall outside his cage to entertain him and tied the remote to it. The little shit's all-day goal was to grab that remote. He must've thought he was John Wayne in another life, because when he got his hands on that thing, he flicked straight to the first western he could find. All the TVs in the house were tied into the same cable box. Once he tuned in to *Bonanza*, we were going to be watching Ben Cartwright and Hoss and Little Joe for a while, because he wouldn't let us change the station.

That kid was something else. He held up his little cup for a drink. He stuck his tiny hands between the bars so we could wash them with a cloth. He made his own bed. When his blankets were dirty, he gathered them and passed them to us. He was so intelligent that we had to create complex treat puzzles to keep him occupied. Coco knew how to open doors. He escaped and ran around the house, screeching and digging through drawers and cupboards, just like Charlie raccoon.

I loved Coco to death, but he was a nasty little creature. He masturbated in public all the time. If he was mad, he didn't hide it. He knew breakfast was served at eight; he'd be furious if we missed that mark by just a minute or so. We had to remember who we were messing with, too, because that guy had big canines. A bite from him would send you straight to the ER.

Coco could see the kitchen from his cage; every time I opened the refrigerator door, he screamed for a snack, like he was saying, 'Hey, what're you eating? I'll have some of that.'

Giving Coco junk food made Dr. Burton mad, but to keep the irritable little brat quiet, we gave him one Popsicle a day. He sat there just like a little kid, the treat hanging out of his mouth, watching cowboy movies. He was hilarious.

We cut holes in the cage so we could slip treats in. I was giving him a snack one day. He sat there playing it cool, until I got too close. His hand shot out through one of the other holes. He snatched a handful of my hair and slammed my forehead against the cage so hard that stars burst around my head. While a hot lump rose over my eye, he sat back and looked at me like, 'Yeah, I did that, bitch. So what?'

He had more doctor and dentist appointments than a sickly 5-year old. He finally had a seizure, and we rushed him to the clinic. I watched Dr. Burton work on him through the window. They had him on a warm blanket on what looked like a baby-changing station, surrounded by people in scrubs and masks, electrodes attached to him, machines beeping and blinking. They worked hard, but they couldn't save him. Coco was a great little guy. We treated him like he was Prince Charles; he treated us like a retinue of body servants.

Like an idiot, I let the state of New York talk me into taking Misty, Nannouk and Yukon, three alleged Artic wolves who had been confiscated from a private owner. Wolves are very beautiful and very shy, but it's hard to tell if they're purebreds or hybrids. The wolfdogs can be super dangerous. They're usually crossbred with German shepherds or malamutes or husky-type breeds, so you end up with an animal that has the lethal bite pressure of a wolf and the aggressiveness of an attack dog. They're almost impossible to place, so the New York people were calling all over the country trying to find anyone who would take them. Eventually, they tapped some vine and ended up with our name.

The first time they called, I turned them down. Dr. Burton and Dr. Markin were all over me about being too heavy on animals, and I didn't even have a full compound to hold the wolves, just the enclosure where we kept Nakomas. When they called about a week later, I refused again.

They went all Floyd Wells on me: "Oh, we'll just shoot them, since there's no place for them to go."

I knew if they really wanted to kill those animals, they'd have done it already. They kept bugging me, and I kept saying no.

Finally, they said, "We'll neuter them and give them all of their shots and provide transport."

The moment was right. I wouldn't need Dr. Burton to examine the wolves. Dr. Markin had done her walk-around recently and wouldn't be back for a long time. I thought I could just hide the wolves under my skirt until I either moved them to a safe place or had to face the music. David put up the enclosures, and we moved them in. They wanted nothing to do with anyone. They hid when any of us approached the enclosure; they wouldn't even come out to eat the treats I threw over the fence.

I never got another dime from New York to help care for

them. In fact, I never did get any money for saving animals. We could've used it, of course, but who would I bill for services rendered? A kid? The judge who ordered the animals seized? Angela's job was never to turn a profit; it was to provide answers, to say, "Okay, everything's fine. I got this." Heather was supposed to come up with the operating capital.

One winter night, it was snowing so hard that Lisa couldn't book any appointments. I was in the log house, trying to catch up on sleep. Just after 10 o'clock, the doorbell rang, which was very strange, since the weather was so bad and we usually kept the gate across the driveway locked at night. I went out onto the porch. There were footprints in the snow. I heard something, looked up and saw a pair of high-topped white basketball shoes running down the hill. Everything else the person had on was black.

"Hey, what the fuck do you think you're doing, motherfucker?" I yelled.

Whoever it was kept running. He must've been a neighbor, because he knew exactly where he was going.

A green three-gallon plastic bucket was sitting at my feet. I looked into it and saw what appeared to be one of those little rubber alligators kids take into the bathtub to play. I figured one of the volunteers was trying to pull a stupid prank. I was mad enough to take someone's head off. Then the toy started squeaking and moving around. I grabbed the bucket and carried it inside.

I thought it was a crocodile, about eight inches long; however, when I called Dr. Burton and described it, he said it was an American alligator, probably a female. He told me to put her in warm water right away and in the morning, buy 40 goldfish at the pet store to feed to her. I set her in the bathtub and ran water so she could warm up.

The next morning, I brought the goldfish back. When I threw them in the tub, the little gator went ballistic. She ate 80 goldfish a week. They weren't cheap, and I hated sentencing those poor fish to death, but that's what I had to do to keep her alive. To be honest, though, watching her catch and eat them was fascinating. She amazed David. He sat watching her by the hour. He reached in to pet her once, and she gave him a pretty good nip.

We moved her to the Jacuzzi just off my bedroom. Dr. Burton gave me a little heater to keep the water at the right temperature, and we brought in some rocks for her to climb on. She sat on those rocks, tripping out for her mother in the most heartbreaking, squeaking cry.

She stayed here for about five months, before Dr. Burton could arrange for her to catch a ride to a gator rescue in Florida. She was one of the lucky ones.

So was Jake the Snake. Jake was a boa constrictor about 15 feet long, a very hefty, impressive guy: coils of muscle giftwrapped in copper skin, watchful rubychip eyes, darting tongue tasting the world. Some nitwits had abandoned him in an apartment. He showed up in a big aquarium, and we put him in the living room.

He was pretty and cool, but I knew less about snakes than I did about bears or alligators. A few weeks after we took him, Jake's eyes went murky blue. He didn't want to eat his live rats. That was cool for the rats, but Jake seemed miserable. Feeling bad for him, I reached down to pet him. I didn't realize he was in a shed cycle, when you best leave a snake alone. I also didn't know he had a lot of spikey teeth that slanted backward. He stuck those teeth in me. It felt like a bunch of red-hot needles had been jabbed into my arm. I freaked out so bad that I can't even remember how I got away from him. I never touched Jake again, just stood by the aquarium and talked to him.

Everybody was so frightened of Jake that we were barely maintaining him. Reeni and Steve's daughter was 17 at the time, a very responsible, curious girl. She wanted Jake, so Dr. Burton gave them a crash course on how to take care of boas. Jake moved into an even bigger aquarium in her bedroom. He became her prized possession. She had a regular schedule for him and didn't mind feeding him live rats, which I despised doing. Once a week, she ran water in the bathtub and let him swim around. He really prospered there. She's married now and lives in Colorado and still has Jake. Reeni says he's gigantic.

We had JC, a pure black Asian jungle cat someone found wandering around New Orleans after Katrina. They stuck him in a shelter where no one knew what he was. A volunteer from Columbus saw him and gave the shelter our number. We went and picked him up.

Tyson the Siberian lynx almost got me arrested. He bit

someone, and his owner asked me to stash him here. Some undercooked douche from the state who thought he was large and in charge showed up at the gate, demanding that I turn him over so they could cut his head off to check for rabies. He ordered me to bring the cat out immediately, or he would arrest me.

"Screw you," I said. "Get the hell off my property and don't come back until you're taking me to jail."

I never saw him again. Tyson is buried out back.

Foxes, dozens of dogs and cats, a three-legged coyote – the animals kept coming, and the bills kept piling up and I kept degrading myself and putting myself in peril to care for them. Things got so insane that I was tempted to join Sheep World and become a wage slave for the rest of my life. Something wouldn't let me do it, though. Sometimes, I think I'm like those wolves – the exact opposite of everything that's "tame."

CHAPTER SEVENTY-ONE

The Boys

Mom and John called David one evening while Heather was out hunting money to talk about Johnny. They said Johnny had come back from Florida. He was unemployed and homeless and stranded down around Athens, Ohio. They asked if we could help him out. When I came home the next morning, David told me the story. I still felt bad, in a way, about Buddy, I missed Johnny's humor and lopsided grin and Mom and John had helped us with bingo.

I called Mom and said, "Sure, he can stay out back and work here. We're always looking for people. David will jump right down there and grab him."

I figured we could get some badly needed help; at the same time, I'd take care of my stepbrother. It was the exactly the kind of generous thing Granny would've done. I came home after work one morning, and the same giggly, fun, sweet, eager-to-please Johnny I remembered was sitting there at the table. He never mentioned Buddy.

He stayed out back in a camper and helped cut grass and weed whack and fix simple stuff, freeing David to do more important tasks. We paid for everything: electric, heat, TV, his groceries, even some dental work. Johnny had become an expert outdoorsman who loved to archery hunt for deer. Rescue One was out in the country, so that was ideal. David started teaching him some big cat fundamentals. I thought Johnny might even make a career out of working around animals.

I kept some coolers stocked with beer on the front porch so everyone could sit around and have fun after workdays were done; of course, Johnny was the star attraction, telling wild stories and acting out all the parts. His favorite was about the time he and Luke ran across an unattended, beat-up Moped somewhere on West Broad. They managed to start it and putt off down the street, Luke driving and Johnny hanging on. In that 'hood, streetwalkers worked every corner. The boys pulled up to an intersection, where a toothless crackhead crone tried to bum a cigarette from them. They flipped her off and pulled away. That Moped was such a piece of junk that the geriatric pipehead ran them down, screaming. Johnny said he was flinging cigarettes to get her off their asses.

For six months or so, the arrangement was perfect, but Johnny couldn't stand to be separated from Luke. He asked if Luke could stay with him and help us, too. Johnny had worked out well, and I still remembered Luke and him as sweet, stoned kids happily scarfing Big Macs and fries in the z-28. Besides, they stood up for me against that stalker, and Luke had almost been killed.

As soon as Luke moved in, they began taking advantage of the fact that Heather was away so much. Every night, rowdy strangers showed up for loud parties. Things escalated into fistfights, huge bonfires, garbage thrown everywhere. It was like weekends back in Lockbourne.

Some of our volunteers were spending more time partying in the camper than caring for the animals. David should've stopped it, but he let it go. The cats were always edgy. It was only a matter of time before some drunk got mauled or left a gate unlocked so an angry predator could escape and wreak God knows what kind of havoc. I warned Johnny over and over to stop the nonsense. He laughed it off every time and promised to change, but the nightly chaos kept rolling.

I was showing two potential donors around the compound one afternoon. I walked them back to check out the cats and our enclosures; they were impressed and ready to write a fat check. When we came around the corner to the front of the log house, Johnny and Luke were sitting on the porch, loaded, beer cans scattered around them. I ordered them off.

Right in front of these lovely, rich, old people, Johnny shouted, "Fuck you! You don't tell me what to do, bitch! Kiss my ass!"

I went after him, meaning to kick the shit out of him right there. Luke restrained me.

I pushed him off and yelled, "You two idiots get your asses off my property now!"

The old people hurried to their car and sped down the driveway. Luke dragged Johnny away. The boys left and never came back. When Arletta found out what had happened, she stopped speaking to me again.

Only then did Mom and John slowly reveal the whole truth: Johnny had worn out his welcome with them and everyone else, except Luke. He had an explosive temper. When he drank, he was destructive and dangerous. They had to call the cops and have him removed more than once. He could never keep a job, never had a permanent home and was getting into deeper trouble with the law. I think he and Luke had been up to a lot more in that camper than swigging Little Kings.

'Thank goodness I threw them out of here before something horrible happened,' I thought. 'At least that's one problem I don't have to worry about anymore.'

CHAPTER SEVENTY-TWO

Big Fish

I should've seen the boys' behavior and the Imara incident as what they really were – omens. Rescue One was turning into a snake pit of anarchy and treachery. In the beginning, when I was there all the time, I made it very clear to everyone: 'This is my gig, mine!' Everything cruised along beautifully. Who knew that I'd have to become a full-time whore? I was distracted and absent, and the staff started taking advantage of it. They wasted my money, disregarded my orders, didn't show up for shifts, trashed my house. Although I wasn't directly paying them, I provided everything from gas cards to free use of any of my possessions. I genuinely cared about them, until they started treating Rescue One like a never-ending frat party and sending the bill to the kids.

David saw what was happening and, once again, did nothing to stop it. In fact, when I needed him most, the ego he'd kept buried for so long popped up. He started acting badass in front of the volunteers, openly defying me and threatening to leave me and the kids high and dry.

"To hell with this! I don't need this shit!" he'd shout and stomp down the driveway, forcing me to placate him in front of everyone.

He played 'poor me' in front of the staff and acted like

everything I'd worked and suffered and risked my life for was his now. I'd even become suspicious that Ellen, whom I'd trusted with my life and the lives of my kids for the past 15 years, was conspiring with him. 'I have to juggle all these balls and walk a tightrope alone, day and night, and you're challenging me?' I thought. 'Oh, hell no!'

I confronted David but got nothing but lies, excuses and denials. Had Dr. Burton seen that side of him years earlier and tried to warn me? I don't know, but I'd also ignored my own advice again: 'Be careful of the monsters you create or don't be surprised when they show up.'

I lived by one guiding principle: protect the kids at all costs. Once I got to that place, I had tunnel vision, and woe be unto the creature that wandered into my garden. However, by the time I saw the true faces of the people around me, I was too busy to stop and set everyone straight. I'd hooked another Big Fish and was busy reeling him in.

The first time he called Cherry Angels, the Big Fish sounded like a jerkoff. Lisa almost hung up without booking an appointment; however, when he said he was staying at the Sheraton Columbus Hotel on Capitol Square, a four-star place, she sent Heather on the call. He gave her $1000 just to go to dinner with him at Mitchell's Steakhouse, a pricey restaurant on North 3rd.

Once things got rolling, he called two or three times a week. The Ohio Theatre was right around the corner from Mitchell's, so we went there a lot, and then to the restaurant. Since I barely ate, I always had doggie bags of fancy food in my office fridge. Girlfriends kept the microwave humming. The Big Fish tipped heavily and took me shopping and bought me anything I wanted; all I had to do was point at a necklace or ring or broach and it was mine, no matter the cost. I couldn't enjoy any of those outings, though, because every date ended in something far worse than one of Grant's power-trip quickies.

Did you ever wonder what it's like to look a true predator in the face? I'll give you an example. Let's say his name is Arthur*, and he's an executive for an out-of-town marketing firm that has a consulting contract with a restaurant chain in Columbus. He's short, purple veins thread his pinkish jowls, his nose is bulbous, he tries to comb his thin white hair over his bald spot, he has a pot belly. Clothed in daylight, he looks like the average asshole you pass on the street every day; close the hotel door, douse the lights, strip off the business suit, and the predator reveals itself.

Arthur was the exception that proved the Stage Witch rule that every client is looking for something in addition to sex. All that that sicko wanted was sex – as raw and as filthy as possible. He fucked Heather in every hole, as hard as he could. He grabbed her tits and pussy and smacked her on the ass, while he told her what he was going to do to her in the vilest language you can imagine: "I'm going to fuck you dead"; "You won't be able to use that cunt for a month"; "This's the best-tasting cock you'll ever suck." It was like he read that shit in a fuck book or a dirty magazine and then spewed it out all over her in a disgusting shower.

No amount of therapy will ever erase the image of that revolting pervert framed in the bathroom door, naked, his hairy body silhouetted by hazy white light, coming to join me in the dark bed. Arthur the Wealthy Executive was no different than Melvin the Tweeker Sadist or Cyrus the Child Molester. The same beast lived inside them. They all figured they'd purchased me, body and soul, and had *carte blanche* to treat me any way they chose.

Arthur was too old and had too many health problems to perform unless he had an extremely heightened experience, which wasn't easy to provide because that old rooster had been around. Heather had to improvise her own Mata Hari routines: lots of lingerie and perfumes and lotions and dancing around naked without making it look choreographed. It was sickening work, but Heather had to pretend to be into it. Those sessions went on forever; the whole time, she had to tell him how she wanted him to screw her all night, where she wanted him to put his dick, how she couldn't wait to feel him inside her – all that sick garbage. I'd spent my whole life using men's fantasies against them; now, that sleazebag was using his fantasies to torment me.

I needed the money, though, and Arthur was a certainly a Big Fish. Over two years, he wrote me a couple hundred thousand in checks. He bought me a Camaro and lots of expensive jewelry. He took me to Florida for weeks at a time. We stayed at Pier 66 in Ft. Lauderdale and went to lovely restaurants and bars with his buddies from work. All of them were with escorts, too, living alternative lives outside their marriages. I tanned on the beach, mesmerized by the endless roll of waves, chain-smoked Marlboro Lights, washed handfuls of Trammies down with flutes of Kir Royale, shopped for shit I didn't need or even want, picked over extravagant lobster dinners and, night after night, searched the narrow, twisting corridors of my mind, pulling open doors, desperately looking for bronze unicorns or goofy stone puppies while a disgusting pig ravaged my body.

Arthur became so blatant that he paid me to come to his home city all the time. He told me his wife was an alcoholic who was abusive when she drank. He said he was going to divorce her, pay her off and marry me. He said we would live in Hawaii, and he'd give me money to send to the animal rescue I'd told him about. I was worn down, sick of the endless hassle. I thought, 'Okay, the hell with it. I'm not going to kill the goose and break the golden egg again. Angela can stay married to David, and Heather can live in Paradise with this old, unhealthy rich guy, who'll probably die soon anyway. If that's what I have to do to keep the kids safe, so be it.'

I'd no sooner made up my mind to jump on that ledge than the economic meltdown of '08 and '09 sapped the final bits of the Fred and Hidden Lake nest egg and cost me many of my heavy-hitter clients. They lost their unlimited expense accounts and stock options and fat Christmas bonuses, if not their jobs. Of course, Dr. Burton was still helping out, but that poor man had done so much for so long that I couldn't ask him for more. Duane was still a regular, but he'd become a dying breed, at best, and he wasn't truly loaded, to be honest.

At least I still had Arthur. He'd been bugging me about quitting nightwork; after the economy tanked, he didn't have to bother. The Cherry Angels phone almost stopped ringing. Arthur kept calling to tell me he loved me. He didn't come to Columbus for months, though, which cost me thousands. I was fighting rush-hour in the city one afternoon, when he called and started blathering about nothing. I was wondering why he was wasting my time, when his wife took the phone from him.

"Honey, you're nothing new," she said, very coolly. "He's been doing this for 20 years. You girls come and go. He's sick. He has early-onset dementia and has to go into a hospital."

The call had been a setup. I just knew that woman was about to put two and two together, drag Heather out into the light and destroy Rescue One. Arthur got back on the phone and said he loved his wife, they were working things out and our relationship was over. That calmly and selfishly, he hung up . . . and pushed me over the edge. The last reliable, substantial fiscal support for Rescue One was gone.

My stomach churned scalding liquid. My heart raced. I couldn't catch my breath. I felt like I was driving through a tunnel of intense white light, blind to the traffic jammed around me. The tunnel kept getting narrower and brighter. Then it went black.

I woke up in the parking lot of a fastfood place miles from downtown, with no memory of how I got there, forced to face the new reality for Rescue One: It was lock-and-load time. Lisa would have to turn every call into a gig; Heather would have to take on all comers; Angela would have to pray that God really doesn't send us troubles that he hasn't prepared us to handle. First, though, we were all three headed to the drive-through lane and a long, terrible night on our knees in the bathroom.

CHAPTER SEVENTY-THREE

Zanesville Redux

I somehow hung on for two more years. I'd always set boundaries for the things I would and would not do with a john; it sickens me to say it, but during that dark time, I was forced to jump over almost all of them. I was standing in the middle of 20 different flavors of fuck spreading away from me in shock waves, when Zanesville rose up out of my subconscious like an angry black dragon.

The night of Oct. 18, 2011, Heather was at her office in Canal Winchester, hoping that Lisa could score a couple gigs. The Nextel started blowing up, not with clients, though. People were screaming that a nutjob had cut open his cages and turned his exotic animals loose. Dozens of big predators were swarming the hills of central Ohio in the dark and the rain. Cops were shooting them.

It was all so unbelievable and confusing that Angela needed a couple of beats to shake Heather out of her head and realize they were talking about the Thompson farm in Zanesville. I turned on the news. Reports said Terry Thompson had smeared himself with chicken guts and blown his brains out in the same driveway I followed up to his house three and a half years earlier. Cats had partially eaten his body, reports said.

God only knows how, but the animals I saw there had hung on

for all that time, then as soon as they were released, cops slaughtered them. 'Surviving in those horrible conditions wasn't enough to earn some justice for those kids?' I thought. 'Now, they have to be frightened and gunned down by maniacs?'

I had to put all my other bullshit aside and rush to Zanesville again. I called Dr. Burton. He said that he and some people from OSU's veterinary school would be right behind me. We were headed to the Thompson farm in force.

I still had Det. Steve Welker's cell number. I started calling him and leaving messages: "Please don't do this! Don't murder those kids! Please stop! We're on our way! We'll speed! Let us save them!"

He didn't return my calls. I soon found out why. The cops already had an "animal expert" on the way: Jungle Jack Hanna. I thought, 'They're going to let that ignorant fool grandstand just so he and the zoo don't come out of this looking bad.'

Jack Hanna had never rescued animals. He actually bred exotics. When he was younger, he displayed cubs in a front window to entice people into the pet shop he owned in Tennessee. His lioness ripped off a neighbor kid's arm. Jack didn't have the experience to know that a frightened animal anywhere near its cage will go back inside. No matter how shitty, that enclosure is its safe haven.

Jack Hanna went to Zanesville that night for one reason: He wanted some face time in the spotlight. Jack made his money and became famous by creating a false image of himself, like

Steve Irwin, or, I suppose, like I did with Heather. I'm certainly not against somebody turning a buck, but Jack should stick to kiddie TV and the lecture circuit and leave the actual animals out of it.

I heard him on the news vowing to help all the poor exotics in Ohio. If he really felt that way, he could've used his star power 20 years earlier to stop irresponsible private ownership. He had to have known that something should be done to avert an inevitable calamity, yet he went on *David Letterman* using animals as props and hosted petting parties and photo-baby shoots for fat cats at the zoo. He talked against private ownership, while sending exactly the opposite message by showing the public how cuddly and cute exotic cubs are.

Long before Zanesville, I called him to ask for help. "Jack, get us on the talk shows," I said. "Jack, engage. You're on these shows. Say something. Get involved. Make this stop."

He sounded like I was bothering him, as he informed me that he was standing in his Montana vacation home. "Angela, you're too controversial, and I'm at the latter part of my career. I'm not getting involved," he said.

Jack signed off on the plan to shoot the animals in Zanesville. Of the 56 exotics Terry Thompson turned loose, 49 were killed, some of them in their cages. A monkey was found later in a lion's stomach. The six left alive went to the Columbus Zoo – on Jack's orders, with no legal authority and no permission from Marian Thompson. Eventually, she got them all back, except for a spotted leopard that was killed when a guillotine gate fell on her at the zoo and broke her neck. Marian quickly dumped those last five animals on another owner.

Let me be fair: Jack wasn't the only one responsible for Zanesville. For decades, the state of Ohio had turned a blind eye to the exotic problem. Anyone who had half a brain and was drowning in the flood of dangerous wild animals, like I was, knew the dam had to break sooner or later. How smart do you have to be to recognize that a pet tiger in private hands is going to turn out bad? The politicians and bureaucrats caved to pressure from exotic breeders and sellers and roadside zoo operators, allowing thousands of innocent animals to be abused, exploited, killed. For 15 years, no one listened when I raved, "What're we going to do about these animals?" They ignored me or wrote me off as crazy or saw me as just another Diana Cziraky. Meanwhile, every time I went out on a rescue, the people who were elected, appointed or hired to deal with the problem were MIA.

USDA was also culpable, of course. USDA has actually done tremendous harm by putting on a fraudulent show to taxpayers to keep the money machine humming. It's just another version of 'Fake it till you make it,' like I learned to do when I was still a kid. Dirtbag breeders gave USDA the finger and kept operating for years, while the worthless simpletons played with their dicks like Coco and collected their paychecks and let me and a few other good guys take it in the face. That statement is no exaggeration. Lorenza Pearson, a breeder and seller from Akron who accessorized his clothing with live boa constrictor neckwear, kept more than 80 exotics on a filthy, rundown property that was somehow USDA-licensed. Pearson allowed a black leopard to roam the house. For some reason, the media reported that it was a tiger, but I know for a fact that it was a leopard. The cat killed his two-year-old son. Fourteen years later, one of his tigers mauled his two-year-old grandson. Nine years after that, another of his tigers bit a USDA inspector. USDA attempted to shut him down, but Pearson kept his permit – and his dangerous wild animals – throughout an eight-year court fight. His animals were finally seized in 2008, mostly because local officials got sick of his ass and jumped into the battle.

I didn't go to Zanesville that night. Once I heard Jack was there, I knew they'd never let me near the property, no matter how much of a fit I pitched. The news photos of dead exotic cats that had been dragged through the mud behind tractors and thrown into piles were heartbreaking.

The official version of "The Zanesville Massacre," which cops and the state pimped, said Terry Thompson was narcissistic and eccentric, a Vietnam vet who was very rogue and felt like he'd been screwed over by the world. The story emphasized that the Zanesville cops, Muskingum County sheriff's office and local humane society had been called out to his compound dozens of times on animal cruelty complaints. His animals were always escaping and roaming around – probably looking for food. Thompson had threatened to shoot his animals or set them on any cop who stepped on his property. Instead, he turned the animals loose and shot himself as an act of revenge, so the story goes.

If that is what really happened, I can understand at least part of Thompson's motivation: He came out of prison deeply in debt and facing the crushing daily grind of finding enough money to maintain what he'd created. His farm was going to hell right in front of him. His wife had also left him. That loss or some other very dark, private thought spooked him. I understand all that, because I went through a lot of the same misery.

Obviously, the Humane Society of the United States saw a connection between Terry Thompson and me, as well. Just after the Zanesville Massacre, HSUS released an updated version of a report called *Ohio's Fatal Attractions*, which was basically a rogue's gallery of terrible exotic owners in the state. My name was right there beside Terry and Marian Thompson. HSUS had culled through years of Dr. Markin's site visits and found enough to make me look like a sadist running a torture chamber, even though my sins were venial: a couple of dirty food receptacles, a rusty piece of fence, a torn tarp and keeping tigers who didn't get along in the same enclosure because I hadn't had time to move them yet.

Ohio's Fatal Attractions was posted on the internet for the whole world to view, forever; it left another stain on Angela Harter's name that is blacker than any could ever be on Heather Smith's.

CHAPTER SEVENTY-FOUR

Endangered Species

After I got over the first shock of Zanesville, I was happy in a way. I thought, 'They can't sweep it under the rug anymore. Now, the whole world is talking about an irresponsible breeder who kept kids in hell. The state and USDA will finally have to deal with this.' My mistake was giving the state of Ohio and the feds credit for having enough sense to tell the good guys from the dirtbags. I was the one dropping her G-string to take in animals that everyone else had allowed to be tormented, so I considered myself a good guy.

Yet again, I was too naïve to sniff out the play. In early 2011, just before leaving office, Gov. Ted Strickland signed an emergency ban on exotic ownership, partly because a bear killed a young volunteer at the farm of a scumbag breeder named Sam Mazzola, near Cleveland. That tragedy wasn't the only one involving exotics to have occurred in Ohio. Another bear escaped and bit a cop in Mt. Gilead. A cougar mauled a girl in Mingo Junction. One of Kenny Hetrick's bears flipped and tore him up to the tune of $170,000 in medical bills. A venomous pet snake killed a fireman in Dayton; another killed its owner in North College Hill. A boa strangled its owner in Cincinnati. No one knows how many other animal attacks went unreported, like the time Jewels jumped me, or misrepresented, like when Serena sliced Denny's leg. Regardless, almost as soon as John

Kasich took office, he let the ban lapse, probably for no better reason than he's a Republican and Strickland a Democrat.

Within months, another young volunteer found Mazzola dead, chained naked and facedown to a bed, a leather mask over his face and a dildo shoved down his throat, and Zanesville exploded. Zanesville was the biggest story in the world, and a lot of people blamed Kasich for it. Since he was planning a run for president, he had to do something dramatic to rescue his reputation. The state immediately began proposing all kinds of strict new regulations to fix a problem about which they were totally ignorant. I realized the fallout was going to hurt everyone, not just the breeders and sellers.

I was the one freaking now. The market crash, the internet and people's screwed-up morals were destroying Cherry Angels. Why would anyone pay Heather a lot of money for sex when he could jump on a computer and find thousands of amateurs willing to do anything, anywhere, anytime, for nothing? I'd become an endangered species who could never afford the extensive improvements to Rescue One that would be necessary to keep my kids.

In the depths of winter 2012, hope finally arrived. Winter is always the most stressful time for exotic animals and their owners. Just when it got coldest that year, some director or producer or something came to my gate. He said he was from *National Geographic* television and was working on a new program called "Animal Intervention." He said they wanted the world to see the difficulties that exotic animal sanctuaries face and how extensive the exotic problem is in America. He mentioned that the host was Alison Eastwood, Clint Eastwood's daughter, a true animal lover.

The guy explained that to help us attract support, "Animal Intervention" wanted to show a day in the life of Rescue One. I listened to the guy's pitch, thinking, 'The state might start seizing and destroying animals any day. You have one of the biggest sanctuaries in Ohio. If they're keeping a hit list, you have to be very high up on it. Extreme situation, extreme measures.'

For the kids, I signed to do "Animal Intervention."

On the day they filmed, Eastwood and her crew were with David around the lion enclosures. I wasn't excited about having my face – and Heather's – broadcast around the world. I put on a heavy scarf, pulled my floppy hat low and slipped away to the other side of the compound. I walked the gravel paths between the enclosures, making sure that the tigers' water containers weren't frozen.

When Rosco tiger saw me, he chuffed and lifted a paw. I made some cat sounds back at him, and he came to the fence. He was rubbing his cheeks against the chain link and yakking away. I was answering him. We had a conversation, not that I understood what he was saying in so many words, but we were definitely communicating on some level.

Until I heard his feet crunch the gravel, I hadn't noticed that one of the cameramen was following me. When I turned around, he was standing there with his mouth hanging open. I thought he was going to tell me how amazing it was to see that kind of interaction between a human and a tiger and how fortunate he was to have shot the footage, but he was upset.

"You talked to that tiger!" he said. "I saw you do it!"

He sounded just like a cop accusing me of a crime and waiting for me to either confess or deny it. Heather flared. I thought, 'Fuck you, jerkoff' and started to go after him. For the greater good, Ang held Heather in check. I kept my mouth shut, walked away and avoided everyone until they left.

I waited impatiently for "Animal Intervention" to air, thinking, 'The public will finally know we're here and see what we do and go through. They'll step up and help us save these precious kids.'

CHAPTER SEVENTY-FIVE

Mommy Will Be Okay

Slow as business was, Heather had to go back to work – at discount rates. Someone called when she was on her way to a gig and said, "Red alert." I flew to Rescue One. When I got there, Jewels was lying in the back corner of her enclosure. Everyone was afraid to go in with her because she'd suddenly turned mean. Something was obviously very wrong. She almost never stood up. When she did, she staggered around like she was drunk, her head weaving and weaving. She drooled constantly. She stopped eating, and that's the beginning of the end for a big cat. I put whole steaks, chunks of horsemeat, deer haunches, fish, chicken in front of her, praying, "Please, God, just let her take one bite. Please." A nibble, a lick, would've been a blessed event. Just like when she was a kitten, Jewels ignored the meat.

I'd been through that exact hell before. Just a few weeks earlier, Apollo fell over and didn't get up. One minute, he was romping around with Zeus; the next, he was on his death bed, suffering terribly. Just like with Sybre that time, we didn't know what happened, and nothing we did helped. We sped Apollo to Dr. Burton's office. His bloodwork came back with an elevated white-cell count, but that was the only abnormality.

We brought him home, and, for weeks, I slept in his den, running med bags and freezing. It sucked: cold as hell;

volunteers all off for the holidays; Apollo semiconscious; Heather unable to make money. I spent Christmas, 2011, crying over a dying tiger that I didn't know how to help. My Christmas prayer was for God to either take Apollo or heal him. I finally nodded off very late one night; when I opened my eyes the next morning, Apollo's face was looming over me as if nothing had happened, exactly as Sybee had done. I thought I was dreaming. None of us could figure it out, but we were overjoyed to have him back.

Less than a month later, the same thing happened to Jewels. She stared, fixedly, at nothing, shaking her head, panting, slobbering. She went down again. I lay beside her as she writhed through convulsion after convulsion, trembling and quivering, her paws thrashing with every wave. I could see the body of a cougar; Jewels wasn't in there, though. Every once in a while, she came back and looked at me, and I hoped desperately that she would miraculously recover, too. Every time, she drifted away.

Things had gone from 'oh shit' to 'oh fuck.' I craved a bushel of sloppy cheeseburgers and greasy fries or a pizza – or two pizzas – bigger than a truck tire, with every topping on them – something to bury the desperation that was gnawing inside me like a dumpster rat. Since I had to hold it together for Jewels, I substituted a handful of Trammies for the food.

Jewels had to go to Dr. Burton. David rolled around a carry cage. We got her in it but not before she broke one of her upper fangs by biting at the chain link. We sped to the clinic. Dr.

Burton met us and examined her.

"Ang, this tooth is broken to the root," he said. "We have to dig it out of her gums and jaw. If we don't, it will abscess, and it will be a painful death."

He spent hours forcepping shards of fang out of her gums and running tests. He couldn't find what was wrong.

We brought Jewels home and tried to feed her liquefied turkey and antibiotics through a tube, just like when she was a kitten. She wouldn't take it. She became weaker. She had to return to Animal Care Unlimited, but David was afraid to touch her. He was outside, preparing her carry cage again and pulling up the van, while I stayed with her. Jewels stood and tried to walk. She was too weak. She sat on her haunches and looked at me. The planet stopped; I was transfixed. I swear I heard the words, 'It's over, Ang. Goodbye.' She collapsed.

I held her and whispered in her ear, "Go, Jewels, just go. Mommy will be okay."

At 11:48 pm, on the last Sunday in February, Jewels went. I watched her lifeforce ebb. Her eyes dimmed and shuttered. Her lungs stopped filling in mid-breath. Her chest collapsed. The tiny kitten who'd snored on my lap and sucked on my ear lobes because she was taken from her mother when she was too young – my joy, my companion, my bedmate, the light of my darkass life – was gone.

The blood drained from my face and froze in the pit of my stomach. My throat tightened, but I couldn't cry. I was numb. If someone had stabbed me in the back with a butcher knife, I wouldn't have blinked. I got in the car and drove to Canal Winchester on autopilot.

Dr. Burton kept calling the Rescue One number. I didn't answer. Lisa took some calls for Cherry Angels. I got up and put on Heather and stood in front of the mirror. She looked haggard. Her skin was as dry and yellow as parchment and creased with worry lines and crow's feet. Her eyes were red and swollen, but they still blazed.

Heather exploded. I stepped back and listened to her motherfuck everybody who'd made it necessary for her to exist: Mom, The Hag, Cyrus Jackson, The Stage Witches, Uncle Bo, the exotic breeders and dealers, Grant Campbell, USDA, the state of Ohio, Angela Harter. Then she hit the makeup kit and got her schedule from Lisa.

The weather had been unnaturally warm for days, but that night, the wind rose around midnight, and the temperature plummeted by 30 degrees in a few hours. Heather didn't even bother to put on a coat, just went out into the blustery cold in the Slutty Professional outfit and worked until almost dawn. I don't recall any details from those gigs and didn't make any notes about them. God only knows where Heather went that night and what she did and with whom.

CHAPTER SEVENTY-SIX

Some Bastard

When I came back to the office the next morning, I collapsed on the couch, still wearing the Slutty Professional getup. I couldn't put two thoughts together, except for the connection between Apollo and Jewels. I thought, 'Those two kids exhibited the exact same symptoms within weeks of each other, and that's a coincidence? No fucking way.'

The answer dawned on me: 'Some bastard is poisoning my kids!'

I was parked outside Animal Care Unlimited by seven. Dr. Burton pulled in. As he got out of his car, I walked up on him, startled him. He spun around and froze. I was a hot mess. I had on pajamas and a robe, my hair was a fright wig, I was smoking a cigarette.

When I came close enough for him to tell it was me, he whispered, "She died, didn't she?"

I couldn't bring myself to say it.

We went inside. Everyone there knew something was terribly wrong. It was hard for me to string sentences together, but I managed to tell Dr. Burton what I thought had happened. I knew by his reaction that he'd never suspected anyone could do anything so vicious. He said he wanted to perform an autopsy.

"No!" I said.

"You've got to let me do this, Ang," he insisted.

I said, "You're not going to cut her up, are you?"

"Ang, I promise," he said. "I'll just make a little incision. I have to get a couple things out, and then we'll be able handle that."

After he was done, David and I brought Jewels home, made a casket out of spare lumber and buried her. She was safe in the ground, at home. Nobody could hurt her again.

CHAPTER SEVENTY-SEVEN

Freefall

I ran back to Canal Winchester, wrung out and in freefall, crashlanded, flat-lined. I could feel this out-of-touchness creeping over me, like I was floating above myself, watching an actor in a movie. My memories had turned into shadows flickering across a faraway desert. My past was gone – no kids, no clients, no family. Light, dark, color, shape, time, sound – none of it meant anything. They all swirled together into a new unreality. I felt like I was trapped in a bummer acid trip that would never end.

I was mute. I couldn't formulate enough clear thoughts even to brush my teeth. I smoked cigarettes, washed down Trammies with Diet Mountain Dew and lay awake on the couch, too unsteady to stand and walk. I cried until I couldn't catch my breath. Even the thought of food gagged me. After a few days, the stink of desolation rose from my body. I managed to stumble into the shower and turn the handle. When I suddenly got wet, I couldn't understand why. I looked up into the spray, trying to remember the word for "water."

Occasionally, I became so exhausted that I fell asleep. Well, I didn't actually sleep. It was like I was in a trance, a fugue state. I couldn't rest. Nightmares shook me awake. I lay there feeling like somebody had wrapped me in a sheet and beaten me with a baseball bat.

One day, I noticed a photo of a tiger hanging on the wall. I had no idea what it was doing there, but it seemed crooked. I got up and tried to straighten it. Every time I adjusted it on the nail and stepped back, it hung off kilter in a new way. For some reason, nothing was more important to me than straightening that picture. I frantically moved it and stepped back and checked it, over and over, cursing; it slid from level every time, like it had a will of its own. I fell back on the couch, sobbing.

Before dawn one morning, I felt people around me. I'm saying "people," but they were more like presences, eight or 10 of them in different parts of the living room. They weren't saying anything or even acknowledging my presence in any way, just staring off in various directions. I didn't know if they were the spirits of people who once loved me and had passed on or guardian angels or what. I didn't know if they were judging me or were upset because I was so distraught.

"I know you're there," I said.

I asked them to help me. They paid no attention, but they kept coming back, morning after morning, ignoring me, which only agitated me more. 'I'm going to lie here and put up with this? For what?' I thought. 'I'm not that kind of dog. You kick me, and I'm going to bite. Don't I have the right to say I don't want to play this stupid game anymore?'

I went out into the garage and sat in my Camaro. I saw that the speedometer registered 180. I thought, 'Man, if I could get this thing up to 200 and hit a bridge, all this pain would end in an instant.'

I almost went back inside for the keys, but something stopped me and made me realize that suicide didn't make any sense, either. For good reason, I've been afraid of the dark since I was a kid. I thought, 'If you commit the ultimate sin, maybe you'll go straight to Hell, and it'll be nothing but darkness. Maybe all the scariest monsters from your worst nightmares will be there waiting for you, and you'll be stuck there for eternity.'

I was just like those poor animals had been at the Thompson farm – caged, helpless, unable to escape even by offing myself.

A week or so later, I was on the couch under a blanket, more asleep than awake, miserable. Dawn was peeking through the sliding-glass doors. I looked up and saw something drifting down from the ceiling. It was a fantastic purplish-blue color, a shade I never saw before or since. It was like a hologram, not any element from our world – not earth or wind or fire or water. It was about the size of a basketball and pulsing, very alive and very real. It drifted down to my feet. It was Jewels. I could smell her and hear her purring. I felt her say, "Get up, Angie. I'm here. Don't worry. I love you." Then she was gone.

I desperately wanted to know where she went and whether she was all right. Nothing except finding her and talking to her was going to make me feel better. I didn't care what it cost – financially, emotionally, spiritually – or who I had to face down, or where I had to go. I had to know whether she was in Heaven, if she was happy or sad or in pain, if I'd ever see her again. I had to know, or I was going to lose it altogether.

"Lily Dale" – the name hit my head like it had been fired from a gun. I'd seen *No One Dies in Lily Dale*, a documentary about a small community of psychics in upstate New York, but I hadn't thought of it for a long time. Lily Dale is supposed to be the most spiritual place in the world, the place where all the good mediums hang out. Then I remembered Grandpa's death and the weird tale about my great grandmother. I have no rational way to explain what drew me to their house that night or how Grandpa had returned to life after Pearl Harbor. ESP? Déjà vu? A sixth sense? I've always believed in them in a vague way, but I saw all spiritualists as grifters preying on desperate, vulnerable suckers. However, as I lay on the couch in Canal Winchester that morning, it was suddenly hell-bent urgent that I get in touch with Lily Dale, even though I had no plan beyond that.

'The hell with it,' I thought. 'At least it's a shot.'

CHAPTER SEVENTY-EIGHT

Lily Dale

Even though my computer skills are limited, I managed to get on the internet and look up Lily Dale. I called the first number I saw. A medium named Sherry answered.

"Oh, oh, I can feel you from here," she said. "What's wrong with you?"

"These presences around me are irritating," I mumbled. "I don't know what they want. I don't know what I'm going to do. My life is a train wreck."

She said, "Okay," and waited for me to go on. I tried to tell her about Jewels. Before I could get it all out, she said, "Honey, you need immediate help. My daughter Robin lives in Wisconsin. I'll give you her phone number. Call her right now. She has the talent. She's in tune with animals more than anyone."

When I reached Robin, I didn't give her any details. I said that I'd lost Jewels, my cat, and I wanted to know where she was.

"Oh, Jewels is a cougar," she said. "Jewels is lying down. She's a big girl. Her front paws are crossed."

I'd never seen another cougar do that, not Sapphy or Montana, none of them.

Suddenly, I was paying careful attention.

"Where is she?" I asked. "Is she okay? Is she happy?"

Robin explained that as a translator in a three-way communication, she could only relay what Jewels was saying. A lot of the time, though, she would have no idea what it meant.

"Jewels is telling me that she remembers you talking to a serpent," she said. "She says you didn't even realize it when you were doing it."

'What the hell? She means Jake the Snake,' I thought.

"Jewels says that when you looked at each other that night on the back porch, you both knew," Robin said.

I was dumbstruck. Somehow, in the crazy spinning of the universe, Robin had found my little girl. I shivered and gripped the phone tighter.

"I miss my baby," I said.

I heard a peculiar, low cackle, and Robin said, "Jewels is laughing."

"Why's that?" I asked, offended.

"Jewels says *you're* the baby," she said. "Jewels is much older than you. She finds it funny that you're calling her the baby when you're really the baby."

When I told her I didn't understand, Robin said, "I don't know exactly what she means, either, but Jewels said a day where she is now is a lifetime here. I can tell you that Jewels is a shapeshifter. She has existed for a very long time and has taken on many forms."

I asked Robin again exactly where Jewels was.

She said, "The best way I can explain it is that Jewels is not a cougar now. Jewels is energy joined with other energy, but she still knows she's Jewels."

"Is she in Heaven?" I asked. "Is she sitting on a cloud? Where is she?"

"It's color. It's light," Robin said. "It's everything great. It's all the happiness and kindness that we can't begin to imagine. She remembers everything. She loves you. She's very worried about you. Jewels is giving me pictures of you pacing on a linoleum floor."

'How could this woman know the floor in my kitchen is linoleum?' I wondered.

"She said you're hoping for some kind of help," Robin said. "She sees you waiting, scared, trying to find a solution to a very big problem."

I'd always hid all the stress I was under from the kids. I never wanted them to see the things I was doing for money or feel the pain I was living with. Jewels, evidently, had known exactly what I was going through.

"She's showing me teeth, teeth, teeth," Robin said. "One of her top fangs is gone. I don't know what that means."

I almost reeled off the chair. No one except David, Dr. Burton and I knew that Jewels had broken a fang down to the root the night we rushed her to the clinic.

"That's what killed her, when she broke her teeth?" I asked.

"Nope," Robin said. "It was her time to go. Jewels says

everything happens for a reason, and she doesn't want you to be upset about her being gone. First, she's not gone. Second, her death had nothing to do with teeth. Third, she said this was all meant to happen."

"What was meant to happen?" I said.

"I don't know," Robin said. "I can only tell you what she said. She says she's so worried about you that she doesn't want to take another form yet. She's going to stay with you for a long time, maybe for years. She'll be even closer to you now than she was before she passed, although you might not know it."

"I don't want her to do that," I said. "I don't want her to worry about me. Tell her to be happy. Tell her I'm happy as long as she's safe."

I offered to pay Robin for her time, but she turned the money down. I said goodbye and hung up. I felt like a house had been lifted from my shoulders.

CHAPTER SEVENTY-NINE

Lightning Strike

Before I could fully wrap my head around what happened with Robin and Jewels, Dr. Burton called and said, "You were right, Angie. Someone poisoned her. I have the proof."

He'd discovered crystals in Jewels' kidneys. Someone had probably soaked meat in antifreeze and thrown it into the enclosure, he said. Whoever did it knew that cats like the taste of antifreeze; they'll eat it like a treat. The active ingredient in it – ethylene glycol – is lethal, the death slow and agonizing, sadistically cruel. The most insidious thing about antifreeze poisoning is that the symptoms mimic many other problems, so it's hard to tell exactly what's wrong, even with bloodwork.

I was certain the murderer had done the same thing to Apollo; Jewels, though, had been the real target. Jewels' enclosure wasn't easy to pick out. Apollo and Zeus were on the northwestern corner of the property, 50 feet or so from the back of the house, while Jewels was right off the porch. David had built a ramp and a swinging door that let her go in and out of her living room enclosure as she pleased, so she spent a lot of time indoors. If you didn't know where she was, you couldn't find her. Plus, the dogs went nuts anytime a stranger showed up, and no one had heard any such ruckus. I loved all the kids, but anybody who knew anything about me knew that Jewels was my first and most cherished. The murderer had to be someone close to me.

I was convinced that Apollo had been collateral damage. Jewels' killer was either doing a dry run on a more accessible animal to see how much antifreeze it would take to kill her or had made several trips to poison her slowly or to catch her when she was outside. Whichever scenario was true, someone had killed Jewels to hurt me as much as possible. At the time, I was too overcome by grief to sort through suspects. Besides, the bulimia had descended on me again, with all its horrid consequences.

Jewels' death had a result the killer didn't anticipate, however: Robin had found her on the other side, and talking to her woke me up. I began to process everything that had happened and honestly assess where Rescue One was. The conclusions I came to were a lightning strike to the heart. For 15 years, I'd saved every animal I could, fixed every mess, won a lot of fights, conjured up a lot of miracles. In the long run, all the money I brought in didn't help Rescue One. I still had to defend my kids from monsters who wanted to destroy or exploit them. My property was vulnerable; I was afraid that someone would sabotage my enclosures and release my animals. I was broke, I didn't have enough help, people were begging me to accept more animals. Jewels was gone, Joshie and Trinity and Imara and Sammy and AJ and Coco and Gem and many of the other Engesser lions were dead, Ellen was very sick with cancer, Grandpa died, Granny was in a nursing home, Don and Marge were dead, Dr. Markin retired, David betrayed me. I was used up.

It was March, but December would surely come again. The vision of being stuck in dead winter, with those precious babies depending on me, and not having the money, being unable to solve the problems, petrified me. I couldn't play Russian roulette anymore. The consequences were too serious.

The shadowy figure of Jewels' killer haunted my thoughts, but I shoved away the question of who murdered her and drove back to Lancaster. I stood in the front yard, just at the top of the driveway, and looked up at the screened-in porch and scanned the enclosures. I was afraid the earth was about to open and swallow Rescue One straight down into Hell.

The state was on a mission to prove that it bore no responsibility for Zanesville, that a bunch of crazed exotic animal owners were the real culprits. I knew we were all about to become object lessons that would demonstrate just how heroic and public-minded the governor and his henchmen really were. Terry Thompson was conveniently gone; I was sure I was next. Getting me would be like getting Thompson after the fact, a move that would wash some of the stigma from Kasich. They were going to rid Ohio of every dangerous exotic, even if they had to confiscate or kill them. Then they would pretend the animals had never existed. Kasich wanted to make them extinct in the public consciousness – out of state, out of mind.

'It's not fair,' I thought. 'It's not these kids' fault. They shouldn't have to pay for human stupidity. I don't care what I have to do to save them. I'm not going to walk away and let them die.'

I didn't know if I could live with the step I was about to take, but if I didn't take it, my kids would be dead, and their deaths would be on me. I knew I could never live with that. I went inside to search for the one agonizing solution that might save them. Fortunately, I kept every scrap of paper having to do with my animals. I found the phone number for the Global Federation of Animal Sanctuaries. GFAS, if you meet their exacting care standards and pay for the privilege, will certify you as a legitimate exotic animal sanctuary. We'd toyed with the idea of becoming certified. Membership in that exclusive club seemed way beyond my means and a practical impossibility, since GFAS almost never certifies small sanctuaries. Ellen, though, was confident she could pull it off, no matter the odds. She'd been working on that project when she got sick, and I was too busy hustling money to pick up the slack.

When I called GFAS, I was so hysterical that I scared the woman who answered. I finally pulled myself together enough to tell her who I was and ask her if it was possible to find reputable sanctuaries that would care for my animals for the rest of their lives. The woman said she would make some inquiries and get back to me. I hung up, then called USDA and surrendered Animal Welfare Act license 31-C-0135.

I prayed again, this time that I hadn't waited too long for GFAS – or anyone else – to rescue my kids.

CHAPTER EIGHTY

Bless The Beasts and Kids

Moving big cats is difficult, dangerous and expensive. I had more than two dozen kids who needed to leave Ohio immediately. The paperwork alone would be mountainous. We needed transport vehicles, drivers, handlers. Before any legit sanctuary would even think about taking them, the animals had to have physicals and shots. Every exotic animal person we knew said the A-list sanctuaries were full. I was afraid my kids would end up in shitholes run by soulless dirtbags. Even if we found open spots in real rescues, transporting the animals would cost a small fortune. I hadn't worshipped Mammon faithfully enough to pay for such a mass move; getting my kids to safety seemed impossible.

GFAS said it took "divine intervention" to locate the spaces and the $45,000 needed to move the kids into them. Bobbi Brink, who owns Lions, Tigers and Bears, a beautiful sanctuary in California, would handle transportation. Bobbi travels all over the country, moving abused and neglected exotics to legitimate sanctuaries, including her own.

Money was an issue, and logistics were an issue, but moving big predators is also straight-up hazardous duty, no matter what. There's only a few ways to get a dangerous wild animal into a transport cage: protect yourself as much as possible while you nudge it along; open the gate and wait until it eventually wanders in out of curiosity or irritation; tempt it with food, which can also take a long time; or sedate it. I owned too many animals – almost all of them big cats – to stand around waiting. They had to be darted.

In the movies, some *bwana* dickhead shoots a lion with a dart gun, and the animal immediately rolls over and goes to sleep. That's not how it happens in real life. A dart gun is reliable only when the animal is contained in a clinical situation so a vet can weigh it and determine the exact amount of tranqs necessary. In an emergency, the animals are so off in the rafters that darting doesn't work predictably. Once an animal tenses up, its body becomes like a sheet of iron. Even if you manage to get a needle in it, the drugs won't take effect for 15 or 20 minutes. Underestimate the dose, and it doesn't knock the cat down at all. The animal gets hit, freaks, does its damage and then hides somewhere and hunkers down, causing a new – and worse – set of problems. Overestimate the dose, and the animal goes into cardiac arrest. Even very experienced veterinarians like Dr. Burton have a hard time judging the correct amount for each animal. We had to say our prayers, wing it and take our chances.

Over two carbon-copy days in May of 2012, GFAS, Bobbi Brink, Dr. Burton and his staff and a volunteer group from Dayton showed up to move the kids. I'd be lying if I said I was coherent for all of those two days. The move tore me up so bad that I can recall only flashes and pieces:

The sunlight is not golden or even yellow, but greenish, like absinthe I drank in France, and so bright it hurts my eyes and makes the bare tree limbs look like they're etched into the bone-white sky. The sun is so bright I feel like nature is giving me the finger.

Dr. Burton hits Sapphy cougar with a dart in one of the dens we built into the living room, among the tiger throws and framed lion photos and cougar figurines and feeding and medication charts. She's been high-strung since some pimply-faced teenager driving a rattletrap Chevy dumped her on my doorstep, and she's scared. Searching for a way to comfort her, I say, "Sapphy, I'm right here. Calm down, Sapphy. You're fine, hon." The drugs turn her into a double armload of slobbering cat, dazed and twitching in a wheeled transport cage that looks like something from a circus clown routine. Her golden eyes are open and glowing, without seeing. Because of the way I raised her and all my kids, Sapphy and I have a very deep bond. I feel it snap, and just like that, I sense her spirit leaving her body. She's not Sapphire anymore. She's a mountain lion on drugs. We don't know each other.

Gage wakes up while we're moving him into a transport cage and turns into a roaring, struggling monster. The former cop who runs the rescue group throws a blanket over Gage's head, and he and David and I pile on and wrestle the stoned-out tiger into the cage. Gage jumps up, runs and smashes his head into the bars so hard that he bends them and scares the piss out of a volunteer standing there.

Zeus is sitting on one of the concrete culverts we put in the twins' enclosure, his nose in the air, blithely watching everyone bustle around the property. He looks regal, godly, like he has the final say on everything that happens. He doesn't.

Misty, a white hybrid, barks and barks, as if she's calling a volunteer to the wolf compound; when he walks toward the cage, she tucks her tail and scurries into her den.

A veterinarian from the Cleveland Zoo says Jabouhti is beyond help; his fate had been sealed from the day he was born; no sanctuary can care for him; he has to be put down; I have to be "reasonable." I call the death card for my special-needs boy.

Sugar Bear lies in his shady corn crib like a lazy fat dude loafing on the couch while everyone else works their asses off.

Someone with that crew from Dayton is creeping around, taking pictures of his buddies holding up the heads of unconscious cats, like my kids are hunting trophies. I stare at him until he feels the daggers in his neck and slinks away.

I'm all over the property, telling Dr. Burton which animal to dart next, lining up the correct transport cages, straining to help lift massive cats. If I can just keep moving, maybe I can avoid the misery that I know is stalking me.

The fire whistle in downtown Lancaster sounds, signaling noon, and the wolves howl – their eerie, daily choral recital.

I'm so tired that I feel myself wilting. I catch my reflection in a window. My hair is soaked with sweat and hanging from under my pink Superman ball cap and plastered against my neck. My bra straps have slid from my shoulders under my wet grey tank top. I pull a Marlboro Light out of a pack and take a lighter from my shorts. I remember not to smoke around the kids and put the cigarette and lighter atop an air-conditioning unit and go into an enclosure to knead Skin-So-Soft into Apollo's ears so that fleas and gnats don't swarm him while he's unconscious.

A volunteer is carrying a gun, a big .45 automatic in a holster. I start to jump him for daring to bring a firearm around my kids, but I realize that this guy has no idea that by coming to Rescue One, he'd unconsciously agreed that this day could be his last. Every time I was around my animals, I said, out loud, that I might die, and if I did, it would not be their fault. I chose to be around them; they had no choice. I have a lot of other stuff to worry about, so I walk away from the guy without bothering to say, 'You might feel secure with your pistol, but, believe me, it doesn't matter. I don't care how many guns you have, the likelihood of killing a tiger before it gets to you is less than winning the lottery.' I figure he'll learn that lesson on his own. Or not.

I catch a whiff of something wrong – something off-kilter and foul creeping up on me. Strangers are wandering all over my property. Some of them are helping; some are poking their noses where they don't belong.

A film crew from the International Fund for Animal Welfare shows up unannounced and starts shooting. When I ask them what they're doing, they claim that they're documenting the move for an instructional video. Dr. Burton flips and wants them off the property immediately. I'm not happy about it, either, but I think, 'If I stop this now, I'll put myself right in the state's crosshairs, and the last thing I want is those sons of bitches showing up at my gate.' I have one goal – 'Get the kids out of here! Get them out of here! Make them safe!' I tell Dr. Burton to let it slide.

An overdose of trang. We have to perform CPR on Zeus. Scaffold planks and an EMS rapid deployment spine board and IV bags under a sumac, as if we're on a battlefield – my heart is a knot of scar tissue.

I see the guy who was taking pictures of the unconscious cats, walking through the front yard. I jump him and motherfuck him *until he looks like he's going to vomit on his shoes.*

A thought keeps beating inside my head: 'The kids think I don't love them anymore, so I'm sending them away.' I stop and ask Jewels to go to each of them and explain. I hope she heard me and did it. I pray she did.

Sugar Bear – drugged and oblivious to the schedules and plans of the stupid humans around him – finally waddles from a transfer cage into Bobbi Brink's huge, beautiful, air-conditioned trailer. He's dragging long tendrils of slobber behind his fat haunches. The trailer sways down the driveway in the last of that washed-out absinthe light. A message on the trailer says, "BBBFF: Be a bear's best friend forever." That's not what I planned to do, but it's pretty much what happened.

My kids were spread across the country. Sugar Bear rode all the way to California with Bobbi and her dad. She has several girl bears on about four acres. She said she was going to have Sugar Bear neutered and move him into that enclosure.

Maximus, Sheba and the North Tigers went down to Mississippi. Montana and Nakobi, China and Rosco and several young lions went to North Carolina. The twins and Jake went to PAWS, the place in California that Bob Barker donates all the money to. Bobbi said it's incredible. Gage and Sybre live in a 10,000 sq. ft. enclosure in Nevada.

Sapphy went down to Boyd, Texas, to the International Exotic Animal Sanctuary. The guy who owns it is very nice. He doesn't know me, but he's done everything he can to reassure me that she's fine and they love her. Nakia and Neko, the two other cougars, went to another place in Texas. The owner is an older woman, semi-wealthy, and her place is said to be lovely.

Talk about miracles – the Cleveland Zoo took Nyla and Serena. They tested the lionesses and moved them into an exhibit with a big male. To be honest, I didn't totally dig that. Not that I'm ungrateful; I just don't like zoos. A lot of times, when they want to change environments or exhibits, it's all about product, not kids, and there's no guarantee that they won't shove the girls out the back door to another zoo, or worse.

The wolves and the hybrids? Like I said, wolfdogs are very dangerous and almost impossible to place. To this day, they're out back. I love to listen to them howl, but they still won't come near me.

I got the kids out just in time. A few weeks later, Kasich signed the Ohio Dangerous Wild Animal Act. The caging and care standards and insurance requirements are so astronomically expensive that almost no one can comply with them, which is exactly what the state wanted. The new law also gave the Ohio Department of Agriculture authority to charge exotic owners with crimes; ODA could now seize animals, lock them up in a maximum-security holding facility in Reynoldsburg and ship them anywhere they wanted. They started with Tiger

Ridge Exotics and Kenny Hetrick – at gunpoint.

GFAS was right: The rescue was a blessing that God had wrapped up and bestowed upon me and my kids. Or so it seemed.

CHAPTER EIGHTY-ONE

Theater of The Absurd

My animals were barely off the property when Bobbi Brink called and asked if it would be okay for some representatives from the state and the feds to visit. She'd been friendly to me during the move, so I told her it would be alright.

Eight or 10 people in official-looking vehicles and outfits showed up, along with Bobbi. She passed out booklets of GFAS care standards, then they all walked around the enclosures in a cluster, scribbling notes and conferring with each other in hushed voices, nodding and pointing, their heads close together. Except for an occasional stupid question, they ignored me altogether. I didn't know exactly what was up and couldn't catch a lot of what was being said.

I slipped in to listen closer to what these good people were saying. It didn't take long to realize that they were cataloguing Rescue One's shortcomings, which they were double-checking against those fucking booklets. I was stunned. For years, other exotic owners had come to Rescue One to ask my advice on building cages. I told them how we bought schedule 40 galvanized pipe from a salvage company, cemented it six feet into the ground and outfitted it with expensive hardware to create the posts from which we hung fencing. Without exception, the owners, most of whom were still using telephone poles as posts, were impressed with the simplicity, practicality and security of our design. In fact, during the move, a vet from the Cleveland Zoo walked up to Dr. Burton and me, put his hands on his hips, shook his head as if he were amazed and said that my kids were the best-looking animals he'd ever seen in private hands and my enclosures some of the best.

Now, the very people who'd helped drive me into a corner were meandering around Rescue One, clucking their tongues and shaking their heads and wrinkling their noses as they disparaged everything I'd risked my life for. The fact that I was standing right there didn't faze them. Knocking me down wasn't enough for them; they had to kick me, too.

In the midst of this production, Bobbi asked to talk to me in private. We walked around to the front porch. She opened a folder that had some papers in it, handed me a pen and showed me where to sign. I hesitated, confused, and asked her what they were. Very matter of fact, she said they were part of the agreement to move the cats. I studied them for only a few seconds before I saw that she was asking me to promise to give up the name Rescue One, surrender my tax-exempt status and take down our website and Facebook page.

"Wait a minute," I said, "*what* the fuck *is* this?"

She insisted that I sign the papers, and her mask slid off. She went from acting like my friend and confidant to posing as some kind of legal authority with the power to force me to do something that I had no intention of doing. Sixteen years of heartbreak and anxiety and humiliation boiled my blood.

'I'll be damned!' I thought. 'This is the final, outrageous, ludicrous insult.'

That quick, Heather appeared on the porch, wide-eyed and shaking with anger, ferocious.

"No the fuck I *did not*!" she said, getting loud. "This is *not* what I agreed to! Who the fuck do you think you are, bitch?"

She was holding the pen inches from Bobbi's nose and staring her down. Things were about to seriously jump off, and Bobbi knew it. Heather could feel the woman's heart pounding, smell her fear. Bobbi fumbled around for a few seconds, searching for a way to change my mind, then turned around and hurried off the porch toward the semicircle of parked vehicles inside the gate.

Heather's loud voice had attracted the rest of the prickpack to the front of the house. They formed up around her, puzzled.

"How dare you come on my property and criticize me!" she shouted.

For a moment, I thought they hadn't heard her, then their eyes widened, and their faces went ashen with alarm.

"You fucking hypocrites," she yelled. "Get the fuck out of here! Get off my property, Goddammit!"

The flock of presumptuous, self-satisfied backstabbers scattered to their crappy government sedans and flew down the driveway. Before the last one turned onto the crooked two-lane at the bottom of the hill, I realized that by letting those lackey tourists through the gate, I'd volunteered for a feature role in a one-act piece of absurdist theater.

I felt like telling Heather to kick Angela's dumb ass.

CHAPTER EIGHTY-TWO

Earthly Predators

Things only got worse. Dr. Burton told me that he'd attended a high-level meeting that included a lot of people from the state and animal rights organizations and GFAS and IFAW. He said they were going on and on, painting me like an ogre and themselves as heroes. Once again, I was the cold-hearted nitwit who had to be stopped from abusing helpless creatures.

Dr. Burton lost his temper, jumped up and shouted, "No, Angela's my friend! You have no idea who she really is! You have no right to judge her! You leave her alone!"

When I called GFAS that first time, I told the woman who answered, "I'm trying to prevent another Zanesville."

Somehow, my words were twisted to make it seem like I was threatening to turn my animals loose and kill myself and become the next Terry Thompson. I meant just the opposite. I meant that I didn't want blood on my hands and on my conscience.

Now, my kids had become pawns in an old hustle in the exotic world: a "sanctuary" generously agrees to "rehome" an animal. The second they take possession, they claim to have "rescued" it. They set up a fund in the animal's name, invent a tragic history for it and pluck at people's heartstrings for money. I was the perfect mark – a nutty hillbilly hussy whose animals were supposedly suffering terribly. The saviors had stepped up to rescue my kids and protect the unsuspecting public – from me, Goddamnit!

Of course, I'm not saying that exotics aren't abused and neglected and in need of saving. I know they're out there by the thousands; I rescued scores of them. I'm saying that charges that my animals were starved out, denied veterinary attention and tortured with cattle prods and baseball bats were lies concocted to turn a profit.

In October of 2012, I also finally figured out why "Animal Intervention" had come to rural Ohio. The episode about Rescue One was called "Mama's Boys," whatever the hell that means, and it aired on Nat-Geo Wild, not on the *National Geographic* channel. I was far too upset to watch it, but David and a whole lot of other people did, and they told me exactly what was in it. Now, instead of helping threatened sanctuaries, Alison Eastwood and her heroic crew were "confronting" exotic owners to convince them to surrender their animals. They cut all the footage and interviews into a mishmash that made us look like hick hoarders who had no clue what we were doing, while Eastwood and her crew were compassionate counselors trying to talk us out of our madness.

My despair had drawn that sniveling producer to Rescue One like a vulture sensing a rotting carcass. He blinded me with the glowing reputation of *National Geographic* and then tossed the Eastwood name around, suggesting that Clint's fame would attract even more attention. I know damned well that he found my name on that *Fatal Attractions* report, because I heard they tried to run the same shuck on just about every owner on the list. I was the only sucker who was dumb enough – or desperate enough – to fall for it.

In the name of mercy for helpless kids, I risked my life to clean up someone else's mess; in return, I got insults, treachery, worldwide disgrace. I wanted to hunt down that pack of jackals from "Animal Intervention" and punch them until my fist went through their heads. I wanted to sue everyone who'd lined up to fuck me over. The state of Ohio, Kasich, USDA, Jack Hanna, the big animal rights organizations, the lowlife breeders and sellers and roadside zoo assholes, "Animal Intervention" – they're the real predators. They use suffering animals to gain political leverage or swindle five bucks out of every gullible old lady in America or to polish their reputations. I knelt down to whore for kids. What the fuck do I care about reputation? I wanted them all arrested for fraud and prosecuted. I wanted their heads stuck on spikes in front of my gate.

I knew that was a fantasy, though; no matter how much I raged, I would have to swallow the injustice or end up in jail for a very long time. What those "Animal Intervention" phonies don't realize, however, is that Duane, who was suspicious of them from the beginning, followed them around and filmed their whole song and dance routine on a little camcorder, including yuck sessions when they snickered about what they were really up to. Somehow, the discs were misplaced. I'm hell-bent determined to find them. I know the Bible says that vengeance belongs to God, but when I get my hands on that raw footage, I'm going to shove it up someone's ass.

CHAPTER EIGHTY-THREE

The Road to Hell

Granny used to say that the road to Hell is paved with good intentions. I didn't start Rescue One for money or because I thought owning lions and tigers made me cool or because I was trying to score brownie points with God to make up for my sins. I did it because nobody wants to stand up and be responsible for the on-going horror in this vicious, abusive world. My only intention was to help as many innocent animals as I could. In return, I got fucked in a thousand different ways.

I had to get away from Lancaster before I melted down. Over the years, I came to know some people who owned an exotic rescue in Arizona. They kept telling me I should come out and visit, maybe even stay and help them. I woke up one morning and threw a bag in the back of the Camaro. I didn't tell anyone I was leaving and didn't tell the people in Arizona I was coming. I just cranked up the '80s jams and headed southwest, fueled by Marlboro Lights and caffeine.

I sped along the interstates, hypnotized, interrogating myself about what had happened to me and to Rescue One. I couldn't understand how everything had gone so terribly wrong. Had Dr. Burton been right when he warned that Heather's whoring and lying and conniving were courting Satan? Had the abortion condemned Angela's soul to the flaming pits of Hell, like that preacher outside the clinic kept shouting? Had the universe lured me into a trap and pounced on me, just to have a little fun?

Or was it even more serious? Had I brushed up against some ancient evil that day in the Vatican, when I yelled at the nun and tried to steal the Holy Water? The Vatican sits on pagan burial grounds, a bunch of mausoleums that are thousands of years old and temples where animals were sacrificed and sex rituals took place. Did I awaken some demonic energy that had slumbered for centuries in the stone ruins of the City of Blood and Terror? Had it caught my scent and started dogging me as I followed Grant through the museums and chapels, scared out of my wits? Had it been trailing me ever since, anticipating my every move and jumping in at just the right moment to step on me, time after time? As I drove, I felt that dark entity listening to my thoughts. It made me shiver. At some point, I became obsessed with the absurd notion that if I cut my own head off and threw it out the window, it would just roll over and lie there on the side of the road, still wondering how everything got so fucked up.

Drained and haunted by my own mind, I'd neglected the gas gauge. I urgently needed a *grande cappuccino* and a tankful of super-premium. Somewhere in northwest Texas I got on Route 54, a string-straight two-lane as dark as an abandoned coal mine. I blew past a lighted gas station but figured I'd come to another town in a few miles. I was right – a ghost town of boarded-up storefronts and abandoned houses. Then there was nothing but sand and sagebrush and tumbleweeds and rattlesnakes and hills that were even blacker than the night.

Cherry Angels and Earthly Predators 461

Growing more anxious by the mile, I ran up on a long-haul trucker, who decided to fuck with me. We were the only two vehicles on that Godforsaken road. I'd catch up to him and try to pass, and he'd bury the needle and pull away. Then he'd slow down until I was almost up against his tailgate and do it all over again. I could feel him looking in his rearviews, laughing.

He must've been talking to other truckers, because a second jerkoff got into the game. They boxed me in. When I tried to pass, the one in front drifted into the left lane and cut me off, as the second one ran up my ass. Enraged, I grabbed third gear and whipped around the truck in front of me. Those jackasses must've invited some eastbound drivers to play, because another big rig was coming right at me. He was blowing his horn. His high beams blinded my good eye. Neither of us budged.

I thought, 'Fuck it! This is where you've been headed since Lockbourne, bitch! It's time to knock on God's door and get some answers, face to face.'

I calmly dropped the shifter into fourth and stood on the gas pedal, summoning every bit of horsepower from the big V8. Everything slowed down and flickered, frame by frame. The semi's lights grew brighter, its horn louder. I thought we'd passed the point of no return, but the guy punked out at the last instant. He jerked the wheel and passed so close to me that the big rig's draft yanked the nose of the Camaro to the left. I felt like I was being sucked backward. I downshifted and steadied the car, watching in the mirror as the tractor trailer barreled off the road and exploded in a cloud of dust and sand. The two rigs behind me slowed down to check on him. I'm sure those halfwits were talking about the Blond Bitch in the Black Camaro for a long time. Fuck them.

CHAPTER EIGHTY-FOUR

Lithopolis

I spent a couple weeks in Arizona, but I was too agitated to be of much help there. I thought being around the animals would help, but it just made me more miserable. When I came back to Lancaster, I had no one to talk to, no one to comfort me. I'd run Johnny and Luke off, Arletta wanted nothing to do with me, Ellen was fighting her lung cancer, Dr. Burton brought back too many memories of Rescue One and I was furious at David. Granny was in a nursing home and had dementia. She went in and out of reality. She'd wake up briefly, take my hand, mutter a few words, then disappear again into her memories.

Late one afternoon, as daylight was slipping into dusk, I drove up to Lithopolis Cemetery to visit Grandpa's grave and cry on his shoulder like I did when I was a kid. I parked the Camaro and walked through lines of tombstones that looked like blocks of rose gold in the fading sunlight. Many of the markers I passed were for soldiers, dating all the way back to the Civil War.

I located the place where a big tree grew over a corner of fencing and walked another 20 steps or so to Grandpa's grave and knelt on the grass, bone tired. I wept until I was dizzy. My head hurt like someone was tightening bolts into my temples. I crumpled forward onto my hands and knees, panting, trying to catch my breath.

"Why is this little girl crying?" I heard a man ask in a deep, resonant voice.

I looked up. He was sitting on a limb in the big tree, several feet off the ground. His back was against the trunk. One knee was drawn up to his chest; his other leg dangled from the limb. I couldn't understand how I didn't see him on the way in.

He hopped down and strode from the shadows toward me. He wore shiny black shoes, creased olive-drab trousers, a tan tie, an olive-drab jacket with military patches on the chest and shoulders and an old-fashioned, olive-drab cloth cap cocked over one eye. I blinked tears away and tried to see his face. I couldn't make it out.

He raised his head as if he were talking to someone behind me and demanded, "Whose little girl is this? Who does she belong to?"

I looked over my shoulder. There was no one there, just rows of stone markers. When I turned back and looked at the soldier, he stopped abruptly, stiffened and put his hands on his hips, as if something had startled him. I wanted to read his expression, but it was like his face had been purposely obscured.

Then he was gone.

My body tingled. Everything was so quiet that my ears rang. I scanned the darkening cemetery with my good eye, searching for the soldier. He'd vanished. I looked down between my hands at Grandpa's grave. Robert Flowers's headstone sat next to one that read:

Alice Marie Flowers

January 17, 1925 –

When I stood up, rubber-legged, fireflies were glimmering over the dark gravesites around me.

CHAPTER EIGHTY-FIVE

Real Evil

For a long time after that, I avoided everyone. To be honest, I was afraid I was losing my grip on reality. I hid in the log house, so no one could see what was happening to me except David, and I ignored him. I didn't talk to Dr. Burton for months. One of the dogs got sick, though, so I had to drive up to the clinic for a prescription. I went in through the staff door and walked into the radiology room. He and another vet were reading a set of x-rays. I waited for them to finish. He coughed twice. The sound hit something in me – a strange vibration, some weird frequency. I distinctly heard serious sickness.

Louder than I meant, I said, "What's wrong with you?"

The room went quiet. Everyone turned and stared. Dr. Burton walked over, grabbed the back of my neck, shook me playfully and said, "Ang, I'm okay. Don't worry about me."

He said, "Come over to the house so we can talk."

I called and drove up to Dublin. We were sitting on the patio in his backyard, just around the corner from the Columbus Zoo, on a beautiful summer day. He coughed again, and I could tell by his expression that he was hiding something. Because he'd always been so honest and direct, it scared me.

"Is something wrong with you?" I asked.

"Oh, I'm just getting older," he said. "I'm having a little bit of trouble breathing. I'm going to the Cleveland Clinic in a few weeks. I'll be fine."

For several months, he dodged my calls. When I did manage to reach him, I couldn't make him tell me what was going on. Then I started getting bunches of calls from his number. However, he was never there when I answered. He didn't leave messages; when I called back, he didn't pick up. I was perplexed. Finally, Susan called and said he wanted to see me.

When I got there, she told me her husband had ALS, and the disease was progressing rapidly. She showed me to his room and said, "I'll leave you guys alone to talk. I'll be in the kitchen."

I walked in and was stunned. Dr. Burton was gray and skeletal and stuck in a wheelchair. He looked helpless. I sat on a chair a little to his right, so I didn't have to look directly at him while I tried to control my emotions. He was pixilated in my damaged eye. He had some kind of computerized device that allowed him to communicate in an unnerving, herky-jerky, synthesized voice. He said that thing had been calling my phone by mistake.

While we talked about my kids and his daughters and what we tried to do at Rescue One, I choked back tears of frustration and anger. After all of the impossible rescues I'd done, I was incapable of saving my closest friend – my father, my guide, my protector – from his own broken body. After a while, he reached out with both hands and gripped my wrists. He pulled me around so that I had to face him. The effort must've been agonizing.

He leaned in close and in that harsh robot voice, said, "Be careful. There is real evil in this world."

Just then, Susan brought his lunch. She had to feed him liquefied food through a tube. I couldn't bear to watch. I hugged him, kissed him, told him I loved him and left. I cried all the way back from Dublin.

I had no idea what evil Dr. Burton was referring to. I didn't even know if he was talking to Angela or to Heather. Did he mean his disease? That miasma from Roma? Was someone threatening him or me? Was it another Bible lesson? I vowed that on my next visit, I would compose myself and ask him to explain. I didn't get the chance. Dr. Don Burton died on November 18, 2014. He was only 63. Believe me, the whole world was diminished that day.

When I heard he'd passed, I remembered the big fundraiser they threw at the Columbus Zoo for his Ohio Wildlife Center, years before. It was a black-tie, $500-a-plate gig, outdoors, with linen tablecloths and beautiful place settings – a fancy gala in a lovely garden. It was so important that I dressed appropriately, pulled my hair into a ponytail and arrived on time. Ellen and I sat at Dr. Burton's table, just in front of the podium.

Pointing out all the wealthy people, he said, "Ang, baby, we're going to teach you how to massage your connections. You have to finesse them and network with them."

I behaved myself while a bunch of boring, pompous speakers droned on. Of course, Jack Hanna was there, and he could never resist a microphone and a crowd. He got up, completely unprepared, and started blabbing. He glanced down, noticed Dr. Burton and me and, out of nowhere, said, "I just want to give a shout out to our good friends at Rescue One in Lancaster. They do a really great job. They're very professional. Angela, please stand so we can recognize you."

'What the hell?' I thought. 'It would've been nice to tell me that this was going to happen.'

I wanted to slap Jack off that podium, but Dr. Burton grabbed me and pushed me to my feet. The crowd applauded. The look on Dr. Burton's face was precious. He was as happy as if those people were cheering his own daughter.

CHAPTER EIGHTY-SIX

There's Johnny

Robin told me that Jewels would be dropping by to check up on me. She was right. Jewels liked to lean against me while I petted her; every once in a while, I feel that exact weight and pressure on my lower leg, or I glimpse her in the cage that takes up a big part of the living room. As always, she is sitting on the corner of the ledge, facing the door, with her paws crossed, watching everything, her tail moving in a casual, full, gentle swish, like she's daydreaming. I'll see her out of the corner of my good eye, but when I try to focus on her, she isn't there.

She isn't always so passive, though. About six months after Dr. Burton died, I was driving around in the Camaro, still heartbroken, still trying to clear my head, fighting the compulsion to pull up to a drive-through window. Again, I was just in the car; I wasn't making decisions about where to turn or anything. It was happening automatically. The funny thing is I could smell Jewels and feel her beside me. Her presence was so strong that I kept glancing over at the passenger's seat, expecting to see her sitting there, looking out the window, just like she used to when I took her for rides in the Cruiser.

I ended up on the main drag in Lockbourne, a place I hated, where no one I cared about lived. I heard someone call my name and slowed down to look. It was Stevie, an old boyfriend. He and some of my other former hoodlum buddies were milling around in the front yard of a rundown house. I parked and walked up on them, smiling. There in the middle of the bunch, sitting on a lawn chair, was Johnny. I didn't even know he was still around, but I thought, 'Let bygones be bygones' and kept going.

An overwhelming information/energy vibe flashed on me. I knew in that brilliant fraction of a second that it was Johnny who'd poisoned Jewels to get back at me for turning him out and, probably, for putting Buddy in a new home.

Johnny must've felt it, too, because he stood up and backed away, his expression shocked and frightened. I watched him rush out of the yard and down the sidewalk. Before he even reached the corner, I understood what Dr. Burton had meant by the "real evil" he'd seen on his deathbed. I never saw Johnny again.

That day in Lockbourne, the Camaro behaved just like Mitzi had on the night Grandpa died. This time, though, I knew exactly what – or who – had been controlling the car. Lily Dale, teeth, Lockbourne – Jewels had left a trail that led directly to her murderer. She was wiser than I am, though. If she'd led me to Johnny sooner, I would've killed him where he stood.

CHAPTER EIGHTY-SEVEN

Ghosts of Rescue One

Not long after, Granny died. I didn't go to the funeral. What was in that coffin wasn't Alice Marie Flowers, and I knew the Harters would be there. I wanted nothing to do with them. I also knew that they and other family members would be fighting over the scraps of her life. I already had the only thing I wanted. Before she died, Granny gave me a box that held all of Grandpa's medals and commendations and the love letters they wrote to each other on Salvation Army stationary when he was in the navy. Her death cracked my head. Heartbroken, lonely, guilty, I cursed myself for refusing to heed the person who'd tried longest and hardest to save me from me.

Everything I'd been – kids, job, money, schedule, friends, family, purpose – had burned down. I felt like every cell in my body had been obliterated and rearranged. I looked back at the woman who'd managed to hold Rescue One and Cherry Angels together. She wasn't me. I remembered someone else – a very brave, strong, got-all-the-answers, fears-nothing woman, the one who rebelled against Grant in Dublin and faced down those muggers in Roma and that shit Floyd Wells and that Super 8 creep, the one who was like Heather, not the ghost of her that I'd become. I admired and envied that woman.

For 16 years, I was fully aware that I could die any day – or night. Every tiger Angela rescued could've been her last; every john Heather fucked could've been her last. I began to wish I had been killed, because the spiritual death I suffered was much worse than any physical death could have been. Now, I felt like I was living in a grave.

For a long time, I went down a very dark path. I drifted into my Shadow Self – my morbid, deeply depressed side; to be honest, though, I've always been like a phantom, my true nature visible only to the kids, passing through the 3D world like the hazy memory of a hallucination. I was in my mid-40s, had spent all my money on Rescue One, couldn't unsee everything I'd done. I wanted to lose my anger, regain my equilibrium and go forward, but I was enraged, beyond redemption, tormented by scorching memories, falling through circles of Hell. The dark entity that had been following me since Roma had to be laughing its foul ass off.

I kept imagining Hollywood scenarios that would save the day: founding a church that worships animals and rakes in donations; hitting the lottery and going on a triumphant tour of exotic sanctuaries across the United States, dropping off hefty donations and picking up my kids along the way; recruiting an army of angry whores and leading them on a Wonder Woman ride-for-vengeance/rescue mission.

That's my big mistake – always trusting that fate will deliver me from any problem I get myself into. I'd just known all along that the troops would show up in the nick of time to help lead my innocent kids to safety. Now, though, "fate" sounded like just another four-letter word. When it arrived, it brought pain along for the party. Fate had shaken my faith and turned my world black. All I had left was another four-letter word – hope. And that was fading fast, too. I'd been expecting an archangel wielding a flaming sword; instead, I got Jack Hanna, Alison Eastwood, John Kasich and Bobbi Brink.

My property smelled like ghosts. Apparitions prowled faint gravel pathways and materialized in overgrown spaces that used to house tigers and lions and cougars, then faded away. The most profound loss wasn't all the money; it was the everyday sounds of the kids. Their constant grumbling, snarling, growling, coughing was replaced by wind hissing through the trees. The cat noise had been a precious possession that I'd taken for granted. The kids were all gone, but I still lay awake at night, hearing tigers wrestling and lions roaring. The sounds echoed off the trees, and in my heart. In snatches of feverish dreams, my kids came home, purring and chuffing as I rubbed my face over their cheeks and ruffled their coarse fur and hugged them to my breasts, finally content. I woke up every morning next to my aggravation and stared at the walls, exhausted, convinced that I'd been a fool to believe that the good guys always win in the end, like life is a fucking movie.

I had David take some of the enclosures down and give the fencing to a guy north of Columbus who was fighting to keep his tigers and bears. I let the weeds and bushes grow, so I couldn't even tell where my kids had lived. Deer grazed where huge predators once played and slept.

People kept saying that I had to get over my loss, but how do you recover from extinction? Years before, I told Arletta that we had to move past our "procedures"; now, I was the one stuck in the past.

One year, we had a late-winter blizzard that kept me snowed in for several days. I needed meds for the dogs, so when the roads were finally clear, I went to All God's Creatures, a veterinary practice in Lancaster. A very sweet older lady was there with a shepherd/retriever mix on a lead. I listened as she told the vet she found the dog outside her house during the storm. The dog was trembling, his belly on the floor, his head and tail drooping.

"Do whatever he needs done," the lady told the vet. "My husband and I will pay for it. We have to take him to the pound when you're finished, though. Our Bichons won't tolerate a new dog in the house."

As she talked, the beaten-down mutt crawled slowly toward my feet. I reached down to pat his head. 'No, get what you came for and get out of here!' a voice warned. 'You've been burned once. Don't let it happen again.'

Unable, as always, to fight my heart, I knelt and petted the stray.

I looked up and interrupted the lady: "Wait a minute. There are no other options for this dog, right?"

She and the veterinarian both sadly shook their heads.

"Let him stay right here until he's completely better," I said, standing up.

I turned to the nice lady and said, "It's okay. I got this. I'll take care of this kid. I'm Rescue One."

CHAPTER EIGHTY-EIGHT

Angela Marie Flowers

I was only willing to go so far, though. A few months after I adopted Toby, a woman called and asked me to take in a female wolf that had fallen into the hands of the local humane society. The caller said the wolf was probably about two years old and very sweet. Nannook and Misty had died, so I had space in the wolf compound; nonetheless, I turned the caller down. Saying no to a needy kid almost killed me, but I couldn't invite the ODA and USDA bullshit back into my life.

I was sitting on the porch one evening, wondering as I had so often since visiting Grandpa's grave, about the faceless soldier who came out of the twilight and then vanished so mysteriously. I pictured him striding toward me – irate, demanding answers to his questions, dressed completely in olive-drab; then I remembered Granny's headstone next to my hand. A revelation jolted me: 'You're not Angela Harter. There's no such person. Your mother hung that Harter name on you when she married John. Angela Harter is like Heather Smith. Neither of them ever existed. Your name is Angela Marie Flowers – always has been, always will be.'

After that, I slowly began to comprehend that when Jewels died and the kids left, my mind had willed itself into amnesia as a defense against overwhelming pain. While it was happening to me, I was sitting in a front-row seat, watching my subconscious throw up barriers, rip down road signs and burn maps, without my permission. That phenomenon had allowed me to survive the shitfest without even realizing it.

As my unconscious mind began to trickle through the defensive wall, I awakened to a new reality and a new woman. I wasn't completely over the burndown yet – I'm still not – but I started to recapture my memories and my will. I quit smoking, went vegan, gave up my beloved Diet Mountain Dew. I joined a gym and had David turn the loft into a meditation suite. I gradually became more attuned to the natural world and the spiritual realm that most people ignore.

Material things didn't interest me anymore. I've been rich. I traveled the world, drove cars that cost more than houses, owned so much jewelry that I could've slept on a different bed of gold and silver and gems every night for weeks. I still have closets jammed with $2000 outfits that smell like mothballs. None of it ever made me happy. I sold the Camaro and the Range Rover and bought a little used Honda.

By accident, I came into contact with Ellen again and was overjoyed to learn that she'd beaten cancer and that, all along, my suspicions about her had actually been the Trammies whispering their devious bullshit. I scoured the log house for rest of the pills and flushed them.

I also came to understand what Jewels meant when she told Robin that this was all meant to happen. Nothing in my life was an accident; saving animals has always been my calling. To survive and provide for them, I had to be resilient, resourceful and unselfish. My life had all been part of a divine plan to prepare me to do that. That Beach Hustler in Jamaica turned out to have been right all along: God does love me.

This is no resurrection, however; it's a rebirth. I have to catch up with all the changes that come with living in a new skin and getting on with a new life. I don't know exactly what form that existence will take, but I can say this for sure: It's going to be a one-woman show.

I think about Dr. Burton and the kids all the time. I have no regrets. Rescue One Exotic Cat Sanctuary was a blessing. I swear, unequivocally, that I would do it again, even if I knew it would lead me to the same Heartache from Hell, and I know Dr. Burton would say the same thing.

I'm finally learning to leave the past where it belongs, to stop allowing what I was to manipulate what I am and will be. For a while, I kept waking up in the middle of the night with the same thought burning through my dreams: 'Stay out of the past, and you'll stay away from your pain.' It reminded me of a passage in the Bible Dr. Burton made me study. I took it out one day and found Matthew 8:22, where Jesus says: "Let the dead bury their own dead."

When I'd asked Dr. Burton what it meant, he said, "There's nothing to gain by living in the past. You can't change it. You can't control it. You're still alive, physically and spiritually. You have to trust in God and move forward."

Stop allowing the past to manipulate the present – more good advice, but the problem is letting go of the past without deleting it from my head. The website for Rescue One is still posted, with portraits of all the kids. Removing it would be pretending they never existed, just like the state wants and just like Bobbi Brink tried to bully me into doing. Seeing them, hearing them, smelling them hurts like hell, though. I try to keep them – and my grandparents and Dr. Burton – alive in my memories, while staying in the day-to-day as much as I can. Talk about balancing your pain.

I take in stray dogs and cats, rehabilitate them and find loving homes for the lucky ones. The rest stay here with me. Homeless domestic animals are not as glamorous and thrilling as big cats, but they have no hope of escaping from the gutter without a human hand to help them. The small deserve love as much as the great.

The phone number for Cherry Angels is still listed. Lisa doesn't take calls anymore, however. One night when Angela was at her lowest, Lisa sent Heather to a motel in a very sketchy part of town. The client was a freak who tossed a $50 bill on one of the twin beds, said he wanted to go "round the world" and started ripping Heather's clothes off. When she clawed his face and shoved him away, he pulled a knife. Heather fought her way out of the room, half-naked and bleeding. She hid in Mitzi's backseat while the nutjob hunted the parking lot for her. After that, we three agreed to leave the nightwork behind.

Heather still sees Duane and a few other long-term clients who are safe and generous, and some horny Skype dudes hit her up when the spirit moves them. Otherwise, she doesn't come around much. She surfaces mostly when I'm really angry or allow myself to brood. It happens especially when I'm around David. He lives here in the log house, and we're still legally married. Even though I want to cleanse the venom from my soul, I've never forgiven him for defying me and don't know if I ever will. We exist in a weird, tense limbo, like Grant and I did in Dublin before the final burndown.

I still sense that evil entity from Roma watching me. I believe that because he created us, God can hear the song of our souls. That ancient force overheard my song; now, it can trail me forever. I also never lose sight of my other dark passenger, that hungry being that dwells inside me. Bulimia is always along for the ride, just waiting to be triggered. I try to be vigilant, but helplessness and sorrow feed it and turn it loose. When the urge becomes strong and beats at my head, food is a very attractive release valve.

I'm still curious about the Other Side and working closely with Robin to understand it better. Maybe we'll meet the soldier there someday and find out who he is. Jewels comes and goes. I don't know what the disappearing act is all about, but it's comforting to know that she's around. I never tried to talk to her again; that one session satisfied me. Granny and Grandpa put up with enough in this world, so I let them rest. We've looked for Dr. Burton but haven't located him yet. I'm sure there's a reason for that, although I'll be damned if I can figure out what it is. I'll keep trying. Maybe he's with Jewels and my grandparents somewhere, happy. I hope so. I can't wait to see my friends and family again. I want to introduce them to Angela Marie Flowers. They're going to love her.

THE END

About The Author

Angela Harter grew up feral on the streets of Columbus, Ohio, abused, neglected and frequently in trouble with the law. She began stripping in bars when she was 16 and opened her own escort service before turning 18. For 16 years, she operated two businesses – **Rescue One Exotic Cat Sanctuary** - where she housed scores of abused tigers, lions, cougars and leopards, and **Cherry Angels**, a one-woman escort service that she used to support the sanctuary.

Acknowledgements

All of my kids, gone from Rescue One but ever at home in my heart; Robin Guayasamin-Salerno (innersongsconsortium.com), in touch with this world and others; all of our volunteers and donors, in particular Heidi, Linda and crazy, wonderful Denny; Reeni and Steve Vaughn; Dana Nisely, always there with a helping hand; the incredible Ellen Martin Chester, wearer of too many hats to list; my neighbors, especially Lee Tipple, the coolest friend anyone could wish for; Dr. Don Burton's entire, indispensable staff at Animals Care Unlimited, no matter how much thanks I heap on you for your unmatched caring and medical assistance throughout Rescue One's journey, it's not enough; former Fairfield County Sheriff Dave Phelan and his wonderful deputies, guardians of Rescue One; Miss Betsy and Renae, for reading early drafts of the manuscript; David Ferris, a second generation of astute critic; and Alan Natali, who had the courage to face Heather at her worst and the patience to help guide Angela out of the darkness.

www.ingramcontent.com/pod-product-compliance
Lightning Source LLC
Chambersburg PA
CBHW071801080526
44589CB00012B/634